"This invaluable book brings postcolonial theory to bear on key issues of practical theology, such as the self, family, borders, migration, and ecology. Using 'interdependence of life' as a framework, it offers astute theological analyses and keen pastoral insights, challenging the false binary of practical and 'impractical' theology. This is a gift to students of theology, ministers, and pastoral workers."

—Kwok Pui-lan
author of *Postcolonial Imagination and Feminist Theology*

"In this wonderfully disruptive and transformative book, HyeRan Kim-Cragg breaks new ground, employing interdependence as a plumb line for Christian realignment. Pushing aside the veil of North American colonialism, she deftly reminds readers that all of us depend on the mercy of others for our very lives, and, suddenly, we see anew those repeatedly cast aside—children, mixed-race and queer youths, multinational immigrants, multi-religious persons, and nature itself. A much-needed contribution!"

—Bonnie J. Miller-McLemore
Professor, the Divinity School and Graduate Department of Religion, Vanderbilt University

"HyeRan Kim-Cragg goes beyond borders and boundaries to probe the potential role of Practical Theology in communities often overlooked by our congregations and the academy, offering lament as well as rich insights from an array of scholars. Her postcolonial, feminist theology of interdependence grounds our diverse expressions of humanity with the earth itself and offers hope and compassion for those on the margins."

—Kathy Black
Professor of Homiletics and Liturgics,
Claremont School of Theology

"HyeRan Kim-Cragg is an expert guide to feminist and postcolonial practical theology. Grounded in lived situations and ranging across various contemporary theological challenges, this excellent book is at once exciting, complex, adventurous, and careful—and much to be commended. *Interdependence* shows the promise of postcolonial practical theology. Both wide ranging in its concerns and kept close to lived situations, it is an ideal primer in (or manifesto for) contemporary practical theology that should not be missed!"

—STEPHEN BURNS
Stewart Professor of Liturgical and Practical Theology, Trinity College Theological School, University of Divinity, Melbourne, Australia

Interdependence

Interdependence

A Postcolonial Feminist Practical Theology

HyeRan Kim-Cragg

Forewords by
Mary Elizabeth Moore
and
Musa W. Dube

☙PICKWICK *Publications* • Eugene, Oregon

INTERDEPENDENCE
A Postcolonial Feminist Practical Theology

Copyright © 2018 HyeRan Kim-Cragg. All rights reserved. Except for brief quotations in critical publications or reviews, no part of this book may be reproduced in any manner without prior written permission from the publisher. Write: Permissions, Wipf and Stock Publishers, 199 W. 8th Ave., Suite 3, Eugene, OR 97401.

Pickwick Publications
An Imprint of Wipf and Stock Publishers
199 W. 8th Ave., Suite 3
Eugene, OR 97401

www.wipfandstock.com

PAPERBACK ISBN: 978-1-5326-1724-9
HARDCOVER ISBN: 978-1-4982-4181-6
EBOOK ISBN: 978-1-4982-4180-9

Cataloguing-in-Publication data:

Names: Kim-Cragg, HyeRan, 1970–, author. | Moore, Mary Elizabeth, foreword writer; Dube, Musa W., foreword writer.

Title: Interdependence : a postcolonial feminist practical theology / HyeRan Kim-Cragg.

Description: Eugene, OR: Pickwick Publications, 2018 | Includes bibliographical references and index.

Identifiers: ISBN 978-1-5326-1724-9 (paperback) | ISBN 978-1-4982-4181-6 (hardcover) | ISBN 978-1-4982-4180-9 (ebook)

Subjects: LCSH: Postcolonial theology | Feminist theology | Postcolonialism | Practical Theology

Classification: BR118 K56 2018 (print) | BR118 (ebook)

Manufactured in the U.S.A. 05/18/18

Contents

Foreword by Mary Elizabeth Moore | vii
Foreword by Musa W. Dube | xi
Acknowledgements | xiii

    Introduction | 1
1. Beyond Independence | 9
2. Beyond Homogenous Heterosexual Family | 34
3. Beyond Adult-Centered Worship | 57
4. Beyond Christian-Centrism | 81
5. Beyond Belonging and Borders | 106
6. Beyond Anthropocentric Borders | 128

Bibliography | 151
Index | 165

Foreword

As I PONDER THE rich textures of this book, I am gripped by the fragility of our world and the destruction that haunts our daily experience. We are faced with global warming, increasing poverty, blatant and extreme racism, violence on the streets, hate talk and hate crimes against faithful religious communities, systemic oppression of persons who identify as LGBTQIA, cruel disruption of immigrant families, war-threats favored over diplomacy, and political actions that escalate all of these patterns and more. As a citizen of the United States, I am devastated by the egregious and destructive actions of our country; however, the patterns extend across the world, and the actions of my country reinforce similar patterns elsewhere. These concerns weigh heavily on my mind; thus, I read HyeRan Kim-Cragg's book as *a life-giving book for a life-destroying time*. Our fragile world needs to be reminded of its fragility and its strength and, most especially, of the deep interrelatedness and interdependence that binds us. We live in a time that calls us to work together to repair, renew, and rebuild our churches and our local and global communities. *Interdependence* offers us that vision.

The title and theme of Dr. Kim-Cragg's book, *Interdependence: A Postcolonial Feminist Practical Theology*, reflects the central motif. From the opening words of the Acknowledgments to the end of the book, she has woven a picture of fragility and strength. She recognizes the fragility of her own life, the lives of others around her, and the life of the church, while also emphasizing their strength. Unfortunately, the strength that indwells these people and communities is often thwarted in a fragmented world of individualism. The strength can actually grow, however, in a context that inspires and supports interdependence. Interdependent strength can nourish each and all to grow into their fuller potential and thus to enhance the flourishing of church and society.

Foreword

Dr. Kim-Cragg pushes her point to greater complexity and depth as she focuses on those who are overlooked or ignored: children in adult-focused worship, youth living in inter-racial and queer families, people participating in multiple religious traditions, immigrants navigating multiple national identities, and non-human beings suffering from selfish human actions. She recognizes the fragility and strength of these communities, as well as the significant potential of interdependent relationships for each of them and all of them together. To address these important concerns, she employs analyses that are interdisciplinary, postcolonial, and feminist, attending to those who are "overlooked," even in practical theology. She is actively *doing* the work of practical theology in relation to issues of urgent existential and theological concern. Thus, she is not focused on practical theology's definitional and methodological debates, but on vocational ones.

Dr. Kim-Cragg's emphases converge with a growing number of scholars who are cultivating postcolonial ground in constructive and practical theology.[1] Her own unique contribution is to probe very particular issues and practices, thus enacting practical theology's vocation to analyze practices and develop insight into the practices (and malpractices) of everyday life. Her critical postcolonial perspective enables her to probe "beyond" the boundaries of dominant social and social-ecological patterns and beyond conventional thinking. She does not assume that the human community has arrived or will ever arrive at a resting point. Rather, she persistently seeks to listen and see the "beyond" the world as it is, and to critique social patterns and theological assumptions that bind the present in patterns of domination. She seeks to stir imagination and open new possibilities for the church and other human communities. These new patterns will draw deeply from the past and present, but transcend the domination patterns therein and point toward a more flourishing future.

Dr. Kim-Cragg's theological method fits her goals and magnifies her contribution. In analyzing social and theological issues, she has drawn on a breadth of literature in practical theology and postcolonial-feminist studies. This choice already pushes the boundaries of domination because

---

1. David Schnasa Jacobsen, *Theologies of the Gospel in Context: The Crux of Homiletical Theology* (Eugene, OR: Wipf & Stock, 2017); Hee An Choi, *A Postcolonial Self: Colonial Immigrant Theology and the Church* (Albany, NY: SUNY, 2015); Sarah Travis, *Decolonizing Preaching: The Pulpit as Postcolonial Space* (Eugene, OR: Wipf & Stock, 2014); Kwok Pui-lan, *Postcolonial Imagination and Feminist Theology* (Louisville: Westminster John Knox, 2005);

Foreword

she is not limiting herself to one thread of conversation, but drawing from multiple threads. She also draws on some historical figures and theological insights, both to mine their theological wisdom and to critique it. Similarly she draws upon case studies, stories from her own experience, and interviews to illustrate and analyze the focal issues. The dialogue between the literature and the social-ecological issues is generative. It illuminates questions of selfhood, time, power, family, home, anthropocentrism, God's mystery (known and not known), and the deep connections of God and creation. The result is a practical theology that decenters dominant ideas and practices. Dr. Kim-Cragg's approach decenters adults in multi-generational congregations, decenters heterosexuality in a world struggling with homophobia, decenters whiteness and mono-ethnicity in an ethnically complex world, decenters Christianity in a pluralistc world of multiple religious belonging, decenters home in a world of migration, and decenters human beings in an interconnected ecology.

Thank you to HyeRan Kim-Cragg for decentering practical theology and for pointing to intellectual and religious practices that decenter the more dominant scholarship and ideas in the field. She has done this work with meticulous care—decentering rather than discounting, critiquing complexities rather than bifurcating, and pointing to what can be. She has thus offered a constructive way forward for practical theology, a field that easily falls captive to dominant streams and oversimplifying bifurcations. Dr. Kim-Cragg has offered an insight-packed exploratory study that opens doors for continuing feminist postcolonial work. Such work will probe ever more deeply into empirical studies and theological analyses that decenter the field and evoke new insight. It will also draw on research forms, such as participatory action research, that assume the interdependence of those who practice faith, those who study and interpret the practices, and those who seek transformation (often the same persons in their different roles).

Dr. Kim-Cragg has not only opened doors to deeper understanding of critical issues, but she has also set an agenda for practical theology that invites others to continue building toward the "beyond." The "beyond" is calling all of us, and her book offers inspiration and frameworks to en*courage* the human family to stretch toward it.

Mary Elizabeth Moore

Foreword

HYERAN KIM-CRAGG'S BOOK IS an invitation to the imaginative space of the beyond, the space of interdependence. The book weaves a postcolonial feminist discourse of practical theology that calls into being modes of community building that are knitted by the values of interdependence. Suspiciously interrogating the discourse of equality, self-sufficiency and independence, the book brings the reader to the space and place of persons with disability, children in worship, interracial youth and couples, queer families, people who practice multiple religious traditions, new immigrants and the Earth as members of our communities—highlighting how the dominant academic and ecclesial discourses have overlooked these groups.

Showing, for example, how the colonial ideology of characterizing the colonized as children and the racial claims of superiority still inform congregations that exclude children from worship on the basis of age and disapprove interracial couples. In modern colonial times heterosexuality and monotheistic Christianity were constructed as the norm, while other sexualities and religious beliefs were suppressed in construction of racial and cultural superiority of the colonizer, a position that has not been fully dislodged in the church and wider communities.

The book returns in every chapter to interrogate colonial and patriarchal foundations of exclusive discourses and how they interlock with other social categories of gender, race, class, ethnicity and religion, while challenging readers to move to the beyond and embrace interdependence. Similarly, in the last two chapters the book returns to suspiciously interrogate the ancient and modern colonial ideologies that shaped immigration and attitudes towards the Earth. Just as the Earth is viewed as a woman; colonized countries were constructed as female to legitimize their subjugation. And so is the taking of the Earth and its resources from the colonized linked to intensified immigration of our age, for as the dispossessed and

Foreword

the disempowered become dislocated, they seek means of survival in other countries and confront racist policies/immigration laws upon arrival. Yet interracial families and interreligious relationships are on the rise due to migration in the religiously pluralistic postcolonial condition, calling for welcoming communities of interdependence.

HyeRan's postcolonial feminist practical theology of interdependence invites readers and ecclesial communities to move across multiple boundaries to the beyond—to imagining a place and space where community can be built upon the foundations of interdependence by disavowing discrimination based upon race, age, sexuality, disability, ethnicity, colonial ideologies, nationality, immigration statues, religiosity, and non-human status.

Musa W. Dube

Acknowledgments

December 12, Monday, 2016 was the first day of the final exam week at the University of Saskatchewan. It was around 8 am when I left for work at St. Andrew's College. I usually walk to work. It takes only twenty minutes on foot. It was an ordinary day, though it was dark and cold, typical of the Advent weather in Saskatoon, one of the most northerly cities of Canada. I took the path I have always done for the last decade. I was crossing the street just five minutes from the College when suddenly I felt myself flying through the air. The next thing I knew, I was face down on the pavement. I was not unconscious, though I could not comprehend fully what had just happened. I heard a voice, "Sorry, sorry, are you okay?"

I was bleeding heavily because my nose was broken and my eyebrow was deeply cut. Within five minutes, I was in the care of nurses who cleaned my bloody face and helped stop the bleeding. I called my husband. It was our wedding anniversary day and we were planning to go out that evening. He came over right away. The police also came in an hour. The ER doctor came in two hours. I was scheduled for tests with CT scan, MRI, followed by a quick stitching surgery in the afternoon. There was no bed for me since the ER was full of patients more critical than me. I was in the ER room for eight hours.

I learned only a few days later that my proposal for this book was accepted. It was a bitter-sweet moment in my life. I had been painfully awakened to the truth of the fragility of life and of the ways we depend on others, especially in times of crisis. I didn't need this accident to prove my point of the book!!

Every moment of our life we are dependent on others. Thus, to acknowledge all the people and all the things that help me to write this book is an immense task which I am incapable of properly doing. From my partner, my children, my friends, my colleagues, my students who have all given me

Acknowledgments

support and encouragement in countless ways, to my college and those in it who staff and maintain it with books and journals, as well as computers, desks, chairs, office spaces, quiet environments, I am also deeply indebted. I am grateful to the authors of the books and journals I have read that have inspired and challenged me. I am also grateful to my academic mentors, among who kindly wrote the foreword and endorsed the book.

Most of all, I am tremendously grateful for my very body that is healthy enough to think, read, write, and give birth to this book. As a practical feminist theologian, I know theoretically how the body is important. However, the experience of feeling my own body being healed, and working so hard to heal from the wounds has been incredible. It has been one of the most miraculous and mysterious experiences of my life. Healing takes time. Different parts of the body draw strength and help from other parts. The body never rushes. The body never gives up healing either. Its sustaining, persisting, constant, and ever-present balancing power is indeed an amazing gift. I believe it is a gift from God, and it is to God that I offer my ultimate thanks of acknowledgments.

Introduction

As a way of an introduction, I will introduce the questions, key terms, and approaches integral to this book.

Why Interdependence?

This book is concerned with the problem of life that is individualized and fragmented. One of the challenges that Christianity in North America in the twenty-first century faces is that established churches are dwindling. That the world is becoming more secular is not a problem, but that one of the primary communities in society is becoming weakened and disappearing is problematic. The communal way of life that Christian churches have modelled is at stake. This book highlights the interdependence of life as a way to explain the importance of community. The book challenges and contests the notion of independence, self-sufficiency, and self-control as the desirable goal of the human being. The attempt to interrogate the logic of independence is mainly discussed in Chapter 1, and the issue of independence will be dealt with again when we examine children as dependent beings in Chapter 3. The indispensable reality of interdependence will be finally articulated in Chapter 6, as we study non-human ecological problems.

Perhaps, it may be most helpful to share my own reflection on the accident in order to demonstrate the importance of seeking interdependence. In the eight hours following my accident, there were so many helping hands for my wellbeing—from many nurses, doctors, health professionals, police, and my immediate family. Even the woman who hit me helped me. She did not run away but drove me to the hospital. She was a University student who was late for the final exam that morning so she was rushing to the intersection, failing to stop and see me crossing. Even though she harmed me, I was dependent on her. Even though I did nothing to deserve the suffering, I was also the one who received amazing care and support from so many people I did not know. That is the irony of gratitude. That is the paradox of joy and sorrow.

To seek the truth of interdependence by drawing wisdom from our interdependent lives is not to gloss over injustices against people and other living creatures that are vulnerable and dependent. There are important consequences for our actions. The number of pedestrians being hit by cars is increasing.[1] It is a public problem that must be addressed. Our car-culture makes those who walk or bike vulnerable to injury or death. Education and policies to ensure safety of pedestrians is needed.

My personal traumatic experience vividly and successfully tells the truth of how vulnerable our life is and at the same time, consequently, how crucial it is to know that we are interdependent. Our lives are at the mercy of others. Not a single day can we live without others' help, care, and support. Thus, to seek to ensure that people who need help receive support is important. To learn to give support, if and when we can, to those who are in need is also important. All of these give-and-take interdependent ways of life must be sought as a life-long learning and teaching, as well as theological and religious practice in communal, systematic, and public ways.

Why the Overlooked?

The book focuses on those who have been overlooked in dominant academic and ecclesial discourses. They include (but are not limited to) children in adult-centered worship, youth in inter-racial and queer families, people who practice multiple religious traditions, new immigrants who belong to more than one nationality, and the non-human species that suffer from the selfish acts of human communities. However broken and fragile the groups named above are, they are important members of the community, without whom the community that God calls us to create, remains broken. Lifting up the experiences of these ignored groups in academic discourse, the book contributes to expanding practical theology engagement by fulfilling its goal of creating a healthy community for all human beings and non-human

---

1. http://www.cbc.ca/radio/thesundayedition/features/michaelsessays/too-many-pedestrians-are-hit-by-cars-in-our-cities-michael-s-essay-1.3868068?autoplay=true

living beings. The book seeks to illuminate new possibilities with a claim that church communities that are dwindling may be renewed, even transformed by embracing these groups with whom God is already present.

Why Deal with Multiple Sub-disciplines of Practical Theology?

The book covers more than one sub-discipline of practical theology. It discusses worship and Christian education as well as religious pluralism, migration, and ecofeminist theology. The book critiques the compartmentalized hierarchical academic approach and calls for a more interdependent one. A more robust interdependent multi-disciplinary engagement is necessary for the good of academia, but it is also much needed for current theological education and ecclesial realities.

Due to the dwindling numbers of churches and Christian seminaries in North America, compartmentalized disciplinary boundaries are blurred. For example, those who teach religious education are being asked to teach spiritual formation and ministry leadership as well. A biblical scholar may be called to serve as dean for religious life or teach homiletics. This challenge, however, offers positive insights. Blurring the lines between disciplines opens alternative paths. The challenge of moving across disciplinary boundaries prompts students, teachers, and staff to work together, fostering collaboration, learning to be interdependent, which is key to creating a healthy community for all.

It is my conviction that learning to navigate and make connections between different disciplines contributes to a better outcome for learning. Scholars and teachers are also better equipped to engage in the Christian life and the world, deepening their own respective disciplines and traditions. This facilitates better diagnosing and problem solving. It means such changing and challenging contexts can enhance the ways we teach and do theological and biblical studies. The most recent feminist biblical commentary series, the Wisdom Commentary Series (Liturgical Press),[2] intentionally makes a point of drawing from different disciplines that are not traditionally regarded as biblical studies in order to embrace different voices. It invites different authors who are not in biblical studies as a way of promoting a multidisciplinary approach. I have been fortunate enough to join in this ongoing project as co-author of two volumes (working with

2. http://www.wisdomcommentary.org/

biblical scholar Mary Ann Beavis on the book of Hebrews and 2 Thessalonians), Our *Hebrews* commentary received an award from the Catholic Press Association as one of the best Catholic academic books published in North America in 2016.[3] I believe the very act of crossing and engaging different disciplines through the collaboration of scholars from different disciplines helped enhance the content of the commentary. Receiving an award was evidence and recognition of multi-disciplinary interdependent efforts.

Why a Postcolonial Feminist Approach?

My postcolonial and feminist commitments are deeply felt and are one of the most important motivating factors for writing this book. I try to demonstrate an urgent need for practical theology to utilize postcolonial feminist approaches. Practical theology has paid attention to the issue of "race, ethnicity, gender, class, and sexual orientation arising from the situated and embodied character of human life," as Kathleen A. Cahalan and Gordon S. Mikoski have argued.[4] However, these issues are not unrelated to colonialism. Yet, colonialism is absent as a concern in practical theology. This book not only calls for the inclusion of colonialism as a critical optic for practical theology but also demands a close look at how colonialism is entangled with issues of race, ethnicity, gender, class, disability, and sexual orientation. In order to examine them intersecting in interconnected ways, we need to engage in a self-critical theological reflection with a postcolonial feminist perspective.

Let me articulate this point using a concrete example. The book discusses migration in Chapter 5. We cannot fully understand migration without understanding postcolonial conditions and considering the impact of colonial legacies. In this regard, migration could serve both as a context of practical theology and as a content of practical theology. Migration is a source of practical theology that provides important matters to chew on. But it is also the very context practical theology must address. Taking on migration from a postcolonial feminist perspective, we may be able to more fully analyze the entangled contexts in which race, ethnicity, religion, and gender become forefront issues of migration. As a content of

---

3. http://www.saintjohnsabbey.org/old-news-and-events/liturgical-press-earns-top-spot-among-book-publishers-2016-catholic-press-awards/

4. Cahalan and Mikoski, eds., *Opening the Field of Practical Theology*, 3.

Introduction

practical theology, migration helps draw the biblical wisdom of pilgrimage or sojourners for Christian vocation. It also lifts up a valuable insight on vulnerability as a prerequisite of interdependent relationships.

Let me finally delineate the main point of each chapter. Chapter 1 claims that a person is an interdependent being, whose existence and growth toward maturity is dependent on others. Interdependence as a key approach to practical theology will be informed by feminist theology as the chapter criticizes the individualized notion of the self as well as its gendered and racialized underpinnings. The notion of adulthood, which is mostly associated with self-sufficiency and independence, will be debunked and the idea of young people, as passive and dependent, will be challenged. It also examines disability and independence by challenging the colonial myth of progress. Finally, a close reading of a church event in thick description will demonstrate what it means to live interdependently in communities, while exploring a goal of practical theology, namely, a restoration of broken relationships towards an interdependent life. The reflection upon a particular church community offers unlearning as an intentional discipline of practical theology. Chapter 2 deals with the role of the family as a basic unit of human relationships. Building upon the criticism of self-autonomous individualized culture from the previous chapter, Chapter 2 investigates the heterosexual white nuclear family as the norm that is promoted and dominant in our religious communities. It attends to the experiences of mixed race and queer families. The ethnographies and interview methods employed by sub-disciplines of sociology affirm the importance of listening and of narrative agency, especially among youth and teens in practical theology. Listening to many stories and showcasing examples of these groups from these interviews contributes to a theological exploration of family beyond blood and binary gender. This exploration undertakes an investigation of the myth of purity and an examination of gender as a social relation maintained by human practice and performance. It unravels the biases, prejudices, and fears that are prevalent and operative in churches and most communities in society, but at the same time we note the minoritized family's agency working for positive changes. A practical theology takes the interracial and queer family seriously as interdependent relationships of love.

Chapter 3 examines children in worship or more to the point, their absence. By closely looking at a Sunday school program in a local congregation, the chapter questions a certain normative activity that privileges one group, while excluding other groups. It addresses the limitation of the age appropriate separation educational model at the cost of the absence of children in Sunday worship. Such age-separate practice reinforces the notion of independence. The exclusion of children in worship, in part, is due to the habitual and historical practices rooted in Reformed traditions. Contesting these dominant practices of worship as orderly and penitential piety, the chapter affirms positive aspects of chaos, as the tumultuous activity of daily life. Finally, a discussion of children at worship opens up a discussion of the inclusion of other minoritized groups in worship, such as those with different physical and intellectual abilities and racialized groups. It is imperative to embrace and expand these groups in worship and other church practices if we are to honor the inclusive nature of the body of Christ and the communal relationships within it.

Chapter 4 examines religious plurality and contests a notion of God in Christian teaching as status quo, while rediscovering its syncretic and hybrid practices in Christianity. Religious communities, including Christian communities, are changing. This chapter reviews multiple religious belonging issues that ecumenical churches around the world, including the World Council of Churches, have been dealing with. It probes a postcolonial concept of hybridity as a way to lift up people who belong to more than one religious and cultural tradition, especially as this pluralistic practice has been judged as unorthodox. Similar to interracial families, interreligious relationships are on the rise due to migration in the religiously pluralistic postcolonial world. The chapter examines the pitfalls of the logic of the One, which embeds Christian supremacy, while also critiquing the very notion of religion from a postcolonial optic, as we explore a theology of multiplicity. It argues that practical theology must heed the challenge of Christian-centrism by appreciating religious plurality and multiple religious belonging within Christian practices and traditions as well as religious pluralism on the level of daily life.

Chapter 5 investigates the notion of belonging and border in the context of migration. Identifying migration as a postcolonial condition, it first of all showcases Canada as a space of migration, informed by my own situation in Canada as a recent immigrant. The historical social policy on migration review reveals how Canada's construction as a White nation, to the exclusion of non-White people, has shaped its history. This particular examination connects with the developed world because critical learnings from Canada are applicable in varying degrees to other western nations. Implementing a hermeneutic use of Scripture, the chapter interprets the present human reality of migration in relation to the stories in the Bible, the family of Jesus as refugee in particular. The issue of migration as journey on the move will be explored theologically. Finally, migration is presented as a challenge and a promise for human communities.

Chapter 6, the final chapter, builds on previous chapters to get an idea of the horizons of Christian life within a cosmic community. It raises awareness of ecological and environmental realities as a critical and emerging area of practical theology. While contesting anthropocentric worldviews rooted in Christian tradition, the chapter examines human dependence on nature including animals as it is described in the Bible. Attending to the interdependent relationship between humans and non-humans, the chapter explores animal-human-divine triads deeply embedded in daily life and religious experience in the Bible. To deepen the conversation around this theme in terms of postcolonial ecofeminist and eco-theological insights, the meaning of Sabbath within the biblical vision of Jubilee will be explored. Circling back to the first chapter's exploration of interdependency, which is the central theme throughout the book, the final chapter suggests that practical theology must engage and learn to respect, restore, and recreate human and non-human communal relationships of interdependence. Such engagement involves the constant and conscious work of challenging the status quo from postcolonial feminist perspectives by attending to overlooked groups' experiences and struggles.

Note on the Term "Beyond"

The title of each chapter begins with "beyond." This word implies multiple meanings. It seeks to evoke a vision of a place that transcends or overcomes present injustices and problems. Yet, as with the conceptual problem of "postcolonialism," it does not assume closure. Colonialism has not ended.[5] In postcolonial understanding, the prefix 'post' indicates "a notion of time that is not linear but constant, marked by events that may be technically finished but that can only be fully understood with the consideration of the devastation they left behind."[6] Current events cannot be fully understood or properly solved without engaging colonial legacies of the past. The reality of "beyond" is in constant tension with the present challenges. "Beyond" points to "spatial distance, marks progress, promises the future, but our

---

5. McClinctok, "The Angel of Progress," 295.
6. Chow, "Between Colonizers," 152.

intimations of exceeding the barrier or boundary—the very act of going *beyond*—are unknowable, unrepresentable, without a return to the 'present' which, in the process of repetition, becomes disjunct and displaced."[7] "Beyond" in this sense is more than surrendering to the past time and current events. It is "hope to transcend its shortcomings."[8] It has "a spatial connotation that underlies the side of coloniality."[9] It is hope to "create a little more space to imagine that an alternative world and a different system of knowledge are possible."[10]

---

7. Bhabha, *The Location of Culture*, 4.
8. Rivera, *A Tough of Transcendence*, 10.
9. Mignolo, *Histories/Global Designs*, 91.
10. Kwok, *Postcolonial Imagination and Feminist Theology*, 3.

1

Beyond Independence

How does a person become a whole self? How can a person become an agent of personal and social transformation? Can we achieve the human virtues of equality and freedom alone? This chapter ponders these questions. It contests the notion that a person can be totally self-sufficient and self-reliable. A whole self, as the chapter seeks to demonstrate, is achieved only through the support of communities and multiple tangled and situated relationships. A wholeness of personhood is only formed and sustained by depending on others. And yet, society, especially Western society since the modern era, instills the myth that we can and should be independent. The modernist notion of the self, which is determined by individual freedom, goes back to the European Enlightenment of the eighteenth century. John Locke, among other philosophers, for example, contends that ideal society is built upon a contract between and among "free, equal, and independent" persons.[1] As it happens, Locke's philosophy assumed that the participants in this social contract would be European white wealthy males whose wealth, education, and class gave them a sense of independence and control. Postcolonial theorist Frantz Fanon argues how European individual freedom was used as a colonial strategy to divide colonized groups in the colonial process in Algeria.[2] This sugar-coated idea of freedom forms the basis of Europe's pretensions to being a universal standard of culture and civilization while dismissing the culture of the colonized and labeling it as uncivilized.

---

1. Locke, *Second Treatise on Government*, chap. 2. par 4; chapter 4, par 98.
2. Fanon, *The Wretched of the Earth*, 107.

The other problem with this myth of equality and freedom was that it presumed that every person was essentially the same. To state that people are equal may speak to a sense of fairness but it also tends to disqualify real differences from consideration, forcing all to conform to standardized conventions. Writing a theology of disability, Tom Reynolds successfully exposes the myth of equality, arguing that "among the vulnerable in society not everyone is the same. For instance, [a person] with disabilities has specific needs that cannot be addressed adequately if all are treated equally as cases to be handled impartially. . . . [I]n the name of equality a social power can be bandied that pressures minorities to accept the dominant culture's definition of who they are."[3] Feminist philosopher Eva Kittay makes a similar point: "the ideology of equality relies on a vision of autonomous individuals who stand outside relations of dependency."[4] Thus, a liberal notion of a personhood based on freedom, equality, and independence needs scrutiny.

To scrutinize such a notion we need, first, to critique independent selfhood through a gender and disability analysis. We will do this in the first part of the chapter. In the second part, we investigate the pitfalls of a notion of adulthood as independence as we also address the problems of patronizing attitudes towards children and young people. The third part includes a case study of a local congregation's communal supper event. This case study demonstrates the importance of unlearning, the practice of taking risks for new learning, and being open to unfamiliar practices. The final part of this chapter includes a reflection of a practical theology of interdependence.

Gender and Independence

John Locke's notion of personhood is gendered. When he spoke of individual independence he had men in mind; European, educated, wealthy men to be exact. Using the lens of gender and the critical tools that feminism affords, it is possible to show the ways Locke's ideas about equality and independence mask real inequality and exploitation. This is not to say that the gender category is more important than other analytical identity categories such as race and class. But it is fruitful to discuss gender because the polarized dichotomy of women and men is reinforced by other

---

3. Reynolds, *Vulnerable Communion*, 81.
4. Kittay, *Love's Labor*, 47.

categories: nature/culture, experience/reason, domestic/public, profane/sacred, emotional/rational, weak/strong, and dependent/independent. These binary polarizations create a gender hierarchy where women are subordinate to men. In this dualistic view, women and men are fundamentally and irreducibly born as unequal. This deterministic outlook justifies men's superiority as ontologically given, thus rendering any attempt to reverse that order unnatural, i.e., against the nature of things. Feminist scholars suggest, however, that gender hierarchy is constructed by society rather than a biological and ontological reality that is given at birth. Philosopher Judith Butler argues that gender only exists in a heterosexual society based on gender binary.[5] It operates "within the terms of a hegemonic cultural discourse predicted on binary structures that appear as the language of universal rationality."[6] Gender roles are "transmitted, learned, and upheld by social institutions such as education, the media, religion and family," as Elaine Graham notes.[7] This transmission is a process of gender construction and socialization. That is why feminist philosopher Simone de Beauvoir claims that "one is not born a woman, but, rather, becomes one."[8] Gender is cultivated and practiced. Gender as an act is learned and repeated. Gender is a product of human action and social relations. In light of how gender is constructed, it is false to claim that humans are independent. This critically informed understanding of gender allows us to look at the importance of relationships formed in social interactions. Humans are made in their interactions with one another.[9]

Selfhood, generally understood as a separate independent state of being as a goal of personhood, is another problematic concept. Separation coupled with independence has operated well for many centuries to promote the status of men's selfhood, representing masculinity and privileging male gender. Selfhood, when it is gendered, meaning feminized, is viewed as the lack of independence. The ideal of independence has resulted in separation and sexism, the two notions, which together have functioned as one of the most fundamental self-shaping assumptions of our culture.[10]

---

5. Butler, *Gender Trouble*, 146.

6. Ibid., 9.

7. Graham, *Making the Difference*, 216.

8. Beauvoir, *The Second Sex*, 301.

9. The early church father Tertullian made a famous remark, "Christians are made, not born."

10. Keller, *From a Broken Web*, 2.

Autonomy based on independence and separation has been regarded as a human virtue. Catherine Keller connects the particle *"vir"* in the term "virtue" to masculinity pointing out that *"vir*ility" is another sign of autonomy. However, the irony is that the concept of autonomous masculinized personhood needs a concept of the other. "He" is dependent on its complementary opposite. He needs her in a possessive and oppressive sense in order to be autonomous.[11] There is an incongruous juxtaposition of what is said (he is independent) with what is true (he is not independent). This, albeit flawed, selfhood construction has been in the Western imagination from the time of ancient Greece, as evidenced by Homer's epic poem *The Odyssey*, and still haunts our current culture including economic and political realms. Male selfhood requiring possession and control of women is extended to the dynamics of nations between the so-called First World and the Third World where the former is dependent on the latter, while the latter carries the burden and the cost of the ecological and economic devastation.[12] Many postcolonial scholars have demonstrated how the very identity of Europe is shaped by the need for Europe's colonized Others, and yet this need must be defended, if not denied. Gayatri Chakravorty Spivak clearly articulates this irony: "as the North continues ostensibly to 'aid' the South—as formerly imperialism 'civilized' the New World—the South's crucial assistance to the North in keeping up its resource-hungry lifestyle is forever *foreclosed*."[13] Here being foreclosed means a kind of "energetic and successful kind of defense" where "ego (the First World, the North, Europe) rejects the incompatible idea *together with the affect* and behaves as if the idea had never occurred to the ego at all."[14]

Disability and Independence

The irony of independence that is dependent on a gender hierarchy is made even more obvious in the irony of the claim that disability is an individual problem. It is a false notion to locate disability solely within individuals. Disability is not an individual issue but a social experience, because it is only presented as a problem when society negatively reacts to impairments that a person may have. In this regard, John Swinton

11. Ibid., 9.
12. Keller, *Apocalypse Now and Then*.
13. Spivak, *A Critique of Postcolonial Reason*, 6.
14. Ibid., 4.

Beyond Independence

attempts a definition of disability as "people's status as a *minority group*" with "a recognition of a shared experience of oppression, marginalization, and injustice" rather than as being defined by any particular impairment or difference. However, this definition of disability has a limit, he continues to argue. It is influenced by liberation and political theologies based on the notion of a just God who takes sides with the oppressed, the marginalized, and the disabled, and assumes that people with disability could organize themselves to be politically active in order to "achieve autonomy, freedom, civil rights, self-representation, and political access."[15] It seems that his attempt to proactively define disability makes use of the flawed logic of independence. In another writing, Swinton provocatively notes that "people with dementia might be better off without the language of personhood." Why? Because, he explains, people with dementia are nonproductive, their time and life is wasted. Not being of worth is being useless, thus, they cease to be persons.[16] However, the logic of personhood based on independence is unhelpful because these goals of autonomy, freedom, and political access are unobtainable by people who have intellectual disabilities such as dementia.[17]

Further interrogating independence logic, Swinton challenges the very notion of progress as a linear sense of marking the time, which has a detrimental effect on people with disability.[18] Many postcolonial scholars have also contested the myth of progress as a colonial project. European epistemology of "a temporal lineality" views history as an ordering of time, where ancestry and the past become major references for their identity.[19] Thus when your ancestors were slaves, you are still slaves, even though you are not legally so in the present. That marker of ancestry follows like a shadow. The experience Fanon had is revealing. When he travelled to Paris, the colonizers' homeland, his identity was "overdetermined from without." His black body was preconceived by white French colonizers, such that mutual recognition became impossible. Speaking in the third person, Fanon expressed his experience as follows, "the environment . . . has horribly drawn and quartered him; he feeds this cultural environment with his blood and his essences," which are "fixed" in deadly histories of enslavement and

---

15. Swinton, "Disability, Ableism, and Disablism," 445. Emphasis original.
16. Swinton, "What's in a Name?" 234–47.
17. Swinton, "Disability, Ableism, and Disablism," 446.
18. Swinton, *Becoming Friends of Time*, 35–53.
19. Ashcroft, Griffiths, and Tiffin, *The Empire Writes Back*, 36–37.

conquest.[20] Once colonized, you do not have a place in the present because you are deprived of both spatial reach (the current state of belonging) and historicity (as the past marker). In Fanon's psychiatric practice, "the colonized are vampires, a figure for this condition of non-existence, a non-existence which is not death but which is rather the undeath of vampire."[21]

The imperial idea of time is also linear, as it assumes that history progresses and develops. There is no return of history. In this notion of historical progress in a teleological sense, any kind of disability becomes a burden because it retards the progress of others and becomes a barrier to efficiency and productivity in society.[22] Here the progress of life for individuals and societies is only measured by its accomplishment and productivity. Living life in this sense is like running a race. One must run fast to the finish line. Being slow does not count as success. Not making it to the final line is deemed a failure. However, for those with developmental disabilities, the goal of life is more or less a process rather than a race to the end or a problem to be solved, approaches which seem to get in the way of "authentic ways of being human."[23]

Pertinent problems to the liberation-theological approach to disability include the assumed status quo of autonomy and independence. Liberation theologies argue that with political will and by removing barriers to social access, all may be able to ultimately achieve autonomy and independence. While the agency of people with disability is critical and the role of defending and the empowerment of the people with disabilities is also important, there is a danger with such an approach to disability, for it may become self-congratulatory and overly triumphant. The goal of autonomy forecloses the possibility of human nature as interdependent. Most of all, an appreciation of human vulnerability is missing in this approach. Vulnerability is a condition, the only human condition that belongs to everyone; nobody escapes it. In this regard, vulnerability makes us the same. Butler helpfully articulates the irony of how being the same in this regard becomes the necessary condition of our difference: "we are alike, only in having this condition separately and so having in common a condition that cannot be thought without difference."[24] We are the same as long as we are vulnerable,

20. Fanon, *Black Skin, White Masks*, 116, 216.
21. Kawash, "Fanon's Spectral Violence of Decolonization," 249.
22. Swinton, *Becoming Friends of Time*, 52.
23. Swinton, "Building a Church for a Strangers," 25.
24. Butler, *Precarious Life*, 27.

yet one's vulnerability comes to oneself and reaches to others differently at different times and in different places. That is where vulnerability requires interdependence, a need to receive life from each other in our difference. "Vulnerability," Reynolds writes, "creatively holds together equality and difference, common sharing, and the gift of distinctiveness, and opens out into a relationality of interdependence."[25] Disability in light of vulnerability consequently means "a shared *continuum*" which "might disrupt disability as a form of *Othering*, while also denouncing the myth of progress as a racing to the ending point.[26] This shared continuum must be practiced and lived out together among those who are identified as "normal" with those who are labeled as "abnormal." This living is in opposition to competition. Life in a shared continuum is not a race. It does not have to go fast. It does not have to reach to the end line since there is no end. This living with face-to-face relationships is a way to create a space of interdependence. Jean Vanier, sharing his experience in the L' Arche community, writes, "'To live with' is different from 'to do for.' It does not simply mean eating at the same table and sleeping under the same roof. It means that we create relationships of gratuity, truth and interdependence."[27]

Adulthood and Independence

Like the myths of selfhood and independence, there is also a myth of adulthood. Religious educator Gabriel Moran laments the fact that once a person reaches adulthood it is assumed that they no longer need to learn. He poses a poignant question: "If one has been (an) adult, that is, a worker, but is no longer working, what does one become? . . . The simple fact is that old age is an insoluble problem for our image of what it means to be adult. Children can grow up. . . . But there is nothing one can do to 're-adult' the old."[28] The etymology of the Greek term of pedagogy (*pedo*, meaning boy + *agogos*, meaning to lead and teach) implies the out-of-place-ness of adults in the learning process. Pedagogy, another word for the art of teaching, assumes that children (and not adults) are the ones who need to be taught and led.[29] Teachers today are challenged to imagine what it means to teach those who

25. Reynolds, "Invoking Deep Access," 221.
26. Fulkerson, *Places of Redemption*, 228.
27. Vanier, *Community and Growth*, 109.
28. Moran, *Education Toward Adulthood*, 20.
29. Moore, *Teaching as a Sacramental Act*, 12.

are already grown up. That is why the late adult educator Malcolm Knowles named the adult learner "a neglected species."[30] Given the widely assumed child-focused concept of education, scholars such as Knowles have proposed and developed "andragogy" with the hope that such a shift would properly address the importance of teaching adults.[31]

What does being an adult mean? What kinds of meanings and misconceptions are generated by the notion of adulthood? For the purpose of answering these questions, one may need to address two related issues: one is that adulthood is often thought of as synonymous with independence; the other is that an adult who is dependent is somehow regarded as deficient. There is an assumption that adults should be able to support themselves by being productive and competent. Underlying the logic of independence that is imposed upon adults is an understanding that dependence is a sign of failure. Dependent adults are deemed irresponsible and immature. There is this sense of shame or guilt generated by society regarding adults who depend on others. The logic of independence creates a stereotype or a false ideal of adulthood as "the rational, autonomous, economically productive individual," as Moran points out.[32] In this stereotype of adulthood, old people, adults with disabilities, and adults who are unemployed are regarded as a problem and a burden to society. Examining time in light of intellectual disability, Swinton astutely diagnoses the problem of time when it is understood as money and speed, combined with an awareness of the nature of our linear, progressing temporal direction. "Thinking, speed, self-awareness, and autobiographical identity," he writes, "all become entangled in what personhood is assumed to be and what is presumed necessary to retain such a status."[33] In this view of time, a normalized personhood, adulthood in particular, is about living your life as productive, as competitive, as quickly, and as efficiently as possible. Adulthood means having gained enough age; being old means you have spent a lot of time on this earth; spending a lot of time also means you should have earned lots of money because time is money. However, if as an adult one is poor, or unemployed, one is regarded as having wasted one's time; your life is a failure. If you did not work and earn enough money, your life is not successful and efficient enough. Thus, although people without wealth may be adults by age, they

---

30. Knowles, *The Adult Learner*.
31. Knowles, *The Modern Practice of Adult Education: from Pedagogy to Andragogy*.
32. Moran, *Education Toward Adulthood*, 105.
33. Swinton, *Becoming Friends of Time*, 31.

may not quite be adults because they did not meet the status quo of adulthood: money or status quo. But they are not children either. Consequently, they are out of place and outside of the norm. Unable to see dependency as a natural and necessary part of life, many adults are driven to despair. In the thought of theologian and philosopher Søren Kierkegaard, society has created and suffered from "the despair of manliness."[34] Here man in *man*liness refers to adulthood. Under the binary gender construction, Kierkegaard saw that human society was sick unto death, wrestling with these two modes, an arrogant masculinity seeking to be independent and a docile dependent femininity.[35]

Postcolonial scholars Gaile Cannella and Radhika Viruru make interesting points regarding the work and play binary which was implicated in shaping colonial and Western capitalist views of the world. Contesting predetermined childhood normality, they interrogate play as the work of children.[36] Even well-meaning educators, who promote the importance of play as a creative process of children's development and learning, think of play as a normal and natural way that children progress toward being adult. Conversely, it implies there is no place for play once a child reaches adulthood. They write, "Binary interpretations of the world are perpetuated in at least two ways: (1) the separation between the child and adult is widened because child is grounded in the discourse of play while adults must function in the world of work. (2) Younger human beings are again treated as ahistorical, universal objects who are ignorant."[37] This work-play binary belittles the role of play as unproductive, the thing to be grown out of once children reach adulthood. It also makes adults who value and practice play out of place because it is an activity that only belongs to children. According to practical theologian Jaco Hamman, playing also poses a problem for practical theology when practical theology is preoccupied with "a definite *telos*, or end . . . or a specific (ortho) praxis of the church such as mission, formation, or justice." It is a problem, Hamman continues to explain, because "playing is nonpurposive and autotelic. . . . It is engaged for its sake."[38] Putting Cannella and Viruru in conversation with Hamman, one may ask if practical theologians unintentionally race into the world

---

34. Kierkegaard, *The Sickness unto Death*, 200–203.
35. Cited in Keller, *From a Broken Web*, 34.
36. Cannella and Viruru, *Childhood and Postcolonization*, 105.
37. Ibid., 107.
38. Hamman, "Playing," 43–44.

of academic work, boasting about their productivity that is "built around clearly defined, repeatable processes, and lucid description." The point is not to dismiss this work of practical theology's academic vigor but to nuance it by juxtaposing the role of play that "thrives on ambiguity, paradox, and multiplicity in meaning" because this, too, is the role of practical theology.[39] Another practical theologian Bonnie Miller-McLemore makes this point by blurring work as adult and play as childlike binary, as she shares her experience of playing with her children. In that chaos of playing, as an unstructured activity, hanging out with children, adults actually begin to appreciate meanings of life, even priority of life. The practice of play in the complexity of play holds paradoxes and creates liminality.[40]

Once the idea of adulthood as independent, strong, and capable is established, the flip side of the idea with regards to children can also be established. Children and young people (before reaching adulthood, though it is debatable at what age one reaches adulthood) are helpless and unable to contribute. All they do is play. Modernity as an outcome of the Enlightenment privileges adults, specifically adults who work, accomplish, and compete. An influential Enlightenment theologian Friedrich Schleiermacher wrote a seminal book, *On Religion*, which opened up the study of comparative religion. In it he claimed that only Christianity is worthy of "adult humanity," while other religions are "childlike."[41] Here religious hierarchy is established based on ageism. Postcolonial theorist Ashis Nandy who studied human development points out the same problem with colonial hierarchy. Reviewing the writings of the missionary David Livingstone and Spanish Europeans, he reveals how these colonialists concluded that African peoples' development remained in childhood or developed to the stage of adolescents but never reached adulthood.[42] Colonial conquest, as the impositions of power, has been justified as the work of looking after children—"to ensure a better future for them, to save their souls." That is why Cannella and Viruru call for an examination of childhood as a "colonizing construct."[43]

One use of the age hierarchy is to dehumanize people who are colonized, who are intellectually challenged, those who are younger and who

39. Ibid., 44.
40. Miller-McLemore, *In the Midst of Chaos*, 127–50.
41. Schleiermacher, *On Religion*, 238–41. This book was published in 1831.
42. Nandy, *The Intimate Enemy*, 15–16.
43. Cannella and Viruru, *Childhood and Postcolonization*, 3, 83.

are dependent of others and society, due to economic and other reasons. We live in the postmodern, postcolonial era, yet children as a marginalized group, and nations that are represented as children, are still ignored and not valued except for what they can become. The only thing that matters about children is that they "[need] to be made into adults," religious educator John Westerhoff criticizes.[44] Again what is implicit is a violent myth of progress. Adults and developed countries are still on center stage, while others are pushed aside. This refusal to recognize what young people are capable of results in a refusal to acknowledge the wisdom and value not only of children but of whole cultures and communities.

The issue of the value and the role of children will be further elaborated in Chapter 3 when we deal with children at worship because among many aspects of church life, it is the worship space where children are most invisible and excluded.

The false notion of independence is an intimidation bumped against as a thick wall. To break it down there is much work to be done. For this task, I suggest a practice of unlearning, a necessary step for affirming an interdependent way of life. The following case study of an event in a local mainline congregation explores this practice. The participants in this event engaged in an unlearning process, meaning they undertook things that they have not done before. Instead of repeating the cliché, "we have always done it this way," they took a risk of unlearning familiar things and ventured into new learnings. This case study loosely utilizes the "participatory action research" method of practical theology.[45] Practical theologian Elizabeth Conde-Frazier articulates this method, citing Cornel West who urged people in the academic and professional life to "give up their search for the foundations of truth and the quest for certainty and to shift their energies to defining the social and communal conditions by which people can communicate more effectively and cooperate in the process of acquiring knowledge."[46] West calls us to pay attention to the dynamic of ordinary people's lives as an important epistemological and hermeneutical source for doing practical theology. Conde-Frazier argues that this method is helpful when we diagnose and attend to the situations of a specific faith community. It is particularly important when we address a social injustice that excludes and denies the dignity of people. Participatory action research

---

44. Westerhoff, "Foreword," 11.
45. Conde-Frazier, "Participatory Action Research," 234–43.
46. West, *The American Evasion of Philosophy*, 213.

method enhances "a capacity for networking and for facilitating the formation of relationships."[47] The following case study demonstrates such capacity, while revealing challenges to cultivate just relationships. My position in describing the events and reflecting upon them is that of a participant-observant, although I did not formally conduct a qualitative research there. This participatory-observation method includes simply participating in a group's life and reflecting on that experience. The following description and reflection are a result of attending a church supper program for a year.[48]

Case Study: The Monthly Friday Community Supper

From 2013–14, the church I attended regularly tried something that they have not done before. It was called "the Monthly Friday Community Supper." This supper had no purpose other than to gather people for a shared meal. It was not a fundraising event or an education program. Nor was is an outreach supper, like a meal for the homeless. There was no "big" agenda and it did not require "huge" preparation. Instead the supper simply aimed to cultivate a desire to get together and eat as a church community. There was a self-identified cook (not a professional chef but a volunteer) who willingly offered his gift to prepare the main dish for the whole group so that people could just come and enjoy. Those who wished to bring them provided small side dishes. An offering basket was made available to help cover the cost of the main dish. The food that was left over went to homeless people through local organizations.

I would call this supper faithful, following the wise words of the homilist of the Letter to the Hebrews, "Now faith is the assurance of things hoped for, the conviction of things not seen" (11:1). It was faithful because nobody exactly knew who would show up or how many would come. There was no guarantee that there would be enough food or sufficient donation to cover the expense. They had to learn to trust God who would assure them of things that they hoped for out of this gathering. Not only did they have to trust God but they also had to depend upon each other.

---

47. Conde-Frazier, "Participatory Action Research," 237.

48. Fulkerson, *Places of Redemption* in which she lays out her own experience of being participant observant at Good Samaritan United Methodist Church. She has conducted interviews, attended Sunday worship services, Bible studies, meetings, and every kind of church event for more than two years.

The church was in Canada, near a university. Among those who attended from time to time was a PhD student from India. He would come early to help set up the tables and chairs. He did not have any official position in the church. But he was eager to help and his help was greatly appreciated. When it was time to eat, he would disappear for an hour and reappear with a big pot of savory curry. While most people by this time were finished eating and their stomachs were quite full, they were happy to taste what he brought. While he had to eat mostly left-overs, people were eager to serve him and share what they had. This disruptive, even disorderly but generous act taught the rest of the participants to value different contributions. This incident taught about the interdependent life of the church, serving and being served.[49]

To our surprise, this supper gathering grew from twenty people to forty to sixty people. The people who came out included seasoned members and new comers, even a few visitors. The supper in itself was a community-building event, strengthening existing relationships in the church, while expanding the relationships to others who were not church members. When some in the church wanted to organize an evening event for seniors aged ninety and up, it was decided to do so in combination with this event, due to its success. In this celebration of honoring elders, we had eighty-two people who came and shared the meal together (this church usually has about 120 people for the worship service on regular Sundays). Some of those who were in their nineties and unable to come to church regularly for Sunday worship service made an effort to come out with the support of their families and church members. It was quite a feast, not only from the food perspective, but also from the variety of the people who came out. The church noticed the importance of the event and decided to keep it going the following year of 2014–15, even though the volunteer chef (who had only committed for one year) was not able to do it. Someone else had to step up, and the church was convinced and believed things would continue to work out.

A Critical Reflection of the Case Study

As mentioned above, this monthly Friday community supper had never been tried before in this particular church. One of the challenges of ministry

---

49. Kim-Cragg, "To Love and Serve Others," 24–32 where I have shared this story and the theological reflection upon this story.

in the mainline churches these days is resistance to change. People seem to be afraid to try new things. This is a sad sign of "the sanctioned practice of unlearning," as I call it. Play writer and essayist Carl Hancock Rux offers salient advice in this regard: "True learning has to involve unlearning—we all have to 'forget what we think we know' in order to arrive at the next relevant idea. And this is extremely dangerous, because knowledge means death."[50] Rux describes the danger (of forgetting) and death (as unlearning). His work points to the ways learning can be both a barrier to transformation and a gift. Such gatherings as the Friday community supper inevitably involve new encounters with others and lead people into unfamiliar spaces.

New encounters can feel strange. The feminist queer theorist Gloria Anzaldua speaks of this risky encounter as the borderlands. The borderlands are "physically present wherever two or more cultures edge each other . . . where under, lower, middle, and upper classes touch, where the space between two individuals shrinks with intimacy. . . . Ambivalence and unrest reside there and death is no stranger."[51] Practical theologian Mary McClintock Fulkerson offers her uncanny experience of such encounters when she, as a white and able-bodied woman, entered the Good Samaritan church in which a good three-fourths of the people were non-white and another big portion of the members were people in wheel chairs, with Down syndrome and other disabilities. "My feeling of strangeness in response to the unaccustomed 'blackness' of the place and the presence of people with disabilities at that first visit, suggests that my conscious commitments to inclusiveness were not completely correlated with my habituated sense of the normal."[52]

Venturing into new things with new encounters can indeed feel strange and abnormal. It can also be risky. Not knowing what to expect when such encounters occur, trying new things that we have not done before, can be fearful and scary. However, learning always involves such risks. Taking on new things and learning new skills and new ideas require departure from comfortable and familiar spaces of previous knowing. Often newness cannot be learned when old knowledge and old ways of doing and thinking take up too much space in our educational realms. However understandable and even natural it is to hesitate to give up familiar and comfortable

---

50. This is shared by Carl Hancock Rux, who was interviewed for the season preview conversations. http://www.tcg.org/publications/at/2001/carl.cfm accessed July 26, 2014.

51. Anzaldua, *Borderlands/La Frontera*, 4.

52. Fulkerson, *Places of Redemption*, 15.

ways, the knowledge that was learned and accumulated in the past inhibits new growth. However, in seeking interdependent ways of life, death of the familiar can lead to life, and life too narrowly defined by what is normal can lead to death. Growth happens not only through gains but also through losses. Thus we must practice unlearning in order to grow. We must lose in order to gain. Unless the old habitual ways are dismantled, new learning or new practices may not be possible to crack open.

Reformed theologian Karl Barth, advocating the vocation of youth, says "[t]hat the young person still relatively without experience means that he [sic] is not in such danger of already being the slave of habit, chained to a routine and therefore traditionalistic.... He [sic] should not be the victim of boredom because everything is so familiar.... He [sic] is also lacking in material to ... learn it off—notions which he might be tempted to make normative for his future."[53] Barth's warning has a pedagogical and practical implication: it is not good to be too comfortable about ways of being the church and being Christian. To be too familiar is often not conducive to learning. While it is good to cultivate muscle memory through practices of repetition that are formative in faith, it is also critically important to acknowledge when such familiar and comfortable practices prevent us from moving forward, preventing new understandings from emerging. In this regard, the Friday community supper turned out to be a venture into the unknown, ushering into unexpected learning through the practice of unlearning. Practical theologian Mary Elizabeth Moore says that we need power for breaking rules and taking risks for this kind of new learning.[54]

One of the most unexpected learnings out of the Friday Community Supper was the cross-generational and inter-cultural learning thanks to those individuals' heterogeneous identities and their willing and generous participation. University students came. Young married couples without kids came. A few families with younger children came. Seniors came, many of them who live alone. Longtime white residents of Saskatoon came, but people from China, India, Dubai, Madagascar, Sudan, and England were represented. It was a multi-racial, multi-national, and multi-generational event. Families of different kinds attended as well: same-sex couples, heterosexual couples, and singles with friends, as well as inter-racial families with adopted and foster children. Stalwart church leaders and those who

---

53. Barth, *Church Dogmatics* 3:4, 607–12.
54. Moore, *Teaching as a Sacramental Act*, 193–94.

were only loosely or temporarily connected to the church broke bread together. In a sense everyone was giving up comfortable and familiar habits around socializing with others and together people gained wisdom in terms of creating a new memory, a new learning, and a new vision of their church.

This memory includes joy. The Friday Community Supper created a sense of joy in getting together, eating together, and simply "hanging out" and "having fun" together. People tasted community. They learned how to play. Children brought games and taught and played with adults. They learned that church can be a place of fun and play, creating an alternative narrative against the dominant narrative that "play has very little to do with faith."[55] They re-learned how crucial that food sharing is to building up the church as the Body of Christ. The theologian Jung Young Lee, sharing his own pastoral ministry experience among Korean immigrants in the USA, argues that it is crucial to Korean American churches to gather together for meals. He claims that the community meal is much more important than communion at Sunday service. In the cell group, as he calls the basic community unit of the church, Lee finds a clue to understanding the growth of Korean-American churches. Lee describes the cell groups that usually meet every Wednesday evening as follows: "Marginal people in cell groups like to eat together.... They prepare a full meal, which is their communion. They avoid a tiny piece of bread or wine from a plastic cup. Just as Jesus ate with his own disciples, they want to eat together in the presence of Christ, the margin of marginality."[56] The table community Jesus created is served with daily food of the ordinary rather than the sumptuous food of the wealthy. The late liturgical theologian and historian James White writes, "The use of common food is at the heart of the eucharist. Christ did not choose nectar and ambrosia, food of gods, but bread and wine, the food of humans."[57] What makes the eucharist sacramental for the church that Lee served is how people who shared the full meal recognize the presence of Christ in their midst. As long as this meaningful recognition is explicit their meal is sacred. He continues, "After a communion meal or love feast [in that cell group gathering], marginal people discuss their social and political concerns, and plan action to improve their community."[58] Gillian Feely-Harnik who studied early Christianity and Judaism contends that food, not

---

55. Miller-McLemore, *In the Midst of Chaos*, 128.
56. Lee, *Marginality*, 141.
57. White, *Introduction to Christian Worship*, 261.
58. Lee, *Marginality*, 136.

symbolic food, but actual daily food, is the most important language in which Jews expressed relations among people and between human beings and God.[59] It is no wonder why the ministry of Jesus was heavily centered around food! He ate and drank with people as a way of showing God's love beyond social boundaries and human-made barriers. This meal sharing became the cornerstone of a healthy and just community.

What was revealed in the monthly Friday Community Supper event was a sense of gratitude, a communal attitude of thankfulness for the food prepared for them and for the time that was spent with one another. The very act of thanksgiving is a form of knowing God. This form of knowledge is spiritual knowledge, which is never purely intellectual but always involves physical senses, as argued elsewhere.[60] It teaches "a capacity for sustained gratitude" and cultivates affections of gratitude, liturgical theologian Don Saliers claims.[61] To learn to be thankful or to deeply embody such gratitude as a way of life requires more than acquiring information about gratitude, or learning about gratitude cognitively or historically. One must experience it. The search for gratitude must eventually lead one to *feel* gratitude.[62] That is why this event created a teaching moment of gratitude and a sense of community in profoundly incarnational ways.

Practice of Unlearning Independence

The practice of unlearning independence is especially critical when we consider accumulated knowledge that has a political weight. When certain knowledge is produced and learned over time, it becomes a gatekeeper that disallows new knowledge from being introduced. For example, the knowledge of self-sufficiency and independence is a result of the idea of individual freedom, equality, and democracy. This knowledge, then, is practiced socially and institutionally over time, and gains political power. When the social problem of poverty, as an example, arises and a growing number of people struggle to get by, the old assumed knowledge about independence can get in the way of dealing with the problem. The ideology of independence is used to diagnose the problem and determines that poor people do not deserve to be helped because they are lazy. This

---

59. Feely-Harnik, *The Lord's Table*.
60. Kim-Cragg, "Through Senses and Sharing," 34.
61. Saliers, *Worship as Theology*, 86–99.
62. Moore, *Teaching as a Sacramental Act*, 145.

socially sanctioned ideology of independence teaches that people living in poverty need to learn to be independent and work harder. The ideology of independence is often applied to support the claim that people with disabilities are a burden to society. In this commodified capitalistic society, people's worth is measured by how capable, able, and independent they are. Certainly people with disabilities are costly, and wasteful of social capital under the logic of independence. It is startling to note that a highly educated person such as Baroness Mary Warnock, a renowned British philosopher and ethicist, promotes this kind of disturbing idea. "If you're demented, you're wasting people's lives—your family's lives—and you're wasting the resources of the National Health Service." She even suggests that people with dementia should be encouraged to take their own lives. What Warnock's dangerous view conceals is a justifiable rationale for killing people, as Swinton rightly points out.[63] Following her logic, if people are not cognitively aware, and are dependent on the support of families and communities, then they do not deserve to live. As I was writing this chapter, there was shocking news in the media about a nurse who killed eight elderly people in three different long-term care facilities. Elizabeth Wettlaufer, who became one of the most prolific serial killers in Canadian history, told the police that she had the "surge" to kill them because she said, "This must be God because this man (who had Huntington's disease) isn't enjoying his life at all." Wettlaufer also thought of another person who had dementia who "seemed to be wanting to die." The last murder she committed was of a person in her care who had been kicking her and yelling at her. She thought to herself, "enough is enough."[64]

Under the guise of independence, freedom and equality abandon the community and society's responsibility for the vulnerable. The apathy of those who are wealthy and systematic social ills are masked. In fact, certain forms of vulnerability become targets of violence serving as a coping mechanism of self-defense. As Jean Vanier suggests, "tears and violence can be ways of protecting ourselves from what is unbearable, from our own vulnerability, from our own pain."[65] When we encounter people who are poor, who are homeless, who are dirty and ugly, and people with profound disabilities, we

---

63. Macadam, "Interview with Mary Warnock," cited in Swinton, *Becoming Friends of Time*, 37.

64. https://www.thestar.com/news/canada/2017/06/01/elizabeth-wettlaufer-woodstock-nurse-guilty-murder.html

65. Vanier, *Befriending the Stranger*, 12.

are faced with our own fragility and vulnerability, which is difficult to admit. We may never find out why Wettlaufer killed these elderly and infirm people. However, one may speculate that if she had seen her own fragility and vulnerability she might have been more sympathetic. Perhaps she was trying to kill her own vulnerability, her own disability by killing them. We are also faced with social limits that counter the never-ending progress narrative, revealing the myth of success, "taken-for-granted perceptions of human flourishing." Unfortunately, this harsh and disturbing reality does not "draw out love and a desire to love" but instead "draws out anxiety and fear." That is why "violence is the inseparable companion of fear."[66]

However, being awakened by this dangerous side of the human condition should lead to neither cynicism nor despair. Unlearning such mystified knowledge of independence can be transformative, for this leads to profound teaching of humility, with a vision of creating a more equitable interdependent society. Of course, this transformation is hard work. It does not happen overnight or occur easily. Such ideology of independence, fueled by ideals of individual freedom and equality creates cultural and social accumulative norms. When individuals practice this ideology as knowledge daily, it is preserved and registered as a normative and collective memory. Therefore, unlearning takes the persistent and patient practice of unwinding the habitual patterns and ideas.

Let us take democracy, one of the most idealized Western values and principles, as a case to make this point explicitly. Fumitaka Matsuoka argues that harm has been done in the name of democracy and freedom especially to racialized and minoritized people. "[D]emocracy should not be essentialized as a universal sacred cow for America. It has its own historical and cultural context from which it originated. . . . That is to say that democracy needs to be tempered by the relational nature of human life that takes into consideration the voices of those who have rights but who are unable to exercise the rights."[67] These voices are the voices of the minoritized. Moore agrees with Matsuoka here. In advocating a theology of paradox and parable, she coins the term, God's "moreness" expressed in Jesus' ministry with children as the little ones (read as the minoritized). She captures this theological teaching of moreness poetically, "God is more than meets the eye—present and visible, yet mysterious and invisible; part of daily life, yet pulling life toward eschatological hope; caring for the smallest and

---

66. Swinton, *Becoming Friends of Time*, 36.
67. Matsuoka, *Learning to Speak a New Tongue*, 14.

humblest parts of creation, yet seeing in them more than others see."[68] This theology of "moreness" is directly connected with the postcolonial practical theology where a sense of being "beyond" is recognized and where belief embraces uncertainty instead of security. One of the enterprises of practical theology is to teach trust. To teach trust is to teach to question. To question is to doubt without falling into despair. Knowing embraces not knowing and learning involves unlearning. In other words, Matsuoka says, "what we believe is not the ultimate. We need the sense of openness and receptiveness to something beyond our own individual values and convictions. What we need today is a recovery of the relational nature of human and ecological life where the values such as caring of others, integrity of self, and trust in the openness of the future are nurtured."[69]

Toward a Postcolonial Feminist Practical Theology of Interdependence

Our very birth is a product of a relationship. No human being can be born alone. When one begins to learn and grow, one needs to depend on others. "We owe everything to others, including the things that we take for granted, such as our ability to learn to speak a certain language," as Joerg Rieger and Kwok Pui-lan claim.[70] To recognize that we owe everything to others means to acknowledge the limits of human existence. Candidly speaking, to have limits is to be human. "Our limits need not (and ought not) be seen as negative, but rather . . . they are an important part of being human."[71] To have limits as a human means that we fully acknowledge the dependence of others. A Korean-Chinese etymology of being human figuratively illustrates this point well. A person "인간," "人 間" (pronounced as *InGan* in Korean) consists of two words, "人(in)" meaning "a person" and "間"(gan) means "between." The character "人," by depicting two lines leaning on one another, suggests that we are persons by virtue of the fact that we lean on each other. It may be interpreted to mean that people cannot stand alone; we need another to rely on. When we put the two characters, "人,"

---

68. Moore, *Teaching as a Sacramental Act*, 99.
69. Matsuoka, *Learning to Speak a New Tongue*, 131–32.
70. Rieger and Kwok, *Occupy Religion*, 64.
71. Creamer, *Disability and Christian Theology*, 64.

(in) and "間" (gan) together we get "person-between" suggesting that what makes us human are the relationships between us.[72]

This Asian anthropological wisdom meets Jewish wisdom. In Hebrew language, the word justice, often translated as righteousness, "*tsedhaqah; tsedheq*" primarily refers to conduct in relation to others, especially with regard to the rights of others. (Lev 19:35, 36; Deut 25:13–16; Amos 8:5; Prov 11:1; 16:11; Ezek 45:9, 10). Justice in the Hebrew understanding is right relationships. The other biblical view of justice is duty; our obligation to others, as the act of mercy. To "seek justice" or "to do justice" (Micah 6:8) means to "relieve the oppressed, give orphans their rights, plead for the widow" (Isa 1:17; compare 11:4; Jer 22:15, 16; Ps 82:2–4). The same idea appears in Deut 24:12, 13 and Pss 37:21, 26; 112:4–6, where the translation is "righteous" instead of "just." The biblical understanding of justice promotes the communal and relational aspect of personhood. In the biblical world, the corner stone of personhood is built upon the right relationship articulated as "the restoration of relationship so that the oppressed are not only included but also seen as essential for the well-being of the community."[73] The self becomes whole and grows into the full personhood as a person works and lives out a restoration of the community through interdependent relationships. Most of all, the health of this community is measured by how the vulnerable are treated, as the apostle Paul aptly illustrates, ". . . Those members of the body that we think less honorable we clothe with greater honor, and our less respectable members are treated with greater respect, whereas our more respectable members do not need this" (1 Cor 12:23–24). In this regard, "Reconciliation without justice is a fiction" as Lee contends, "when the norm shifts from centrality to marginality, the church is placed at the margin of the world. To be at the margin means to be a servant of world, even of the world at the center. This idea is a paradox of the Christian faith."[74] "Justice," according to Rieger and Kwok, means, "bringing those who have been treated unjustly back into the community while challenging those who have promoted injustice and curbing their transgressions."[75]

---

72. Kim-Cragg and Doi, "Intercultural Threads of Hybridity and Threshold Spaces of Learning," 268.
73. Rieger and Kwok, *Occupy Religion*, 99.
74. Lee, *Marginality*, 197, footnote #13 and 146.
75. Rieger and Kwok, *Occupy Religion*, 64.

A postcolonial feminist practical theology of interdependence rooted in these biblical traditions understands that we believe in God who desires right relationships. We also believe that this God is in relationship with the cosmos, a universe made up of relationships of interdependence. We can only know God through the relationships of which we are a part. God is a relational being. That is why God is incarnational, taking on human flesh in Jesus Christ. Furthermore, this God is the God who takes the side of the oppressed, the vulnerable, the weak, and the ones who have to be dependent on others. Our faith deepens when we know that our very life is at the mercy of God, who is wholly the Other. Here God's Otherness is not a matter of detachment from us but a matter of difference from a reality that is often manipulated by human greed and power. God is not an impartial or indifferent being who stays out of our problems but a compassionate being that hears cries and sees our pain (Gen 16:13). God's Otherness points to the uncontrollability and impossibility of limiting God to our own human comprehension. God does not fit in the human box. God will not be found where God can be controlled. Despite the powerful assumptions of modern society, deep in our hearts we know that we are "dependent beings who only can abide in the difference God has made and is making."[76]

In exploring a practical theology of interdependence from a postcolonial feminist approach we also acknowledge a God who is dependent on us. This may be a challenging thought for some Christians, including the eleventh-century Anselm of Canterbury. He asks, "how art thou . . . compassionate, and at the same time, passionless?"[77] Unable to admit that God can be dependent on humans, Anselm concludes that we experience God as compassionate but this does not tell us who God really is. God in essence may not be compassionate. God is incomprehensible. In short, Anselm concludes that God cannot be known through our experiences. If we follow this logic, our experience is denied as a valid form of knowledge. According to Anselm, human experience of God is reduced as an illusion, not an accurate reflection of God's essence. What we know of God is not real because our experience cannot substantiate the existence of God.

Anselm is not alone; many Christians who are particularly limited by modernity cannot accept the notion of God needing us. The nineteenth-century theologian Søren Kierkegaard dismissed the idea that God is dependent on us. He writes, "this is stupidity, for God needs no man [sic].

---

76. Westerhoff, "Foreword," 12.
77. Anselm, *Basic Writings*, 11.

It would otherwise be a highly embarrassing thing to be a creator, if the result was that the creator came to depend upon the creature."[78] Though the theological position of Anselm and Kierkegaard is dominant, however logical it may sound, it does not satisfy some theologians and Christians in the twenty-first century, including Stanley Hauerwas, who challenges overconfidence in the notion of independence as the ability and the product of modernity. Reflecting on the experience of people with profound intellectual disabilities, such as those who have significant learning difficulties, he writes, "the challenge of learning to know, to be with . . . is nothing less than learning to know, be with, and love God. . . . For the God we Christians must learn to know to worship is not a god of self-sufficient power, a god who in self-possession needs no one; rather ours is a God who needs a people."[79]

Feminist, postcolonial, and practical theologians have helped understand the ways in which God is experienced. Of course, we cannot know God in totality, they say, but we can know God through our experiences, however partial and limited. To use Mayra Rivera's words, God is beyond us but "not beyond our touch."[80] Rivera's theology invites human communities to envision ethical relationships between themselves and creation, seeking interdependent relationships. There are a few other theologians who developed their theology based upon interdependence.[81]

Catherine Keller offers an interesting point for understanding theories. The word theory, rooted in the Greek term *theoria*, means vision. "To see connections, we must see connectively."[82] Her insight is intriguing because it denounces the dualism between reason and experience and the binary between theory and practice. If the very notion of theory is experiential, involving practice, theology as theory must also involve experience and practice. That is exactly what John Swinton also argues when he articulates what practical theology learns from theologies of disabilities and vice versa.

---

78. Kierkegaard, *Concluding Unscientific Postscripts*, 240.

79. Hauerwas, *Suffering Presence*, 104.

80. Rivera, *The Touch of Transcendence*, 2.

81. Liturgical theologian Kathy Black develops a theology of interdependence, addressing the issue of disability in preaching. See her *A Healing Homiletic*. Biblical scholar Musa Dube wrote a stellar book promoting interdependence as a goal of the biblical interpretation. See her *Postcolonial Feminist Interpretation of the Bible*; Religious educator Boyung Lee, adopting Dube's biblical hermeneutics to her pedagogy of interdependence. See her "Toward liberating Interdependence: Exploring an Intercultural Pedagogy."

82. Keller, "From a Broken Web," 159.

"When faced with the realities of human experience, the theory-practice gap inevitably closes down."[83] In order to see human connections with God as a task of doing theology and theorizing, we must see how God is connected through our experiences, i.e., our practices and our ordinary experiences. Irenaeus of Lyon lifts up this point: "*Gloria Dei vivens homo, vita autem hominis visio Dei*" (the glory of God is the human being fully alive; or to be alive to the glory of God).[84] The glory of God is known through the joy and the pain of human life—that is, the experiences of being alive. Even in death and suffering, the opposite of life and joy, we can still or even more clearly and intimately see and experience God. The Nobel Prize winner Elie Wiesel illustrates this point viscerally. "Where is God?" a man behind him asked. "He [sic] is hanging here on the gallows," he answered. This conversation happened at a Nazi concentration camp.[85] Wiesel's answer is not a simple answer but an answer pointing to a divine-human connection, which is the work of theology. Fulkerson calls for theology "as a response to a wound" because theology involving "creative thinking originates at the scene of a wound" where theologians are "compelled to find new connections in thought, to brokenness in existence, where creativity is compelled to search for possibilities of reconciliation."[86] To see this divine-human connection as theology is to feel the wounds of living beings. Alice Walker captures this point in the words of Shug in *The Color Purple*, "I knew that if I cut a tree, my arm would bleed."[87] Thus, to know is to feel. To feel is to be in connection. To connect is to recognize others. To recognize others is to practice an interdependent way of life.

Finally, in developing a concept of interdependence in practical theology we must expose the masquerade of equality and individual freedom that perpetuates the status quo, benefitting some, at the expense of others.[88] It draws from postcolonial realities that point to a critical need for creating an interdependent life, while addressing power differentials among people and nations. To teach interdependence means to teach both of these power differentials through critical analysis of systematic oppressions. To practice

---

83. Swinton, "Disability, Ableism, and Disablism," 450.

84. Irenaeus of Lyons, *Against Heresies* 4.20.7. Mary Ann Donovan elaborates his phrase in "Alive to the Glory of God: A Key Insight in St. Irenaeus," 283–97.

85. Elie Wiesel, *Night*, cited in Rivera, 55.

86. Fulkerson, *Places of Redemption*, 13.

87. Walker, *The Color Purple*, 167.

88. Kittay, *Love's Labor*, 184.

interdependence means to recognize each other's differences including inequity and unearned privilege, while affirming needs of each other and yearning for mutuality. It is about attending to those in need for the sake of the empowerment of the marginalized and oppressed in church and society. A postcolonial feminist practical theology of interdependence encourages the community to redress power imbalance and model the practice of interdependence as a communal way of life.

2

Beyond Homogenous Heterosexual Family

BUILDING UPON THE CRITICISM of self-autonomous individualized culture that promotes independence given in the previous chapter, this chapter investigates the heterosexual white family as the norm that is dominant in our religious communities and our secular society. It explores the changing face of the family by navigating three different trajectories: race, sexuality (sexual orientation and gender identity), and age (with a focus on young people) by treating these identity factors in intersecting and interconnected ways. In order to highlight the changing demographics of the family make-up as both problem and promise for practical theologians in the twenty-first century, we will focus our reflections on the reality of mixed-race and queer[1] youth and young adults. We will draw attention to interracial couples, some of which are in same-sex relationships and caring for mixed-race young people. Here interracial families are understood as couples in relationships whose races are different, which includes white and non-white but not limited to that mix. Interracial relationships as a particular form of the family have existed since the beginning of human history. However, this configuration represents a growing proportion of families in the twenty-first century around the world, in part due to global migration in the postcolonial world.

---

1. Here I use the term, "queer" whose identity is not bounded by the gender binary form of male and female. The term queer is used here to include both the members of the Lesbian, Gay, Bisexual, Transgender, and Two-Spirit and those who are questioning their gender and refusing to be categorized into one gender. Such reference is informed by queer scholars; to name just two here: Butler, *Gender Trouble*; Althaus-Reid, *The Queer God*.

We cast a light on the role of family in practical theology by lifting up the experiences of queer and mixed-race youth. This is one way to do justice to a complex matter of studying youth as members of the family and society in practical theology. Qualitative study, using ethnographies and interview methods, stresses the importance of listening and of narrative agency, especially among youth and teenage individuals. First of all, the chapter provides rationales for why queer and mixed youth are important subject matters of practical theology, followed by a discussion of the roles of family and homes in light of these youth. Then, we move on to identify three faithful approaches to family from the perspective of practical theology: listening, checking blood, and seeing/passing. These tasks serve to build up interdependent relationships and create abundant life based upon mutual recognition and respect of difference.

Queer and Racialized Youth: Subject Matters of Practical Theology

There are at least two important justice issues that make it necessary for practical theology to discuss queer and racialized youth. The first being, that some political and legal opposition against and social discrimination of lesbian, gay, bisexual, transgender, queer (LGBTQ) people is based on religious doctrine propounded by Christians. The church has sanctioned "the cultural status quo" regarding sexuality and our education has been functioning as a "cultural captivity."[2]

The discourse on sexuality of the family cannot be separated from the discourse on patriarchy and religions. Pioneer feminist theologian Mary Daly noted the connection between patriarchy and religion almost forty years ago: "Patriarchy is itself the prevailing religion of the entire planet. . . . All of the so-called religions legitimatizing patriarchy are mere sects subsumed under its vast umbrella/canopy."[3] Anticipating the 500th anniversary of the Reformation in 2017, the World Communion of Reformed Churches (WCRC), as the biggest global ecumenical organization in the Reformed tradition, has been raising the ordination of women as something that today has still not been accepted in many reformed churches.[4] To some denominations, including The United Church of Canada, the

---

2. Foster, *Educating Congregations*, 31.
3. Daly, *Gyn/Ecology*, 39.
4. Douglas, "A Turning Point for Reformed Women in Ministry," 9–16.

discussion around women's ordination is almost a century old.⁵ However, the WCRC notes that this is not the case for at least one third of member churches, mostly located in the Global South, but some churches in Europe as well. These churches that do not ordain women are reluctant to open the discussion of the ordination of women, in part because women's issues would lead to a discussion of sexual orientation, thus opening up the door to acceptance and ordination of members of the LGBTQ community. As revealed in the ecclesial and ecumenical movements above, patriarchy is alive and well in churches, and sexism and discrimination on the basis of sexual orientation are different yet interlocking issues.⁶

While it is never too late, it is urgent that we sincerely and seriously examine our theological and doctrinal underpinnings on sexual orientation and gender identity as topics of practical theology, challenging heterosexism. But this task can be greatly assisted if we include the perspective of interracial relationships as well as the children of those relationships. As Kathleen A. Cahalan and Gordon S. Mikoski have pointed out, central to our task as practical theologians today "is an emphasis on race, ethnicity, gender, class, and sexual orientation arising from the situated and embodied character of human life."⁷ While I agree with their emphasis wholeheartedly, it is useful to note that one historical factor that ties all these issues together is lingering effects of colonialism. This reality has, however, been overlooked in theological circles. Kwok Pui-lan sounds the alarm: "While biblical and religious scholars have deployed postcolonial theory to scrutinize their respective disciplines, theologians, with a few exceptions, have scarcely paid any attention to this burgeoning field, though many are interested in the related field of postmodern studies. This oversight is unwarranted, given the lengthy history of theology's relation with empire building, especially in the modern period."⁸ Kwok not only calls for the inclusion of colonialism as a critical theme of practical theology but also takes a close look at how it is entangled with the issues of race, ethnicity, gender, class, and sexual orientation. In another writing, Kwok with Donaldson have shown that gender, religion, and colonialism interconnect

---

5. For example, Lydia Gruchy was the first ordained woman in The United Church of Canada. She was ordained in 1936.

6. Hoeft, "Gender, Sexism, and Heterosexism," 412. Sexuality is beyond the binary category of sexes between female and male, while gender is a socially constructed norm rather than inherently biological and fixed.

7. Cahalan and Mikoski, eds., *Opening the Field of Practical Theology*, 3.

8. Kwok, *Postcolonial Imagination and Feminist Theology*, 6.

in myriad ways. They operate in parallel, separate from and independent of each other, but are intricately enmeshed with one another.[9] In order to examine their intersecting and interconnected ways, we need to engage in a self-critical theological reflection, which allows us to reveal how the church's teaching and tradition function as systems of oppressions. Religious educator Jack Seymour writes, "We need to challenge (to transgress) when systems, even churches, teach us that we are less than children of God. Racism, classism, sexism, and heterosexism are just a few of the ways that the tradition is manipulated to deny to some of our brothers and sisters full life chances and their due status as children and heirs of God."[10] Seymour does not mention colonialism, but I suggest that insights into the problem that he prioritizes would benefit greatly from this approach. This is why practical theology from a postcolonial feminist perspective is urgently needed. Engaging queer and racialized youth by deploying postcolonial theory may bear much fruit for practical theology.

The second reason why we must challenge the white heterosexual norm as a reality affecting youth at the heart of the matrix of family and religions is because it is often when they are in their adolescent years that issues of sexual orientation and racial difference surface. All of the three lesbian young people that Patricia Davis interviewed for *The Sacred Selves of Adolescent Girls,* came to terms with their queer identity when they were fifteen or sixteen years old.[11] The interviewees in Pearl Fuyo Gaskins' *What Are You* shared their struggles of being mixed-race as youth and young adults.[12] This is the stage in life when young people have a sufficient amount of experience to critically reflect and think abstractly about important problems.[13] It is a time of discovery and of crisis. Their various identities are found, confused, sometimes even lost, then hopefully rediscovered and affirmed. Along with other turbulent changes, especially physical and emotional changes, it is at this time that they begin to embrace who they are fully and holistically. Many practical theologians have demonstrated the importance of narrative agency for studying female youth.[14] It is in this

---

9. Donaldson and Kwok, eds., *Postcolonialism, Feminism, and Religious Discourse.*
10. Seymour, *Teaching the Way,* 60.
11. Davis, "Okay with Who I Am," 144, 152, 154.
12. Gaskins, *What Are You?*
13. Parker, ed., "Introduction," 7.
14. Parker, *Trouble Don't Last Always,* Parker, ed., *The Sacred Selves of Adolescent Girls;* Turpin, *Branded;* Baker, *Doing Girlfriend Theology;* Dean, *Practical Passion.*

stage of adolescence that young people form their identity and construct their subjectivity through telling their life stories. It is in this time of identity-formation that youth also search for the meaning and purpose of life.[15] Quoting Walter Brueggemann's understanding of vocation, Joyce Ann Mercer argues that it is during adolescence that the question of "who we are eventually becomes a question about human purpose, a question of *whose* we are; a question of why it should matter *that* we are."[16] Because youth undergo such drastic changes with many puzzling questions, it is critical to have the support of the family who are faithfully and patiently willing to journey with them. If on the contrary, support is not provided, if the family disapproves of their gender and racial identities, it can be destructive for their spirituality since sexual orientation, gender, and racial identity are a core and a part of their sacred and spiritual identity. If such mutual support in the family is broken and lost, the healthy growth of the children and youth will be hampered. The stories of queer youth in *The Sacred Selves of Adolescent Girls*, capture the difficulty of losing the family at the expense of gaining one's identity. All of the girls speak of the importance of their family, including the role of their parents as people they can talk to, rely on, and get strength from. Yet, when they "came out," disclosing their hidden queer identity, these same girls found that their family support was gone (at least initially, though for some it later came back). Most shared that losing their family caused the worst suffering that they had ever experienced.[17] Their expressed experiences provide convincing evidence that the family is critically significant in the quest for gender identity. The family that practices and models justice, furthermore, provides a foundation of building up a just society. Feminist philosopher Susan Moller Okin who probed the connection between gender and ethics in the role of the family argues, "It is within the family that we first come to have that sense of ourselves and our relations with others that is at the root of moral development."[18] Bonnie Miller-McLemore says that the home is a place for doing justice, challenging the split between home and the world and between spirituality and justice.[19]

---

15. Parks, *Big Questions, Worthy Dreams*.
16. Mercer, "Call Forwarding," 32. Emphasis is original.
17. Davis, "Okay with Who I Am," 142.
18. Okin, *Justice, Gender, and the Family*, 14.
19. Miller-McClemore, *In the Midst of Chaos*, 101–25.

Erik Erikson reflects upon the meaning of "fidelity," and suggests that it is a virtue that must be developed during adolescence.[20] From a young person's perspective fidelity means "being there." Kenda Creasy Dean argues that fidelity cannot be taught or known unless it is received and experienced.[21] Fidelity is known by experiencing it in another person who is a part of your life. It requires the epistemology of presence. Fidelity also demands the epistemology of relationship. To be present with another person is ultimately an act of acceptance, to be open to that other person no matter who they are. Families have this quality at their core. Fidelity is only possible to learn and know when a young person experiences it, by being unconditionally accepted. Fidelity, expressed as faithfulness and loyalty, is most influentially cultivated during adolescence. This faithfulness of fidelity practiced in the family and various faith communities offers a glimpse of the steadfastness of God. So knowing and learning fidelity has a theological implication. It is difficult to articulate how we know that God is faithful unless youth experience it through and from others who surround them, especially in the family. That is why the discussion on queer and racialized youth for the role of family is important for practical theology. That is also why queer and racialized youth are important subject matters of practical theology.

Family and Home: Critical Matters for Queer and Racialized Youth

What is family? This question has never been simply answered. In the world where there are so many different kinds of family due to such events as migration, adoption, and same-sex marriage, the question of how to define family is difficult. And yet, almost everyone would agree that family is one of the most important places for the cultivation of virtues and life principles. The study of the family has been a subject matter of practical theology for many decades. Practical theologians have incorporated multiple disciplines, including feminist theory and social policy in their discussion around family.[22] Family is complex and thus it begs an investigation of the various networks and roles of the public (social and religious) institutions in addition to an examination of personal issues that unfold in families.

20. Erikson, *Identity: Youth and Crisis*, 233.
21. Dean, "Somebody Save Me: Passion, Salvation, and the Smallville Effect," 22–23.
22. Couture, *Blessed Are the Poor?*; Miller-McLemore, *Also a Mother*.

Practical theologians have made it clear that family issues are both private and public, personal and social. Interconnections between these arenas are critical. A late prime minister of Canada remarked that "[t]he state has no business in the bedrooms of the nation."[23] Pierre Trudeau's quip was made in order to introduce a family policy reform, basically legitimizing divorce, homosexuality, and abortion. In order to protect privacy and minority groups, the public, including government, has a role to play. Despite the effort of such reform, these issues continue to be relevant a half century later when one looks at the most recent Conservative Party leadership result in Canada where the support of social conservatives (who opposed abortion rights, gay rights and transgender rights) was significant.[24] Such current reality of Canada can be felt in many other parts of the world.

Family is also critical in religious life. Spiritual formation begins and continues in the family. An individual's internal sense (or loss) of identity of who s/he is and how s/he is related to the world and to God is, in part, developed through and in light of how family functions. There is much practical theology research and writing that addresses, affirms, and discusses the roles of the family. However, there are few publications that address the issues of queer families and interracial families from the perspective of youth and adolescence. That is what practical theologian and Christian educator Evelyn Parker noticed when she began her work on the spirituality of adolescent girls of color, of lesbian, and working/poor white girls. While there is a great contribution of Christian feminist, womanist, and *mujerista* theologians who articulated racism, sexism, classism, and heterosexism, she notes, there are much fewer contributions on the adolescent girls who are racialized, poor, and queer.[25]

To adequately study queer youth, practical theology must examine the prevalent notion of the family, whose parameters are often defined in white heterosexual terms. Heterosexism based on anti-homosexuality was also part and parcel of the colonial agenda. The very term, "homosexuality" was created to label the colonized cultures in which various sexual practices occur as barbaric, inferior to European Christian colonial morality.[26]

---

23. http://canadachannel.ca/canadianbirthdays/index.php/Quotes_by_Prime_Ministers_-_Pierre_Trudeau, accessed July 20, 2016.

24. https://www.thestar.com/news/canada/2017/05/28/liberals-brand-andrew-scheer-as-social-conservative-extremist-after-surprising-leadership-win.html

25. Parker, *The Sacred Selves of Adolescent Girls*, 3.

26. Aldrich, *Colonialism and Homosexuality*.

Homosexuality as a construction referred to a form of disorder and was regarded with dread.[27] The demonization of homosexuality was part of the demonization of colonized culture, which led to cultural suppression and served to establish heterosexuality as the norm. The normalization of heterosexuality is another salient example of how religion, colonialism, and sexuality are intertwined.

In order for any normativity to work, there needs to be an imagined reality that is not normal. Normativity requires and depends on abnormality. Heterosexual normativity only works on condition that those who are labelled homosexual and queer not only exist but are understood as some kind of defect or example of excess—viewing them as having either too few or too many hormones and desires. Qualitative research on mixed-race and queer families calls for an examination of this normativity. Several research projects conclude by urging practical theologians to critically examine blood purity and gender binary ideologies.[28] These groups, using lived experiences in these research projects, put forth an investigation of the myth of blood as race and that of gender as a social relation maintained by human practice and performance rather than viewing them as a biological fixed identity.[29] Their stories unravel the biases, prejudices, and fear that are prevalent and operative in the church, and most communities in society. Lifting up these experiences and stories guides a practical theology to a path that takes the interracial and queer family seriously and contributes to affirming the heterogeneous and queer family's agency for positive changes towards transformation.[30]

Additional tools critical for debunking heterosexual normative family ideology include a nuanced understanding of home. Katherine Turpin finds that the most primary and crucial environments that adolescent youth are shaped by and drawn to are the school (and their friends) and the broader culture (media in particular) rather than home. These spaces are the ones that fuel the ideals of life that may often be so different from those imbued by the family. This does not mean that home is unimportant. The practice of love and care in families, she has found, is not in vain.[31] In the

---

27. Kwok, *Postcolonial Imagination and Feminist Theology*, 138.

28. Elam, *The Souls of Mixed Race*; Bystydzienski, *Intercultural Couples*; Senna, "The Mulatto Millennium."

29. Graham, *Making the Difference*; Butler, *Gender Trouble*.

30. Marshall, *Counselling Lesbian Partners*, 131.

31. Turpin, *Branded*, 176.

later years, young adults often remember what was taught and practiced at home and rediscover the practices learned from the church that may have been dormant for a time. Such teaching becomes especially effective and transformative if what they learned at home and in the church is countercultural. Lessons that challenge consumer culture, for example, provide tools to dismantle the idea that a happy life is only determined by buying and having stuff. What has been taught in the home and the church may not always be apparent but it is, in the long term, effective.

In *What Are You?* Derek provides a great example on the crucial role of home.[32] He talks about the power of learning that happened at home.

> It's something that both of my parents had prepared me for. They always made me aware that there is racism out there. . . . When it came about, it wasn't as striking a blow for me as it may have been for others who wouldn't have been prepared for it. I have parents who are willing to teach me what I don't learn in school. . . . At my house, I've always been encouraged to read black literature and to understand both sides of our culture. At home, it's more focused on the African-American side than on the Caucasian-American, because I learn so much about the Caucasian American side in school. . . . It seems like the only time we learn about blacks in school is during February, which is Black History Month. In my house, every month is Black History Month.

Here we see that instruction happens at home as an environment where teaching, learning, and practice are intentionally present. This role of the family becomes especially crucial when the community outside the family is trapped in "avoidance responses" failing to teach critical information and faithful responsibility.[33] What Derek's parents provided is "conscious listening, responding, critiquing and questioning," as Elizabeth Caldwell helpfully articulated when she listed the critical roles of home. How fitting it is that her metaphor of such a model of instruction is "homemaking!"[34] In the home of Derek, a new world was made, while an existing dominant system was dismantled. What went on at the home of Derek became a mirror that reflected the world. Postcolonial scholar Rosemary Marangoly George asks: "When is the word 'home' shrunk to denote the private, domestic sphere

---

32. Gaskins, *What Are You?* 120. Note that I have not preserved Gaskins' convention of putting quotations in italics.

33. Seymour, *Teaching the Way of Jesus*, 136.

34. Caldwell, "Religious Instruction: Homemaking" 79–80.

and when is the 'domestic' enlarged to denote 'the affairs of a nation?'"[35] From a postcolonial feminist perspective, home is never solely private but has a historical reference that involves tribe, community, nation, gender, race, slavery, and colonial trajectories.[36]

Engagement of Queer and Racialized Youth

Listening

In examining the identities of interracial and queer youth as a task of practical theology, it must be stated from the outset that identities are never fixed but in flux. This applies to the notion of family as well. Family that forms, shapes, and influences a person's identity is therefore never fixed because members of the family are never fixed. This fact as realization is of utmost importance to the young members of families based on interracial and queer relationships. These young people engender and embrace the fluid identities of "multiplicity and heterogeneity... contingent, provisional, variable, tentative, shifting and changing."[37] How does a postcolonial feminist practical theology engage the lives of these young people and their fluid identities?

One approach to such engagement is listening. Listening is a common human practice. It is also an attitude, an intentional and deliberate behavior. Listening as *Shema* from the biblical wisdom is both an approach (method) and an instruction (content) for practical theology. The teaching of *Shema* is recognition of our humility, trusting God, who promises liberation and faithfulness in the midst of oppression and injustice. *Shema* requires discernment and discipline.[38] Listening involves hearing and telling. Melinda M. Sharp draws attention to "the postcolonial stories of intercultural misunderstanding."[39] She speaks of the creative narrative agency involved in hearing and telling. Pastoral theologian R. Ruard Ganzevoort acknowledges critical contributions of subaltern voices that challenge the narrative hegemony of dominant groups by telling the stories of personal experiences of women, people of different skin colors, and gay and lesbian

---

35. George, *The Politics of Home*, 13.
36. Kwok, *Postcolonial Imagination and Feminist Theology*, 104.
37. West, "The New Cultural Politics of Difference," 203–4.
38. Seymour, *Teaching the Way of Jesus*, 79–80.
39. Sharp, *Misunderstanding Stories*, 10.

believers.⁴⁰ Listening, as hearing and telling, also requires the humility of the ones who listen.

Listening assumes a speaker, implying that there is one who is willing to tell one's own stories. Listening also implies a learning opportunity for the hearers (audience). Hopefully, our capacity to listen points us to see God at work, even though the stories do not talk about God in any explicit ways. Precisely because God may be hidden and unspoken in their stories, it is critical to listen for how God is present in the work of empowerment and emancipation for these young people. Doris Baker values the importance of listening as a way of encouraging and engaging young people to build up their own lives.⁴¹ This listening Baker and Mercer call "holy listening."⁴² Listening to young people informs interested adults and a wider faith community about the journey with God and also creates a space for other young people to explore their own journeys. In fact, Baker and Mercer suggest that interviewing youth in the significant moments in their lives such as graduation, or losing a family member or a friend, could be a meaningful part of youth ministry.⁴³

As addressed by Parker earlier, there seems to be few studies in the field of practical theology dealing with interracial and queer young people. However, once practical theologians turn to literature in other disciplines, they may find ample materials. For example, one may find Pearl Fuyo Gaskins's work useful.⁴⁴ As a child of an interracial marriage and an award-winning journalist, she listened to the stories of interracial youth and young people over two years in order to validate their experiences through interviews. As a mother of two interracial adolescent youth, I take these stories from the work of Gaskins as a "witnessing bystander" might.⁴⁵ This rather removed yet involved position engages me in "authentic participation,"⁴⁶ which Emmanuel Lartey suggests as a justice-oriented pastoral care approach. As a witnessing bystander, I am accountable to my own bias and my limitation of

---

40. Ganzevoort, "Narrative Approaches," 214.

41. Baker, *The Barefoot Way*, 112. She suggest four approaches that help young people build their lives. "L. I. V. E."—Listen; Immerse in the feelings; View it wider; Explore Actions and "Aha" moments.

42. Baker and Mercer, *Lives to Offer*, 73.

43. Ibid., 79, 81–82.

44. Gaskins, *What Are You?*

45. Baker and Mercer, *Lives to Offer*, 78.

46. Lartey, *In Living Color*, 32–34.

Beyond Homogenous Heterosexual Family

a fragmentary nature of presenting, and even misrepresenting their stories. However, the listening captured in a vignette form below, is a way to lift up their struggles and highlight their wisdoms from lived experiences, as they negotiate interracial family issues including divorces, migration, segregated socialization at the University and problems of mixed blood construction in the name of purity.

The first story I listened to is that of Donna Maketa Randolph. She is a twenty-year-old Korean-African-American whose Korean mother was divorced from her Afro-American father. As an immigrant, her mother felt desperate after the divorce. Donna remembers her mother saying, "I am here in this country. I don't have a job or an education. I can't go home. Oh, my life is over."[47] Due to her unstable status and the lack of education in the USA, Donna embraces her mother's struggles. This experience was influential in developing her own identity. "Because we did depend on each other so much. . . . She was the one who raised me. . . . She's always been there for me. . . . [But] my mom relies on me a lot. I'm like her dictionary."[48] The notion of fidelity from our discussion earlier in the chapter seems particularly salient here. The mom was "there for me," thus I "will be there for her." Here we can also find a development of the notion of "reciprocal responsibility" in a mother-daughter relationship. Theologian Nancy Duff stresses this mutual responsibility between parents and children as she explores the meaning of Christian vocation. God calls not just parents and adults but also children and young people.[49] Love and care do not flow one way only. Children often have the capacity to help and care for their parents. This reciprocity of love in the family may become even more pronounced when the people who need each other are already minoritized in society. Donna's story demonstrates that this interdependent relationship, despite or because of their vulnerable and difficult life, is a key to survival and growth.

While most who were interviewed in the work of Gaskins responded that they had a supportive family, we should not assume or romanticize that all interracial families are more healthy or stronger than homogeneous non-interracial families. In her study of 200 interracial families, Maria Root found that families are diverse in terms of their identity performance, on one end of the spectrum as very able/confident, on the other end of the spectrum, as avoiding the issues of race, and as ignorant/indifferent of

---

47. Gaskins, *What Are You?* 92.
48. Ibid., 89, 92.
49. Duff, "Vocation, Motherhood, and Marriage," 69–81.

racism in the middle spectrum.⁵⁰ So the question remains how to cultivate a family within which complex and ambiguous identities are affirmed. The following stories of young people demonstrate this point well.

Listen to Kurtis Fujita, Japanese-European-American twenty-year-old:

> Sometimes there are questions in my mind about which side I relate to more. . . . I think a lot that comes from my parents' divorce. . . . I guess to some degree I have been trying to force myself to fit into one or the other. Now the way I feel is—I am both. . . . In a way, I'm lucky because I can fit into so many places. . . . I don't think anybody should limit themselves as to what they are. . . . You are always changing, there's a new definition for you every second. You've got to keep learning.⁵¹

Listen to Maya Corey, African-European-American, nineteen-year-old:

> As a biracial person, it's struggling to make people believe that I fit in, or even knowing where I want to fit in. I definitely went through that stage that I think a lot of biracial people go through. It's not fair for people to say that because you're biracial you're not black. . . . They are so many different kinds of black people. . . . I'm part of the whole so-called American black world experience. So that's the point that I've come to. . . . I've got a long way to go, but I've come to a point where I'm comfortable with how I consider myself. . . . Societal definitions and limits regarding racial identity and other labels don't have to have anything to do with the inside of me. I think I just grew up.⁵²

Both Kurtis and Maya seem to be comfortable with their mixed identities without choosing one at the expense of the other. While they are aware of external racial normative pressure, they seem to be able to navigate their multiple identities. However, some struggle with the wall of bias they bump into in the public space. Stuart Hay, a twenty-year old Guyanese-European-Canadian-American, shares an experience of one such wall: "A lot of times we'd be someplace together as a family, like a restaurant, and they'd ask, 'Are you all together?'"⁵³ Stuart takes this to mean that people do not see them as a family because they do not fit the box of a family that looks alike. The following responses from the interviews similarly address more challenging

---

50. Root, *Racially Mixed People in America*, quoted in Gaskins, *What Are You?* 118.
51. Gaskins, *What Are You?* 182, 183.
52. Ibid., 187, 189.
53. Ibid., 106.

Beyond Homogenous Heterosexual Family

issues, a segregated socialization, stereotypical assumptions, and a notion of blood purity.

Listen to Monina Diaz, African-American-Puerto Rican, twenty-year-old:

> I especially see it at Princeton because it's very socially segregated. You have all these different people and they align themselves along with these socially constructed lines. You put them into a dorm. . . . You put them into a cafeteria. . . . You put them into a class, they align themselves. . . . I don't know what it's like not to live in a house where there are different ethnicities, different cultures. My brothers and sisters all look completely different as far as color, and that's normal to me. . . . It's only been a hurtful issue when we step out of our house.[54]

Listen to Denise Hobson, Navajo-European-American, twenty-year-old:

> I don't think people should have to prove themselves. . . . We have a stricter blood quantum. We only go up to one-fourth Navajo blood. It bothers me that there are Navajos who grew up on the reservation but they can't be considered Navajo. . . . In my mind, traditions and culture are what make you who you are.[55]

Monina, Stuart, and Denise highlight the absurdity of superficial and ideological color lines that divide people. "Dividing people up by color is like dividing cars up by color. Color is a superficial add-on. The same is true for skin color in people."[56] However, listening to their stories makes us acutely aware how much society, even universities are still divided by skin color, which construct mixed-race people as out of place because they cannot fit into a box created for the color of their skin. Such division is further marked by blood lines, as if there is pure blood and tainted blood for the perspective of an ethnic community. The false association of blood with race begs a more focused examination. Blood purity ideology is still powerfully operative in the public psyche.

---

54. Ibid., 55, 56.
55. Ibid., 68, 70.
56. Cohen, *The Culture of Intolerance*, cited in Gaskins, 46.

Interdependence

Checking Blood

Blood has been closely linked with family, belonging, citizenship, and one's racial and gender identity. We all share blood as a biological necessity of human survival. However blood has unfortunately been used as a symbol to divide communities and discriminate against certain groups. The use of the language of blood to differentiate between genders and races and assert superiority of white males over others is a deeply seated practice in European society that has been around since ancient times. Aristotle in the fourth century BCE, for example, argued that men's blood is superior to women's blood. He had this idea scientifically "proven" by pointing out that men had sufficient heat to transform blood into semen, whereas women lacked sufficient heat to produce semen, which became the proof of the inferiority of women. Women, in contrast to men, he said, ended up with extra blood and had to expel it during menstruation. He wrote, "the woman is as it were an impotent male, for it is through a certain incapacity that the female is female, being incapable of concocting the nutriment in its last stage into semen owing to the coldness of her nature."[57] This "scientifically" substantiated claim demonstrates the way that the language of blood has been used for centuries to justify socially constructed hierarchies. This claim on the incapacity of women's blood reminds us of the heterosexual normativity's claim on homosexual people's abnormality based on a deficiency or excess of hormones. Here we can also view how gender hierarchy is closely connected to the blood discourse.

Blood donation has also been used to discriminate against gay people in relationships. In Israel, France, Greece, and the United States, gay men are not allowed to donate blood. While Canada banned this rule a few years ago, it still has a rule that only gay men who have been celibate for five years are eligible for blood donation.[58] Why five years? How absurd and arbitrary this regulation is! And how can people in the health profession exactly determine that gay men have been celibate for that period of time? The absurdity continues. Canadian renowned author Laurence Hill has done extensive research on blood as a part of his CBC Massey Lecture series. In these lectures he made a candid criticism that such exclusionary rules as exemplified by blood services in America and Europe are based

---

57. Aristotle, *Generation of Animals*, 1.20.728a16–21, cited in Sharkey, *An Aristotelian Feminism*, 85.

58. www.huffingtonpost.ca/2013/01/12/gay-men-donating-blood_n_2467103,html, accessed September 1, 2016.

on the fear of homosexuality fueled by ignorance. Agreeing with many gay rights scholars and activists, he writes, "a promiscuous heterosexual who does not practice safe sex will pose a much greater risk for the transmission of HIV than a gay male who is faithful to one partner and who uses a condom."[59]

Unfounded theories about the purity of blood as it pertains to race are another case in point. During the Second World War, Dr. Charles Richard Drew, an Afro-American leading expert in blood storage, was in charge of shipping liquid plasma from the USA to Britain for soldiers who were wounded in France. In addition to his own battle against racism, he had to face the racist policy announced by the American Red Cross in 1942 that it would exclude blacks from donating blood to white soldiers. Objections raised to this policy were such that it had to be modified. But it still remained that blood would be processed separately so that those receiving transfusions may be given blood of their own race.[60] Dr. Drew heavily lamented this nonsense: "One can say quite truthfully that on the battlefields nobody is very interested in where the plasma comes from when they are hurt. . . . The blood is being sent from all parts of the world. It is unfortunate that such a worthwhile and scientific bit of work should have been hampered by such stupidity."[61] The differentiation of blood had nothing to do with science, and everything to do with prejudice and discrimination. Dr. Bernard Lown, a white cardiologist and contemporary to Dr. Drew, was one of many who was annoyed by the discriminatory blood donation policy. In his own rebellious and mischievous way, he mixed up the tags on "colored" and "white" blood bags. As a task of practical theology, we may also join in this prophetic even playfully subversive act, combatting racism, contesting notions of pure blood that divide people and discriminate against non-white people. In the story of Denise Hobson told above, it was used to discriminate against people who were "too white" as Navajo indigenous people.

Though blood runs through most of us naturally and impartially, in our mind and social psyche, blood carries rather heavy, often tainted, bias in the way we judge people. Blood discourse is often used to destine a person's ability or gift as if it is fixed and cannot be changed. However dangerous and difficult it is to discuss blood, it is essential and critical to

59. Hill, *Blood*, 111.
60. Ibid., 102.
61. Love, *One Blood*, 155–58.

note that blood is connected to identity-formation in multiple ways. We must contest bloodline as a determined factor of one's particular identity, whether it be a racial, gender, or sexual identity. Instead, the so-called identity of blood can affirm fluid identities. Like blood, identity is fluid. Like blood, identity constantly changes and circulates. The challenge is that such fluid and changing identities are often invisible. We simply cannot know which race one represents by the way the person looks. In the same way, we simply cannot know what gender identity one has by the way the person behaves. Therefore, one needs to learn to move beyond our limited sight, by learning ways to recognize the things that are not obvious. We as people of faith believe in God who is beyond our visible grasp. In fact, "faith," according to the homilist, is "the conviction of things not seen" and "what is seen was made from things that are not visible" (Hebrews 11:1–2). Young people from mixed-race and queer families can teach us about faith, being able to see things that are unseen and invisible. They may be able to tell us how to navigate ambiguous and complicated identity issues in ways that help to transcend conventional and normative ways of looking at the family identity so that we can create new ones. Let us, then, turn to 'seeing' as our third task of practical theology, in addition to the first two, listening and checking blood in engaging racialized and queer youth.

Seeing: Its Power and Pitfall

The question Stuart Hay kept being asked at restaurants, "Are you all together?" is not uncommon among interracial and queer family members. Even if there are growing numbers of interracial couples and queer families on the streets in big urban cities and also small and rural places today, they are undoubtedly noticed. This being noticed in a negative way (passive tense) often involves an unpleasant feeling. Even if interracial couples and queer families are accustomed to this kind of unwanted attention over time, it still makes them feel self-conscious, and often creates anxiety. They feel forced to prove their decency and their legitimacy, as if their relationship needs public approval. Donna, who is mentioned above, shares this: "I never liked being stared at, and I always felt I was being stared at. A lot of them would look at me as if they were thinking, 'Okay, well, obviously her mother slept with a black guy or something.'"[62] Feminist scholar on disability studies Rosemarie Garland-Thomson argues that this experience

---

62. Gaskins, *What Are You?* 90–91.

of being stared at may create an epistemological reconsideration: "We stare when ordinary seeing fails, when we want to know more. . . . Staring offers an occasion to rethink the status quo. Who we are can shift into focus by staring at who we think we are not."[63]

Religious educators including John Westerhoff have powerfully discussed what they call the power of "seeing."[64] Seeing is powerful because "the way we see things is affected by what we know or what we believe. . . . We never look at just one thing; we are always looking at the relation between things and ourselves."[65] This connecting capacity of seeing enables a hermeneutical reflection. Seeing becomes mirroring as people reflect the actions of others.[66]

The power of seeing is not neutral in the same way that interpretation is not neutral. Precisely for this reason, seeing can be positive, in terms of advancing learning and generating effective teaching, and at the same time, it can also be negative, communicating prejudice. Michele Elam, an English professor at Stanford University, has examined novels, drama, graphical narrative, and TV shows, all of which feature mixed-race people and address cultural representation of them. Her analysis includes the material on the front covers of education textbooks of and for and by mixed-race people that are used for courses at college and University. These covers have pictures of "real" people featuring "real" faces. However, they "conceal as well as reveal, and unintentionally narrow as well as open perspective," Elam notes.[67] While they reveal diversity of racialized individuals and their families, they unintentionally limit the reality of these people to middle-class, well-behaved, and attractive. A particular privileged group is chosen to be seen. "The fact that only heterosexual couples appear," Elam continues, "by implication, other, more minoritized families (for example, adopted offspring of same-sex or intersex couple or branded-family) are not deemed as 'representative' of the mixed-race constituency and thus are silently omitted from the field of representation."[68] Her argument resonates with Elliott Eisner's distinction of the three forms of curriculum, as explicit, implicit and

---

63. Garland-Thomson, *Staring*, 3, 6.
64. Westerhoff, *A Pilgrim People*, 8.
65. Berger, *Ways of Seeing*, 8–9.
66. Foster, *From Generation to Generation*, 79.
67. Elam, *The Souls of Mixed Race*, 32.
68. Ibid., 36.

null curriculum.[69] Seeing is one of the most explicit ways to communicate a curriculum. But seeing at the same time implicitly conveys other aspects of reality by concealing them. When only a certain kind of mixed-race family is being seen (explicit) in the public arena and social media, other kinds of the family are to be viewed as insignificant or undesirable by implication and by their absence. But even when a group is made visible in the culture through representation, this can serve to hide unpleasant realities faced by those groups. Historian Kobena Mercer's point on racial inequality is astute here. The modernist view of visibility as empowerment is limiting because "even though media images of blackness are more visible than ever before, we witness the deepening of racial inequalities in U.S. politics as evidence of the structural decoupling of culture and politics."[70] His point can be easily made to other racialized, non-black and mixed-race people. Such racial inequality reaches other places beyond the U.S. context as well.

Here we may ponder the experience of what is called "passing" as a particular way of seeing and being (un)seen. "Passing" as we use the term here is understood not as an inability to see but as an ability to see differently. Passing as a subversive performance is helpful because it allows us to clarify that "determining race is not so much a matter of appearance but one of apprehension, not of visibility but of vision."[71] Passing, according to Homi Bhabha, creates hybridity: "almost the same but not quite" reality. Passing accomplishes both resemblance and menace.[72] It creates puzzlement in the eyes of those who are in power as majority as spectators. Passing can create confusion in spectators of the dominant group as the one who passes performs mimicry, almost the same but not quite. It also enables the one who "passes" to achieve the paradoxical reality of having two mutually exclusive identities at the same time. They can also move beyond given identities. "Those who can pass not only inherit the legacies of mixed-race heritage; they put that heritage into practice in a way that marks transgression of . . . the paradox of unequal entitlement in the land of inequality."[73] It should be noted that this transgression within the passing performance is not totally liberating, as far as the goal of being completely free from the oppression of

---

69. Eisner, *The Educational Imagination*.

70. Mercer, "Diaspora Aesthetics and Visual Culture," 158, Quoted in Elam, *The Souls of Mixed Race*, 158.

71. Elam, *The Souls of Mixed Race*, 161.

72. Bhabha, *The Location of Culture*, 86.

73. Elam, *The Souls of Mixed Race*, 118.

racism is concerned. Passing only works when playing the white race card has power. Passing is still sustained by the complicity in systematic, institutionalized racism with which those who are passing are entangled even in the midst of achieving the goal of untangling and dismantling it. Thus passing as a particular way of being seen must behold "the oppositional gaze," as bell hooks suggests, by both using the performance of staring at strategically for self-critical reflection (confusion effect) and changing the position from being a spectator to a participatory agency, from spectatorship to participation, from bystander staring to ally recognition.[74]

Insights on passing as a subversive act of hybridity are drawn from postcolonial theory and its distinction between essence and performance. The ability to pass is not an individually isolated choice but a highly politically charged and socially located public performance, a performance as "a form of historical engagement, as cultural palimpsest, as continuous negotiation with social practices and norms."[75] Describing passing as a form of historical engagement and negotiation, Lisa Lowe claims that racial "hybridities are always in the process of, on one hand, being appropriated and commodified by commercial culture and, on the other, of being rearticulated for the creation of oppositional 'resistance cultures.'"[76] Being conscious of the ambivalent stance of hybridity as far as passing as seeing and seeing beyond is concerned, it is this resistant and subversive spirit that practical theologians are inspired to engage in in order to work against dominant and oppressive normalization and racial, sexist, and homophobic exploitation. "Resistance," indeed, "is a gift in education because it opens us truthfully to another instead of hiding differences in withdrawal."[77]

Those people of mixed-race can pass as white because white people cannot see past themselves as the norm; they cannot imagine otherwise. Thus it holds true to claim that "whiteness is ex-nomic, characterized by its function as an unmarked—that is, unsaid—norm: to name whiteness is to racialize it."[78] Ironically masking white as "passing" unveils the visual obsession with the mixed-race body. Passing reveals the dominant power's desire to know by staring at them and yet expresses their frustration by

---

74. bell hooks, "The Oppositional Gaze: Black Female Spectators," 94–104.
75. Elam, *The Souls of Mixed Race*, 105.
76. Lowe, *Immigrant Acts*, 82.
77. Seymour, *Teaching the Way of Jesus*, 135.
78. Elam, *The Souls of Mixed Race*, 108.

their failure to know who they are (menace). This secret truth of "passing" sets the racialized and queer group free in their ability to blur the traditional boundaries to break open what has been concealed as the mask of normalized, commercialized, and categorized racial representation framed in the unreasonably narrow and rigidly normative box called the white heterosexual homogenous family.

A final point on seeing as a task of postcolonial feminist practical theology engaging queer and racialized youth is to probe the meaning of recognition. Borrowing from Rosemarie Garland-Thomson, recognition includes but goes beyond a self-realization of someone else. It serves more importantly "as the cornerstone of an ethical political society. . . . Recognition, then, relies on a combination of identification and differentiation. The trajectory of recognition is this: I recognize you by seeing your similarity and your difference to me. . . . In other words, I see you as you are."[79] In the language of sociologist and civil rights activist W. E. B. Du Bois, mutual recognition involves "double consciousness," which means "always looking at oneself through the eyes of others; no true self-consciousness, but only lets him [sic] see himself through the revelation of the other world."[80] As a postcolonial biblical scholar whose hermeneutics is informed by the non-Western non-dualistic notion of seeing with "yin yang eyes," Tat-siong Benny Liew suggests that we have bi-focal visions that "witness both the living and the dead." He explains we see people that are both living and dead because we can see with yin yang eyes things beneath/behind/beyond material visibility.[81] For practical theologian Elizabeth Conde-Frazier seeing with yin yang eyes is to venture into the world of others as our neighbor, because God in Jesus Christ takes on otherness, an identity different from divine identity. This venture is conversion, she argues, because it involves the dislocation of our own familiarity and comfort as a spiritual and educational practice.[82] This is conducive to a postcolonial interest in dislodging our own habitual ways of thinking, and ways of seeing.[83] This intentional attempt to dislodge is necessary because one legacy of colonialism is what Sharp calls "strategic forgetting." Strategic forgetting is facilitated by socially

---

79. Ibid., 158.

80. Du Bois, "Of Our Spiritual Strivings," 615, quoted in Elam, *The Souls of Mixed Race*, 154.

81. Liew, *What is Asian American Biblical Hermeneutics*, 2, 19.

82. Conde-Frazier, "From Hospitality to Shalom," 170.

83. Kwok, *Postcolonial Imagination and Feminist Theology*, 3.

Beyond Homogenous Heterosexual Family

sanctioned colonial rules and policies that constrict possibilities of recognizing the goodness of human beings (colonized), and their dignities.[84]

Here two critical and related kinds of recognition must be noted. First, from the standpoint of mutual recognition, we are not seeing this particular group as if an archaeologist is looking for evidence of human presence. In other words, we are not objectifying people as a category to be studied. We are, instead, shifting our perspective, orienting ourselves to recognize how people see and identify themselves as, for example, racially mixed or queer.[85] This posture is pastoral. As a pastor, we discern the sheep, their unique gifts and abilities as we lead them into safe places. Second, seeing based on mutual recognition is not pathological and paternalistic. We are neither looking for particular problems that are only inherent to mixed-race and queer people, nor patronizing young people as the helpless in need of support. However, we are not in a position of romanticizing them, either. We see them as a distinctive and diverse group that empowers us to unravel monolithic and oppressive norms. Through their struggles and commitments, while recognizing their limits, we can learn to resist stereotyping, profiling, stigmatization and erasure of one's identity. Young people's lives in their different and various ways provide a glimpse of the profound reality of the human family and a view of the splendid complexity of our human selves and identities in interdependent relationships.

Concluding Remarks

The tasks of postcolonial feminist practical theology engaging racialized and queer youth began with listening and ended with seeing, two actions that are inseparably connected. We find an illustration of these two actions in a Buddhist practice called "KwanEum" "Kwan" (觀) as seeing and "Eum" (音) as the sound. It literally means "seeing the sound (suffering)." we "see" (觀) the sound by "listening" (音) to it. This captures the paradoxically related nature of seeing and listening. It also teaches us the importance of a heart that has the capacity to attend to (and be touched by people's) suffering and pain. Such Buddhist wisdom resonates with the wisdom of Jewish neurologist Oliver Sacks. He says, if and when we begin to "see voices,"

---

84. Sharp, *Misunderstanding Stories*, 86.
85. Cahalan and Mikoski, eds., *Opening the Field of Practical Theology*, 6.

we begin to see ourselves and others as both "neighbour and stranger" at once.[86]

This chapter has paid attention to a particularly understudied group, mixed-race and queer youth, as a way of revealing the complexity of family. Understanding this complexity from the point of view of mixed-race and queer families has also allowed practical theologians to uncover white heterosexual family norms. Once we move beyond an understanding of family as a homogenous normative set, we begin to recognize the heterogeneous family and its ambiguous situation in today's society. This is where we find interracial families as a category of rupture while finding the space of queer family structure possible in the realm of hybridity and amphibiousness.[87] Because interracial and queer families disrupt the given homogeneous and heterosexual norm of family, they represent a particularly fruitful site for exploring how families are formed, and interpreted, recognized and negotiated. The attention to these differences and their role in the formation of families is a learning site of practical theology and is linked to the goal of a postcolonial feminist practical theology that stresses the importance of mutual recognition of differences for the sake of the interdependent relationships that God desires.

It is time to broaden our view of the family beyond the heterosexual and homogenous norm to "put out into the deep water and let down your nets for a catch" (Luke 5:4). Life, like the water of the sea, is also deep and wide in its heterogeneous diversity. Unless we learn how to put out our net wisely and to cast our net widely, we will fail to catch an abundance of fish. Cornel West, taking up this teaching of Jesus, reads a sign of non-linear Kairos time: "The time has come for critics and artists of the new cultural politics of difference to cast their nets widely, flex their muscles broadly, and thereby refuse to limit their visions, analyses, and praxis to their particular terrains."[88]

---

86. Sacks, *Seeing Voices*, xiii.
87. McCarthy, "Nuclear Alternatives."
88. West, "The New Cultural Politics of Difference," 217.

3

Beyond Adult-Centered Worship

THIS CHAPTER FOCUSES ON children as a group that is ignored in adult-centered Christian worship in most churches, especially mainline Protestant churches. Critiquing the problem of the Sunday school model of education prevalent in most mainline churches through a description of the scenes of the particular church Sunday school, we will visit unexamined assumptions that are at play. Second, we will draw from liturgical scholarship on the meaning of worship to draw our attention to children at worship. Then, we name the fear of disorderly worship often associated with the presence of children. This leads us to examine the fear of messiness in social and church settings. Finally the chapter suggests that attention to the exclusion of children from worship is connected to the exclusion of other groups, who are also overlooked and invisible in worship.

The critique of Christian education as schooling[1] has been vigorous over the years and yet children's education in church continues to be very much dictated by the Sunday school ethos, its history, and its program.[2] Even if the name of the Sunday school is replaced with other names,[3] its core mode

---

1. I will use Christian education that is related to Sunday school in this chapter because it is "Christian" Protestant churches rather than other religious groups who use "Sunday school" as a place of educating children.

2. Kennedy, *The Shaping of Protestant Education*; Lynn and Wright, *The Big Little School*. While they review the history of the Sunday School that was adopted from England to USA in frontier revivalistic traditions, in the Roman Catholic church contexts, Maria Harris offers contemporary critiques of the pitfalls of catechesis that is detached from the whole life of the church. Harris, *Fashion Me a People*.

3. Two of the United Church of Canada congregations I know have changed the

of teaching and learning has not changed much. This is especially so where children's detachment from the practice of and participation in the wider community of faith is concerned. The rationale behind such separation is supported by the argument that the developmental needs of children are different than for adults and that there is a need for age-appropriate teaching and learning. We do not mean to dismiss the importance of developmental theories, age-appropriate teaching, and peer-group learning needs. The problem is that this becomes the only or the most dominant way of doing children's teaching ministry without considering the importance of intergenerational and wholesome learning opportunities. In regards to intergenerational learning, age-separated education creates a false notion that only children need education, a point raised in Chapter 1 from the etymology of pedagogy. This notion diminishes awareness that education is a lifelong endeavor. It undermines the importance of education for adults and other age groups. While adults are busy separating children from others, and running a separate show, they miss a chance to learn from children in church and beyond.

Children-separate Christian education may be justified by the overstressing of developmentally appropriate needs—that is, children must learn in ways appropriate to their developmental stage and with their own peers. Such claims warrant some investigation. What is learning in religious contexts? One might claim that religious learning is the process of meaning-making, making sense of the world that surrounds and shapes a person. Thus, learning is never individualistic. It cannot happen solely from and independently of others. While one aspect of learning consists in acquiring information and such learning can happen individually in private settings—say, by reading a recipe book to cook a particular dish alone at home—even this kind of learning needs others (the author or the authors who wrote the book, and many others who produced and distributed it). Through relationships and social interactions, a person gathers and internalizes information; furthermore, an individual reflects and makes sense of this information in order to critically engage in action within a particular community. In this regard, Christian education involves identity-formation in the context of communities. Joyce Ann Mercer notes, "to learn is to be changed, to take on a new identity, to engage in a process of becoming. . . . In so far as learning refers to the processes by which persons change,

---

name "Sunday school" to "Grace Land" and "Rainbow Village" as a place and a program of learning for children on Sunday morning when adults worship. Some other churches, in terms of the programs, change their curriculum to "Godly Play" or "Rotation Role Play" programs beyond using a typical Sunday school curriculum.

become different, or undergo transformation, learning centrally concerns identity."[4] However, the community should not be romanticized as inherently good since a dominant community, characterized by privilege, can and have subjugated other communities. The church as a community is not free from such wrong doings.[5] The community is not neutral, just as education is not; it can justify and endorse discriminations and exclusions as well as it can liberate and resist them. As a result we need to undertake the task of "researching our pedagogy."[6] This researching involves a critical examination of our own assumptions as teachers and learners that may insert certain values and views explicitly and implicitly when we consider children's education in church. What would be those assumptions that are at play in the place where children gather for learning in the church on Sunday? Here is one example using a narrative approach of practical theology to analyze these assumptions in verbal forms and human actions. Here actions are considered as texts that generate communications.[7]

A Personal Narrative and Reflection

On Sunday afternoon, after we came back from church, our son Noah said, "I do not want to go down to Grace Land (a different name for Sunday school)." "Why?" I asked. "It is boring. I don't learn anything," he answered. "What did you do today?" I asked again. "Nothing, I mean, other than drawing and cutting stuff." My assumption was that he did not like this activity because it was not using computers for learning. Computers and computer games tend to be his activity of choice when he is not in school. I responded, "What is wrong with drawing and cutting? There are other ways to have fun and learn other than playing with computers."

The conversation ended there. But I was curious to know what is happening on Sunday morning downstairs in the Grace Land, while adults are worshipping upstairs in the sanctuary. So I decided to volunteer to teach in Grace Land one Sunday a few weeks after I had that conversation with my son. There were two age-divided groups, one from Grade 1–4 and the other from Grade 5–8. What I noticed was that both groups focused on learning the Bible stories following the Revised Common Lectionary. To my mind this

---

4. Mercer, *Welcoming Children*, 168.
5. Kim-Cragg and Schweitzer, *The Authority and Interpretation of Scripture*, 30.
6. Hess and Brookfield, eds., *Teaching Reflectively in Theological Contexts*, 4.
7. Ganzevoort, "Narrative Approaches," 216.

was desirable because it meant that both the adults worshipping upstairs and the children downstairs were learning the same text.[8] Instead of simply reading and telling the biblical stories, they were given crayons and paper with scissors to make something based upon the given story. Again I was pleased that the teaching method involved visual and tactile approaches beyond simply listening and speaking. In fact, I felt the approach in the Grace Land curriculum was interactive and creative. What I came to understand was that the problem was not with what was happening downstairs but with what was not happening. That is, while the educational approaches used were thoughtful, they were only meeting the needs of some of the children, those who enjoyed arts and crafts. Someone like Noah, who is not good at fine motor skills, doing crafts is not the best way for him to engage in learning of the biblical stories. This was not the case for Noah's younger sister, Hannah. Hannah was having a great time, proudly showing her parents after the service what she had done with coloring and creating patterns. She was happy to receive positive compliments from her teachers. In this visit, I realized the power of the norm in shaping students' experiences in the classroom. Hannah was a happy student because she was well-suited for the educational activity that was prepared by the teachers. This poses a challenge to the education plan in Grace Land to develop activities that engage a wider range of abilities and learning styles. Gaile Cannella and Radhika Viruru, who study children's education using a power analysis developed by Michel Foucault, warn us to look carefully because sometimes "the language of values, usefulness, productivity, accountability, and even empowerment are used to conceal disciplinary power. What is considered desirable is created by engineering 'practiced docile bodies.'"[9]

Another assumption to be examined is the feminization of the teachers. It is understandable and natural to assume that the way we learn is the way others also learn. But such assumption is a "catch-22."[10] In discussing multicultural religious education, Elizabeth Conde-Frazier points out the following: "The learning experiences of teachers and how they have informed their educational theories and practices are also a part of self-knowledge. As teachers reflect on these, they can see how and why their teaching is accessible or inaccessible to students from different cultures."[11] It is a well-known fact that teaching is often done by women, especially

8. Kim-Cragg, *Story and Song*, 46.
9. Cannella and Viruru, *Childhood and Postcolonization*, 63–64.
10. Tye, *Basics of Christian Education*, 86.
11. Conde-Frazier, "From Hospitality to Shalom," 182.

primary schools. It is also the case at most church schools. One may ask, what are the consequences and the implications of teaching when most teachers are women? Would it be fair to assume that certain activities that female teachers prefer would be used more than other kinds of activities? I am not essentializing here that all girls and women like doing crafts more than all boys and men. Nor am I generalizing that biological women's work is feminine without understanding gender-fluid identity. But since more girls and women tend to enjoy doing crafts as an activity than do boys and men, one may speculate that it is likely that women teachers by default might choose this kind of activity over others. A Chinese saying in terms of teaching is poignant in this regard, though it does not directly point to gender: "Do not confine your children to your own learning for they were born in another time."[12] The critical lesson that may be drawn from my personal narrative of the particular Sunday church school was that any normative approach to learning requires critical scrutiny, asking who benefits from using a particular teaching method and who is excluded from learning when a certain way is imposed and repeated too often.

When a certain teaching or a certain practice done repeatedly impacts our ways of thinking and behaving it becomes a "regulative norm." This can lead to what Sarah Ahmed calls "repetitive strain injuries" in the pedagogical sense. "Through repeating some gestures and not others," this postcolonial queer feminist theorist argues, "or through being oriented in some directions and not others, bodies become contorted. They get twisted into shapes that enable some action only insofar as they restrict capacity for other kinds of action."[13] While Ahmed's argument particularly points to heterosexual normativity and to how sexual orientation functions, legislates, and regulates social spaces that people inhabit, it is a helpful insight to keep in mind whenever we engage in teaching, cognizant of different learning styles and our own teaching practices and preferences.

Multifaceted Aspects of Worship

In the study of American religions, one of the common themes that emerged is that children are sacred. Not only the Abrahamic religions but also Confucianism and Hinduism view children as gifts of God.[14] How

12. Caine and Caine, *Making Connections*, 13.
13. Ahmed, *The Cultural Politics of Emotions*, 145.
14. Browning and Miller-McLemore, eds., *Children and Childhood in American*

can we affirm the sacredness of children in Christian life? And what are the places and times that we celebrate children as gifts of God? One may argue that the worship rituals of the faith community are one place to do so. It is impossible to build up a healthy faith community without robust and sustained worship experience. This is where the role of worship that includes honoring children as sacred and embracing children's full participation comes in.

Ruth Duck's *Worship for the Whole People of God* is relevant for our discussion because she addresses her concern for the lack of effort to involve and include children in worship.[15] A close relationship between the discipline of Christian education and the discipline of worship is critically needed, as I have explored elsewhere, although I have not focused on children only.[16] A close relationship between worship and Christian education in light of children does not mean that they are the same. David Ng and Virginia Thomas clarified this in 1981. The purpose of worship is not education, as the purpose of Christian education is not worship. Yet, they should not be treated as entirely separate because these two mutually inform and shape each other. As Ng and Thomas argue, acts of adoration, thanksgiving, and offering, the essentials of worship, teach children about God and our response to God. Alternatively, children's excitement, and spontaneity as well as their "mistakes" teach adults and the worshipping community about joy, acceptance, and forgiveness, essential to Christian faith and Christian life.[17]

Furthermore, a close look at the place of children in worship from the perspective of postcolonial feminist practical theology demands a critical look at the tendency to compartmentalize worship and education. Some have provocatively suggested that the compartmentalization of these Christian activities and practices, and the creation of children's Sunday school separate from adult worship has been encouraged by the culture of choice. In a lecture, Alasdair MacIntyre makes a point that the current culture has been changed in part due to the influence of compartmentalization and choice. He writes,

> all our lives are compartmentalized, so that as we move from the home to the workplace, to the meeting of the trade union branch, to the sports club, to some religious service in the parish, whatever

Religions, 3.
   15. Duck, *Worship for the Whole People of God*, 27–30.
   16. Kim-Cragg, *Story and Song*.
   17. Ng and Thomas, *Children in the Worshipping Community*, 48–65.

it is, we move into and out of areas each of which has its own autonomous sets of norms, each of which requires of us that we adapt to those norms if we are to be effective in that situation and in such a way that we have to exchange one set of attitudes and norms for the other as we move between them. So it comes about that a new virtue is added to the list of the virtues, adaptability; and a new vice is added to the list of the vices, inflexibility.[18]

When we move from one place to another place, say, from the home to a Christian service, our relationships change in order to adapt a set of norms that includes inflexibility. At home, children and adults co-dwell and do things together, which is autonomous, taken-for-granted norms. In church, however, the operative norm is that adults go upstairs and children go downstairs. We make that choice because we believe it to be effective, following the logic of MacIntyre. What is at stake in this culture of choice, is the splintering and dividing of community into different cells of activity. Practical theology's challenge to the compartmentalization of community is at heart a counter-cultural challenge to a society that chooses to divide into age groups to do separate activities, as MacIntyre has called into question. What we are proposing is a radical reconsideration of the importance and place of intergenerational worship to correct this fragmentary culture. We can adapt a new virtue and resist this compartmentalization. We may need to challenge the very mind set or the very system that hinders this adaptation. After exploring twelve different Christian practices, Dorothy Bass and Craig Dykstra offer salient advice: "Sometimes people cannot enter a practice because the very structures of society oppose it."[19] Perhaps imagining Sunday morning as a time when people of all ages share together in the experience of Christian celebration is difficult precisely because it goes against the societal norm. But it is not impossible.

Seeking to mend this separation, I suggest we revisit the various aspects of the basics of worship rather than reinventing new wheels. This revisiting can be aided by reviewing the recent developments in the reform and renewal of worship. The Second Vatican Council's liturgical renewal movement (1963–65) was a major event that sparked change in Reformed Churches of many denominations. Don Saliers summarizes these changes as following: a renewal of emphasis on the centrality of baptism and the

18. Alasdair MacIntyre, "A Culture of Choices and Compartmentalization," a public lecture delivered October 13, 2000 at Notre Dame. http://brandon.multics.org/library/macintyre/macintyre2000choices.html

19. Bass and Dykstra, "Growing in the Practices of Faith," 200.

Eucharist; a comprehensive lectionary of biblical readings for the Christian year; recovery of biblical preaching; new models of prayer, often based upon ancient Jewish and Christian sources; recovery of senses and bodily participation; vital connections between liturgy and social ethics; and creativity in hymn writing and musical reforms, both ancient and contemporary.[20]

His concise list points to the emphasis on Scripture and sacraments and especially their interplay in worship. Worship needs both Scripture and sacraments. Since the Reformation, Christians have experienced a negative separation of worship practices along denominational lines. The Protestant tradition dismissed the role of the sacraments, focusing more on the role of preaching and biblical interpretation under the banner of *Sola Scriptura*. Meanwhile Catholics deemphasized Scripture and focused more on the Eucharist in worship. This gap widened as the Enlightenment thinking and colonial ideology swept the world in the eighteenth century, and peaked in the late nineteenth and the early twentieth century.[21] The recovery of the ancient practice of prayer is, thus, to some extent, a postcolonial move, denouncing modernist, post-Reformation outlook and practices. The new focus on ancient practices has shown that they tended to involve forms of prayer that maximized human sensory experience. Prayer in ancient traditions involved chanting and communal reciting. Instead of relying on simply using the written text, prayer in orality included silence and maximized human voice.[22] The prayer was also involved in different bodily movements, namely, standing, kneeling, sitting, bowing, and walking around. When human senses are creatively engaged in worship we can appreciate the profound connection between religious celebration and Christian education which encompasses experiential, cognitive, artistic, and reflective ways of learning and teaching. John Westerhoff has constantly stressed the importance of multi-sensory experiences for holistic learning and has pointed out that these experiences are available through liturgy.[23] Stephen Brookfield whose scholarship and research has been dedicated to teaching makes a similar point. He delineated seventeen truths about skillful teaching. For example, he advises, "Attend to how students experience learning; Trust your instincts; Recognize the emotionality of learning; Acknowledge

---

20. Saliers, "Worship," 292.
21. Kim-Cragg, *Story and Song*, 2.
22. Senn, *Embodied Liturgy,* 297.
23. Westerhoff, *Will Our Children Have Faith?* 54–60.

your personality; Reflect on your own learning."[24] This list highlights the importance of the experiential aspect of teacher as learner, while also lifting up the crucial roles of senses, as emotions and instincts that teacher has for students. Insights from both the liturgical renewal movement and from skillful teaching, though they have different purposes, contribute to practical theology whose concern has to do with the well-being of a person and that of a community, especially those experiences of the marginalized and oppressed.[25]

With these insights in mind, let us examine five theological foundations of worship that I call "5 Rs" of worship: worship as Ritual, Revelation, Response, Relationship, and Rehearsal.[26] First, through ritual, we create meanings in our lives and form our Christian identity. Worship as ritual helps mark life passages (birth and death and in-between) and coping with crises and challenges (loss, illness, and transition). Ritual shapes who we are as humans. Ritual, through its repetitive and communal act, creates meaning, not in an isolated, individual way but with others. It therefore promotes Christian learning goals connected to making meaning, making sense of the world and discovering a personal and communal identity. Of course children are also capable of learning through ritual. In fact, there is much about the repetitive, tactile nature of ritual that is ideally suited to children. That is why the exclusion of children from adult centered worship is problematic. The conviction that "education takes place in the ongoing patterns of life together," holds true as Bass and Dykstra have argued: "This is like belonging to a congregation at songs: you learn, even as a child, to take your pitch from others, to clap along or not to, to anticipate certain melodies at certain times of the year. You use your whole body, and you draw on the musical tastes and training you have developed outside the church as well as in it. . . . This kind of learning—communal but unplanned—takes place all the time."[27] What Bass and Dykstra described here applies to both adults and children. Indeed adults also lose out on learning opportunities when children are absent from worship on Sunday.

In such missed opportunities there are consequences for our relationship with God as well. Intergenerational worship and learning can lead to epiphanies of God's presence, which leads to the second "R" of worship:

24. Brookfield, *The Skillful Teacher*, 192–210.
25. Cahalan and Mikoski, eds., *Opening the Field of Practical Theology*, 273.
26. Duck, *Worship for the Whole People of God*, 7–17.
27. Bass and Dykstra, "Growing in the Practices of Faith," 198.

Revelation. Worship as revelation points to God. God is revealed in worship as we sense, encounter, and experience the presence of God. In Scripture the mighty act of God as well as the vulnerable nature of God are manifested. God is revealed individually as a person reads and contemplates Scripture. Scripture is read, interpreted, preached, and performed collectively in community where God is revealed in worship. Through sacraments, we taste and see, touch and receive God's self-giving love. That is why many people of faith give thanks to God before eating. A connection here can be made to the ritual practice of saying grace before meals. We ask God to bless the gifts of food before us.[28] This makes the most mundane act of eating theological. This again connects back to Sunday worship. Each Sunday (or the Sundays on which the Eucharist is celebrated) we are invited to see ourselves as guests at "a hungry feast," as Gordon Lathrop calls it.[29] Bread is given "to those who are hungry and hunger for justice [is given] to those who are fed" as an Argentine hymn teaches us.[30] "Eucharist is the nexus of how liturgy meets food," claimed elsewhere, as eating becomes the nexus of how humans meet the divine in worship.[31]

The third "R" of worship is our Response to God. Worship is about our response to God's self-giving and steadfast love for us. It is God who initiated it first. God created us. God made a promise. God freed the people because God heard them cry. We respond to God because we are "grateful for God's loving action." We respond because "we cannot keep from singing."[32] Here singing as response to God has multiple theological meanings. Singing, according to Saliers, is "a natural language of praise."[33] It is a basic human language to God. The response to God is primarily expressed in our thanksgiving through praising God. Singing, singing together as Christian practice, is one of the most human acts imaginable. That is why Dietrich Bonhoeffer insists that we sing together: "It is not you that sings, it is the Church that is singing, and you as a member may share in its song."[34] This very act of singing together is the very practice of Christian life together, he

---

28. Bass, "Eating," 51.

29. Lathrop, "The Eucharist as a 'Hungry Feast,' and the Appropriation of Our Want."

30. "God Bless to Us Our Bread," English translation by John Bell from Iona Community, Scotland.

31. Kim-Cragg, "Through Senses and Sharing," 34.

32. http://www.united-church.ca/beliefs/statements/songfaith accessed July 29, 2017.

33. Saliers, "Singing Our Lives," 179.

34. Bonhoeffer, *Life Together*, 61.

says. This very act of singing seems to be programmed in the human DNA prior to receiving any form of Christian identity. "There is something about human beings that needs to make music," Saliers writes.[35] Making music as making sound is the first thing that every human does at birth. This is the very first sign of the baby being born alive. But not only the person is born with the sound but also "faith is born and lives in song."[36] When Mary heard from the angel the news of Jesus being born through her, she sang. Her courageous and faithful response to God was celebrated and confirmed in her song, *Magnificat,* as she begins to sing, "My soul magnifies the Lord, and my spirit rejoices in God my Savior . . . for the Mighty One has done great things for me according to the promise he made to our ancestors, to Abraham and to his descendants forever" (Luke 1:49–50, 55).

Why is God doing this amazing thing for Mary and her ancestors? Because this God is relational. This leads to the fourth dimension "R" of worship: Relationship. Worship expresses God's desire to make a covenant with us. It further gives voice to our yearning to be the people of God. Through worship we hear God calling us as God's own, and we are invited to join God's work for justice, peace, and love on earth. This is a relationship of love, where justice and peace kiss. Herbert Anderson, who has written extensively on family, faith, and marriage, calls loving a practice of relationship. "Love in all its forms is a pervasive quality in human relationships."[37] In other words, relationship constitutes love, while love is expressed as the concrete action of mutuality and the practice of faith. God provides a model for love. In fact, the love God shows is inseparably intertwined with the love of self and neighbor. That is what Jesus reminded his followers when he summarized the law in two commandments: "The first is, 'Hear, O Israel: the Lord our God, the Lord is one; you shall love the Lord your God with all your heart, and with all your soul, and with all your mind, and with all your strength.' The second is this, 'You shall love your neighbor as yourself.' There is no other commandment greater than these" (Mark 12:29–31). "Love of God and love of neighbor, are twin elements wrapped in one dynamic," Reynolds continues, "It is a divine liturgy of love where love of one another in vulnerable relationships of giving and receiving is a way of loving God."[38]

---

35. Saliers, "Singing Our Lives," 180.
36. Ibid., 183.
37. Anderson, "Loving," 63.
38. Reynolds, "Invoking Deep Access," 222.

Interdependence

This triad mutual relationship of love between God, self, and neighbor seeks a just relationship towards a reconciled world, bringing the Kin-dom of God on earth.[39] This Kin-dom is already here and now, even if it is not here yet. The final "R" of worship as Rehearsal points to this already and not yet Kin-dom of God reality. As we pray for the Kin-dom to come, we worship because "the gathered church is changed and prepared to take its part in God's drama of transforming life in this world."[40] In worship, we sound prophecy—"to ring out in opposition to injustice," prophesying a just world to come that is already here.[41] The visible and physical sign of the Kin-dom of God is captured well when one thinks of the worship space as a tabernacle, or *mishkān* in Hebrew. This word is translated in the New Standard Revised Version as *tent*. This tabernacle/tent evokes an image of the worship space as movable and temporary. It challenges our tendency to think of church as building and worship space as fixed and permanent. We seek the Kin-dom of God, pray God to bring it on earth, and rehearse the Kin-dom of God in worship. Therefore, we cannot settle permanently in a comfortable place. We must rehearse the heavenly city even as we travel the liturgical road, committed to changing the world and open to be changed by new people and new insights that are wrapped in the movements of the Spirit.[42]

Each "R" points right at the heart of the matter for our interest in children at worship. Children as newcomers on this earth and as new members to a particular faith community learn who they are by observing and participating. Through participating in baptism, for example, children encounter God where God's unconditional love, freely given through water is revealed. In listening to, reading, and enacting the Bible in worship, children learn how their life stories are linked with the divine stories. They encounter and experience the presence of God, who is intimately close to them, as much as they know that God is beyond their knowing. To such an awesome and intimate God, they learn to respond and ascribe their worth—which is where the English word "worship," *weorth-scipe* (worth-ship) comes from.[43] They also learn to value their life, their worthiness because they are all equally created

---

39. This term, 'kin-dom of God' has been coined by Isasi-Diaz. See her article, "Solidarity: Love of the Neighbor in 1980s," 31–40.

40. Duck, *Worship for the Whole People of God*, 14.

41. Saliers, "Singing Our Lives," 190.

42. Kim-Cragg and Burns, "Liturgy in Migration and Migrants in Liturgy," 125.

43. Duck, *Worship for the Whole People of God*, 3.

in the image of God, and called by God who seeks right relationships. As they participate in worship from simply observing and absorbing what others do, they are encouraged to participate more actively in taking leadership roles of offering, reading, serving, and singing, thereby getting a sense of their relationship to others and their gifts in the community. In worship they learn to realize that another world, the world in which God once created, still creates and desires, is possible. They begin to dream and imagine that divisions can be mended, "reversal of fortune"[44] can happen, and where the last shall be first. This will be proclaimed and actualized if we work for it with God's help. The paradox of the already (in the sharing of the bread and wine and singing together) and the not yet (the Kin-dom of God that is coming) is nowhere better communicated than in worship.

The fifth point of worship as Rehearsal resonates with Mary Elizabeth Moore's idea of parabolic-paradoxical theology as far as teaching children is concerned. It is to teach the parabolic theology of the last shall be the first, through embodying that theology through our educational practice, as we cultivate the paradoxical nature of our life and our faith.[45] There is power to oppress; there is power to resist. That is the paradox. Moore writes, "We're never trapped by power: it's always possible to modify its hold."[46] Such learning of parables and paradox along with other transformative learnings can and often do happen through liturgical practice with children at worship. Take Mercer's words, worship as "liturgical practices simultaneously do make a real difference—God transforms us with alternative visions and images that enable us to live differently . . . and yet cannot be seen as completely coterminous with *being* a 'real difference' unless worshippers formed and reformed in Christian faith live the difference."[47] In this worship experience, children and others even touch the future of hope, a changed world, by beholding the eschatological vision, at the very present moment during worship when bread is broken and served by children, despite their inexperienced hands.

In sacramental theology as far as the liturgical leadership is concerned, it is God who is the subject of the sacraments that make things holy (*ex opere operato*) rather than the goodness or the ability of the person who presides

---

44. Turner, "Reversal of Fortune," 87–98. She offers Miriam's song in Exodus as an example of a prophetic preaching, titled Miriam's performance as "reversal of fortune."

45. Moore, *Teaching as a Sacramental Act*, 91–120.

46. Foucault, *The History of Sexuality*, 13.

47. Mercer, *Welcoming Children*, 226.

at the sacrament *(ex opere operantis)*. During the Donatist controversy, Augustine of Hippo argued that sacraments depend not on humans but on God, and developed an understanding of sacrament as a visible sign of an invisible grace, as the historian of worship, James White, explains.[48] While it is important that whoever is called to preside and perform sacraments must learn well and practice with care, it is also important to note that ultimately it is up to God as the divine agency. Therefore, any excuse to prohibit ordinary people from participating in sacraments is theologically unwarranted. We cannot faithfully claim that certain sacraments are more valid than others (e.g., Roman Catholic or Mennonite baptism) or certain liturgical practices are open only to some (e. g., only the baptized receive communion), although the church has sanctioned this view throughout the ages. Education is needed in order to receive God's gift and share it with others. Regardless of the sacrament itself or the leadership that presides at it, we know that through sacraments, God's self-giving love is made visible within the community. There is much to explore about sacraments in relation to religious education, and there exists a strong literature on the subject already.[49]

In order for the five "Rs" to be fully taught and practiced in actual worship, Duck says that two additional important groups must be considered. These are first of all, people with disabilities and second of all, people from minority cultures. Worship and disability, like worship and children, are unstable allies.[50] It is not simply about addressing the issue of physical accessibility to the space, though that is important and the church has still ways to go (i.e., accessible lecterns, pulpits, bathrooms, meeting rooms and social halls, as well as mobility aids, listening devices, sign language services, braille and large print literature).[51] People with disabilities is more than an accessibility issue. It is a theological issue. "A particular gift persons with disabilities may bring is the grace of facing and affirming life with its

48. White, *Introduction to Christian Worship*, 183.

49. Edie, *Book, Bath, Table, and Time*. He uses baptism and Eucharist as valuable educational practices. Mary Elizabeth Moore *Teaching as a Sacramental Act* provided educational clues for sacred teaching by studying and analyzing the theories and the practices of sacraments. Robert Browning and Roy Reed spoke of a paradigm shift in liturgy by attending to a phenomenological approach to sacraments in connection to religious education. See their *The Sacraments in Religious Education and Liturgy*. Susan Ross provides a feminist analysis of sacramental theology as she emphasizes holistic and bodily dimensions of human experience in *Extravagant Affections*.

50. Jobling, "The Bible and Critical Theology: Best Friend or Unstable Ally?" 154.

51. Eiesland and Saliers, eds., *Human Disability and the Service of God*; Foley, ed., *Developmental Disabilities and Sacramental Access*.

goodness and its limits in finding God's presence in it all, in contrast to the promise of perfect lives and perfect bodies that is the stuff of fairy tales and television commercials," Duck writes, taking the insight from Nancy Eiesland who extensively wrote on disability and theology.[52] Tom Reynolds, calling for "deep access," suggests "spirituality of attentiveness" which requires paying attention and minding differences. Dealing with disability in worship and congregational life, for Reynolds, is dealing with differences.[53] Affirming difference involves affirming an irreducible dignity of each person created in the *Imago Dei*. Theological anthropology of *Imago Dei* points to a common yet diverse nature as human beings in relation to God. Disability is a part of this human nature and a feature that emerges in and through bodily difference. In short, disability is not an additional and extra (outside) human problem but a limit that includes susceptibility and a possibility that enables different gifts to be shared. However, in order for such understanding of disability to be fully appreciated, Reynolds contends that "cult of normalcy" must be questioned.[54] Under the cult of normalcy disability is viewed as a lack of ability, a deficit to be filled, a paternal problem to be accommodated, and an extra service to be provided. He scrutinizes the very positive term, "inclusion" when it actually privileges the dominant group by universalizing their experiences at the expense of the denial of difference. What this inclusion does is to set those labelled "disabled" apart from the normal in society, identifying people with disability as the other, making them out of place, making disability abnormal.

Furthermore, disability is an educational issue as far as education is regarded as "leading out"[55] the potentials that people (children) already have and the truths that they already know. Those of us who are minoritized, including children and people with disabilities, are not simply the ones that are supported unilaterally by those in power. Members of the disabled community are not only receivers, but they are the givers who suggest and model different kinds of values, priorities, and meanings of life. Education goes both ways. Learning happens in mutuality. If education goes only one way, it becomes an imposition and it is used to oppress and control. The

---

52. Duck, *Worship for the Whole People of God*, 33.
53. Reynolds, "Invoking Deep Access," 214.
54. Reynolds, *Vulnerable Communion*, chapter 2.
55. Groome, *Christian Religious Education*, 5.

presence of people of diverse and different abilities in the community of faith "surely increases its faithfulness."[56]

Similar things could be said of racial and cultural diversity. Duck urges us to move beyond Euro-American white-centered traditions of worship as norms: "The European and White North American measure of what is adequate liturgy must be decentered, so that Christians of many backgrounds can learn from one another and the Spirit, ways to worship and to honor one another more deeply and fully."[57] Non-European cultural elements will necessarily change "normal" Euro-American ways of worshiping. Often what we see happening in worship that seeks to be culturally conscious entails the addition of a song or a prayer in a different language to an order of service that remains largely unchanged.[58] Such inclusions risk becoming tokenistic gestures if they do not move beyond this to include more radical change. A change of worldviews and values happens by changing practices. This is a complex and sensitive job[59] as we pay attention to the difficult realities that members of non-white ethnic minority cultures often face due to poverty, immigration, racism, cultural and linguistic difference. "To integrate worship and culture," especially the minority cultures, Duck advises, "the congregation will need to consider its attitudes towards diversity and change, address prejudice and racism, and give voice to the mix of feelings members and newcomers are experiencing."[60]

Fear of Being Disorderly

Keeping in mind the five "Rs" and committing ourselves to ability and cultural diversity, we have the essential rational for moving beyond adult-centered worship. Fear, however, may still hold congregations back from a shift that would see worship geared to a more intergenerational and diverse community celebration and gathering. The belief that worship must be decent and orderly may be behind most of the reluctance to change. The influence of the apostle Paul is detrimental in this regard. Addressing the disputes of the church in Corinth regarding the ways people worship and prophesy gave the following advice: "So, my friends, be eager to

---

56. Mercer, *Welcoming Children*, 228.
57. Duck, *Worship for the Whole People of God*, xviii.
58. Kim-Cragg, *Story and Song*, 91.
59. Black, *Culturally Conscious Worship*.
60. Duck, *Worship for the Whole People of God*, 54.

prophesy, and do not forbid speaking in tongues; but all things should be done decently and in order" (1 Corinthians 14: 39–40). A few verses earlier Paul had spelled out one aspect of decency and order as follows: "As in all the churches of the saints, the women should keep silent in the churches. For they are not permitted to speak, but should be in submission, as the Law also says. If there is anything they desire to learn, let them ask their husbands at home. For it is shameful for a woman to speak in church" (vv. 33b–35). This text made a huge impact on women in the church in terms of their ability to fill leadership roles but also contributed to shaping the notion of worship as something that should be solemn and orderly. This text that was used to control women can be extended to those who are deemed disorderly, children and people with mental illness.

Then, there is a problem with the verb we use to indicate "worship." The word "observe" conjures up certain meanings that are associated with "commemorate" and "solemnize" in a public, official, and even legal sense. A typical example of such a view of worship as observance is Remembrance service. It is definitely observed in order to commemorate and solemnize the ones who lost their lives in war. Cannella and Viruru draw our attention to another meaning of observation in terms of obeying rules. "Observation" they argue, "which sounds apolitical and innocent, could more accurately be termed surveillance because it has become an unquestioned method of categorization, judgement, and control."[61] Michel Foucault makes a similar point that observation, meaning "keeping an eye on" is necessary for adults to gaze over children in the name of regulating their sensations and assessing social behaviors.[62]

The view that worship is orderly and something to be observed has become dominant, though it is hard to pin point how and when such a view began. However, we can say that penitential piety is one of the most powerful essential elements that influenced such a view of worship. "Certainly," White contends, penance "became a lasting part of Protestant piety."[63] That worship must be orderly constrained the thinking of the baby boomers who grew up as Christians since the 1940s in North America. They also include people in the Global South who were missionized by North American Christians around the late 1800s and the early 1900s. To them, worship has had to be reverent, solemn, and ordered. Spontaneous responses (clapping, laughing,

---

61. Cannella and Viruru, *Childhood and Postcolonization*, 108.
62. Foucault, *Discipline and punish*.
63. White, *Protestant Worship*, 27.

singing, or praying) are disapproved of in order to maximize reverence and avoid disturbing the order of godliness. Natural human noises (e.g., children crying or people with cerebral palsy moving around) must be controlled in order to create solemnity. Movements (dancing during hymn singing and action prayer) are discouraged because it leads to uncanny emotions.[64] Such fear of movement and noise is not limited to the issue of children but extended to the dance of indigenous and colonized people.

A Cherokee postcolonial scholar Corky Alexander has provided an interesting example of the way the demand for order and solemnity has affected indigenous participation in and exclusion from Christian worship. He explains how "The Stomp Dance," a tradition that belongs to many indigenous tribes, was banned by the early missionaries and American Holiness Movement group.[65] This example shares features in common with another colonial case. According to Charles Kraft, who examined Nigerian dances and their exclusion from Christian communities, the move stems from both a sense of superiority for solemn worship, as well as from "the fear of syncretism."[66] Dance, he says, was considered inferior to Christian culture and worship by European colonizers and missionaries and thus disallowed in Christian worship. Furthermore, the notion of mixing indigenous forms of worship with the colonizers' forms was seen as compromising the purity of the colonizers' worship practices. Many Christian colonial missionaries fiercely rejected and censored any mixing of the local ritual practices with Christian liturgy. We will examine this religious hybridity further in Chapter 4.

From a pedagogical point of view, the control of worship by banning dances is more than a fear of bodily movement. It is also about the control that leaves little room for learning through spontaneity. However, education, despite its nature that arises from a deliberate and intentional effort, as Pierre Bourdieu and Jean-Claude Passeron argue, always produces unintended practices.[67] Theologically and biblically speaking, we as teachers are those who only plant the seeds of learning. The growth is ultimately beyond our hands. "So neither the one who plants nor the one who waters is anything, but only God who gives the growth" (1 Corinthians 3:7). Growth is a surprise, a mystery; it can be a delight or a disappointment. In

---

64. Miller-McLemore, *In the Midst of Chaos*, 1–20.
65. Alexander, "The Cherokee Stomp Dance," 268.
66. Kraft, *Anthropology for Christian Witness*, 259–60.
67. Bourdieu and Passeron, *Reproduction in Education, Society and Culture*.

that sense, Moore claims that teaching is about expecting the unexpected. She guides us through the meaning of Advent, a central practice of expectancy.[68] Christian education depends on the work of the Spirit. What an absurd idea to contain and control the Spirit, in the name of education! The result of education is ultimately beyond our control. It does not mean that we as teachers do not have to design any planned educational activities. Such effort is necessary. Without such effort, we cannot call it education. Often deliberately (systematically and sustainably) designed educational work leads to effective learning which is conducive to transformation.[69]

Finally our approach of practical theology in terms of worshipping with children, is not either-or but both-and beyond. We need a Sunday-school as a place and a mode of teaching where children can be themselves with the assistance of adults who share and learn what they know. But we also need to create a space where children and other groups can interact and negotiate, gaining from each other's insights, and where they can be guided by the gift of the Spirit. Worship is one such space. Even though we plan our educational activities well and anticipate certain outcomes we need to make room for unexpected learnings, spontaneity and unintended practices. This attention can also contribute to debunking the generic notion of the development of the child. Cannella and Viruru examined the theory of Jean Piaget on children's cognitive development. They challenged his underlying view that the child must learn to be in control, demonstrating autonomous, rational and contained behavior.[70] Once we let go of the fear of being disorderly, and instead trust in the work of the Spirit, we may receive delightful surprises out of the participation of the worshippers.

These delightful even uneasy surprises may also lead to much stronger and more effective learning, yielding healthy fruits. Such a both-and-beyond approach cannot happen unless we open up children to join in the worship fully. In order to have both Sunday-school-like, classroom, age-appropriate learning and intergenerational, interactive learning with others, it is clear that separate times are needed for both. But a drastic change, countercultural and habitual change may meet strong resistance as Sunday morning is restructured. It may need a gentle (but persistent) approach involving small and

---

68. Moore, *Sacramental Teaching*, 40–64.

69. Cremin, *American Education*, xiii. His definition of education is "the deliberate, systematic and sustained effort to transmit or evoke knowledge, attitudes, values, skills, and sensibilities."

70. Cannella and Viruru, *Childhood and Postcolonization*, 94.

steady steps. For example, we may try once a month to worship without Sunday school, or decide to try worship together for the duration of the summer. Or we could set aside an intergenerational service at the beginning of each liturgical season (Advent, Christmas, Epiphany, Lent, Easter, and Pentecost) for the same experiment. Preaching could focus on the beauty of surprise, and the freedom of letting go of control or fear as a barrier to faith, hope, and love. A lesson could be prepared for teachers to learn about disciplinary power, the limitation of observance understood as worship, or insights of regarding worship as joyful (making noises) celebration.

Pastoral and Liturgical Implications: Where Do We Go from Here to Move Forward?

Worship is a radical Christian practice. No one needs a passport to enter worship. There are no prerequisites to worship. All those who want to worship God are welcomed. That is why liturgical theologians name worship as the rehearsal of the Kin-dom of God. However, there are ways in which worship accommodates only some and excludes others. In reality, worship is not radically practiced. In reality, certain ways of doing worship prevent others from glimpsing the Kin-dom of God. Children are among those who are excluded when we consider all the aspects of worship, from praying, to singing, to preaching, to sharing communion, that are geared to adults, especially those adults considered normative.

My overall approach throughout the book is an invitation to attend to the groups that have not been adequately studied and recognized as the subject matter of practical theology. This chapter has focused on children and people with disabilities, as the previous chapter has focused on queer and racialized youth and young adults. Attention to children in worship unveils the power structures and social systems that corrupt our vision of what a Christian church should be. The Power Flower exercise can be an excellent tool for uncovering those structures and systems. This exercise is developed by Canadian educators for social change to help people become self-aware of the power differentials in personal and social levels.[71] The center of a daisy type flower is divided into sixteen segments including race, ethnicity, language, religion, family, class, age, denomination, education, ability, clergy/lay, geographical region (origin), geographical region (current), sexual orientation, and sex. It leaves one petal open so that the one

---

71. Arnold, Burke, James, Martin, and Thomas, *Education for a Change*, 87.

doing the exercise can include her or his or their own identity of special importance. These segments constitute at the center like a pie, which is surrounded by the two sets of petals, the outer one describing the dominant identity in society, and the inner one filled in by the participant. The object of the exercise is to discover one's social location in light of power dictated by society.

Let us look at the congregation closely in using the Power Flower. Who chooses hymns? Who chooses or creates prayers? Who chooses and reads Scripture passages? Who leads the worship? In short, who make decisions on worship matters? Are children involved in any of these? Are the needs or interests of children reflected in the decision making? As long as children are not considered as valuable participants of the worship, the worship experience may alienate them. As long as children's needs and interests are not included in various times during the worship, it makes it difficult to motivate children to engage and learn. It is an educationally critical task to raise awareness of the actual practice of power within a congregation, and begin to change aspects of decision making that honor all, while addressing unhealthy patterns that privilege only a few. "The phrase, 'we never did it that way before' must cease to be a discussion stopper as we consider worship," Duck contends.[72]

Looking at worship through the lens of children and utilizing the Power Flower exercise helps us to notice other ignored groups. Children enable us to look beyond what we "normally" see in our worship. Since the worship leadership, through the worship committee or the ministerial and music team, is often concerned with the existing and established members of the church, the choice and the decision that they make often represent the styles, habits, and interests of the dominant, normative group. That is what I mean by structural and systematic power that lies in the politics of worship in congregations. Even though they see the new comers and non-established members who regularly worship with them, established members do not actually see them when they plan worship.

Speaking of seeing them but not actually seeing them, it is useful to introduce the term "color-blindness" as often discussed in the discourse on critical race theory. Sociologist Eduardo Bonilla-Silva argues that the myth of color blindness is used by white people as a means of avoiding the topic of racism and accusations of racial discrimination.[73] Patricia Williams puts

---

72. Duck, *Worship for the Whole People of God*, 54–55.
73. Bonilla-Silva, *Racism without Racists*, 53–54.

it this way, "'I don't think about color, therefore, your problems don't exist.' This naïve utopianism, combined with motivated ignorance, does nothing to disrupt hegemonic whiteness." What is needed, she continues, is "a more thoughtful, albeit more complicated, guardianship."[74]

Given that newcomers (who appear but are not seen in worship these days) in the postcolonial era of massive global migration are often racialized, people of color, from the global south, the insight from critical race theory on color-blindness bears some weight for Christian educators and worship leaders who must consider and make some changes around worship. These newcomers are often people with children. We are talking about racialized children, and their families, along with other people of color who have crossed borders, seeking to find new religious homes in the church. By simply welcoming them in worship, without concerning ourselves with their participation, interests and needs, we create "children-blind" and "color-blind" worship. While it may engender an unhelpful bias against people who are blind, the concept of color or children "blindness" bears a useful tool to expose our own hidden prejudices and unexamined practices.[75]

Furthermore, the issue of intersectionality must be added into this discussion on the different groups who are not adequately addressed in worship, Christian education, and practical theology. Dale Andrews calls for practical theology that addresses "duplicitous forms of oppression."[76] When advocating the gifts of children in worship or promoting inclusion of the newcomers of the racialized non-European descent, or accommodating the needs of those with disabilities, it is unhelpful to compartmentalize one oppression over the others, as if they are in competition. So called identity politics is at work here. A more pastoral and faithful approach is to connect the issues of age, race, and disability as interlocking oppressions that people experience differently yet concurrently. In that way, we can see each person as different, as the one who has multiple and complex identities, while each person also shares certain similar identities with others. For example, the heavily word-rationalistic centered worship makes it difficult not only for young children who have not quite grasped cognitive skills, but also for

74. Williams, *Seeing a Color-blind Future*, 4.

75. Kathy Black in *A Hearing Homiletics* investigates various aspects of worship, especially preaching and biblical interpretation, which condone and justify social stigma marked on people with disability. Such justification is most dangerous when it is theologically charged as theodicy or God's punishment due to the lack of faith, or scapegoat as sinner to be cured. Black, *A Healing Homiletic*.

76. Andrews, "African American Practical Theology," 27.

adults with intellectual disability to participate in worship. The message of the preacher whose voice diction is not clear will be inaccessible not only to the newcomers whose first language is not English, but also those who have a hearing disability.

A less overt but equally damaging and harmful issue related to the task of engaging children and other minoritized groups at worship is paternalism. Let us conjure up the biblical metaphor of the lost sheep to illustrate the problem. While the lost sheep has often served to symbolize groups who have been ostracized by society, it is important to avoid regarding them as utterly helpless victims that simply need to be restored to the normative group. If we identify children as the lost sheep, the ones that are excluded in worship, the lesson of the parable is that they are nonetheless precious, worth finding and including. Paternalistic attitudes towards them are unhelpful and even harmful for their identity-formation and full participation in worship. A paradigm shift needs to occur to avoid paternalism. The ninety nine sheep need to see themselves as restored when reunited with the one as much as the other way around. Those in the majority may be deprived of something crucial, if they miss the important opportunity of learning from the minority. Those who enjoy white privilege can learn from those whose identity has been always regarded as suspect. Minorities have something important to teach us because they know how to navigate and affirm their racial, ethnic, and cultural identities. Those in the majority need to learn from those with different abilities, who daily experience discrimination based on their difference, yet embody the vulnerability and resilience of life.[77] Those of us who are adults need to learn to honor children's gifts of spontaneity and honesty. Children, racialized new immigrants, and people with different abilities may as well teach the ninety nine sheep, and restore them to an exciting, surprising, and delightful fullness of life. Perhaps through the lost sheep, their struggles, their resilience and resistance, their graciousness and humility, we, as the rest of the sheep, can encounter God and learn what it means to be the people of God.

Concluding Remarks

While "worship" stands as "the heart of Christian education," as Debra Dean Murphy claims,[78] worship does not stand alone in the life of the church. It

77. Butler, Cambetti, and Sabsay, eds., *Vulnerability and Resistance*.
78. Murphy, *Teaching That Transforms: Worship as the Heart of Christian Education*.

cannot solve the problem of schooling only with the remedy of the full participation of children in worship. As critical as it is to increase the participation of children and the other ignored groups in worship, increasing their involvement in other areas including mission and outreach, for example, as a way of honoring their thoughts and initiatives, is equally critical. Mercer further elaborates on this matter. Her reading of "legitimate peripheral participation"[79] suggested by Jane Lave and Etienne Wenger resonates with my argument on attention to the ones whose positions are structurally and historically marginalized. By peripheral they mean an initial space, though legitimate, which is not at the same level as what "old timers" hold in terms of responsibility, understanding or skill. This peripheral space becomes a marginalized space if they are not encouraged to move to the next stage which is integral inclusion in the practice of the church. Mercer puts it thusly: "for children to gain an identity as members in the community of practice, they must have access not only to its edges but also to its core, in the form of access to its centrally defining practices."[80] Moving beyond legitimate peripheral participation, though necessary, takes patience, requiring some fundamental changes of how we engage practical theology.

The full participation of children every week at worship may be difficult to achieve and even harder to imagine, because no one has actually witnessed this given our flawed and broken experience of church. So here "full" should not be understood as "perfect" or "total" but as "partial and imperfect though nonetheless wholesome." Wholesome worship allows us to glimpse a worship where all participate. It is practice we need to cultivate with conviction and humility. To know that it is not impossible is liberating and powerful enough to motivate those of us who take this path. That is where we begin. That is where the horizon starts to open up towards a new possibility. After all, we are on the journey.

---

79. Lave and Wenger, *Situated Learning: Legitimate Peripheral Participation*.
80. Mercer, *Welcoming Children*, 201.

4

Beyond Christian-Centrism

SIMILAR TO THE INTERRACIAL family issue discussed in Chapter 2, interreligious relationships are on the rise due to migration in the religiously pluralistic postcolonial world. Acknowledging this interreligious reality, this chapter explores a Christian theology of multiplicity and religious hybridity.[1] It argues that practical theology must endeavor to decenter Christianity by appreciating religious plurality and multiple religious belonging within Christian practices and traditions. Such a decentering posture contributes to building up interreligious relationships and practices.[2]

The landscape of Christianity in the twenty-first century has been shifting. Christians in Europe and North America who have enjoyed its power and privilege for centuries have struggled with the minority status of their religion in a predominantly secular and multi-religious society. On one hand, Christians lament the loss of privilege and try to reverse the current shift. On the other hand, other Christians argue that even though Christianity is becoming a minority as a religion, it is not minoritized on the global scene. The Christian sun has not yet set. Christianity continues to carry its colonial and imperial legacies even as the church in the Global South is growing. These Christians argue that religion never exists in isolation but is always inseparably connected to other factors including economy, politics, culture, gender, and race.[3] As long as Christianity is as-

1. Schneider, *Beyond Monotheism*.
2. Kujawa-Holbrook, *God Beyond Borders*.
3. Russell, "God, Gold, Glory, and Gender; Kwok, Compier, and Rieger, eds., *Empire and the Christian Tradition*.

sociated with economic, cultural, and political power, compared to other religions, Christianity still plays an influential, potentially even destructive, role. Practical theologians have a role to play to critically engage this issue.

Given Christian responses to the secularization of both European and Western societies, practical theology could do more to fully study religious plurality within its own tradition and religious pluralism around the world. Religious plurality is not simply an abstract concept but the lived experience of many people. It is also an unfolding context in which different religious practices occur today. This reality was showcased at a conference on multiple religious belonging co-sponsored by The United Church of Christ in the USA, The United Church of Canada, Seattle University and The World Council of Churches. This chapter is informed by that conference and argues that religious hybridity is a way to lift up those who belong to more than one religious and cultural tradition, especially when these traditions have been judged as unorthodox and labelled as syncretic. First, we will talk about the conference and some of its results, followed by a critical examination of a theology of the logic of the One. This examination is necessary if we want to address the problem of Christian-centrism that often results in an attitude of Christian supremacy. Once the logic of the One, referred to as theological monotheism, is challenged, multiple religious belonging can be affirmed. The metaphor of leakage and the permeable nature of Christian identity and practice will be proposed to enhance affirming Christian hybrid traditions and practices which help us decenter Christianity and open up genuine respect for other religions and sincere self-appreciation of Christianity's own pluralistic and heterogeneous traditions.

Descriptions of the Multiple Religious Belonging Issues in Christian Communities

In 2015 I was asked by my church, The United Church of Canada, to present a paper at a consultation on Multiple Religious Belonging which The

United Church of Christ in the USA[4] had organized in partnership with The World Council of Churches.[5]

My denomination was aware of the article I had written and published in *Liturgy in Postcolonial Perspectives,* where I argued for an understanding of baptism as not only belonging but also crossing.[6] I examined Galatians 3:26–28, which has been used as a baptismal formula, to show how belonging to a community has been a central and important meaning of baptism. At the same time, the formula points to the experience of crossing over to other communities and identities. The story of Thecla informed my study. My exploration of baptism as crossing is an attempt to reflect the experience of many Christians affected by migration and interreligious realities who come to terms with the complex and unsettling realities of belonging and crossing.

The gathering at Phoenix, November 2015 was challenging. I met a woman who is a priest of the African Methodist Episcopal church and a Muslim at the same time. She wore a hijab and a clerical shirt. There was a minister who works with families who are both Jewish and Catholic Christian. I also met an interracial woman who grew up with parents of different faiths, one practicing Hinduism and the other practicing Christianity. I got to know an ordained clergy in a Protestant church who is married to a practicing Muslim who raise their interracial children in both religions. They opened up the question of what it means to be Christian while at the same time embracing other religious traditions. Such encounters are not unlike what Kathleen Greider shared from the discussion of diverse students in her classroom. This discussion reflects the complexity and the challenges of the Christian centrist view as much as the religiously pluralistic realities that are on the rise in globalized faith communities.[7] It is a critical issue to those who belong to more than one religious identity due to their relationships either as couples or as children of parents of different faiths. At the

---

4. http://www.ucc.org/news_multiple_religious_belonging_04212015. The first meeting in the USA was "Exploring Religious Hybridity and Embracing Hospitality," Cleveland, Ohio, April 20–23, 2015. It was hosted in conjunction with the World Council of Churches. Later in the same year in November, another consultation "Living Across Religious Traditions: Multiple Religious Belonging and the Changing Religious Landscape," happened at Phoenix, Arizona, 2015.

5. https://www.oikoumene.org/en/press-centre/news/churches-enter-dialogue-on-hybridity-hospitality-and-multi-religious-belonging accessed on November 3, 2016.

6. Kim-Cragg, "Baptism as Crossing beyond Belonging," 201–11.

7. Greider, "Religious Pluralism and Christian-Centrism," 452–53.

next consultation following the conference of 2015, at Seattle University in October, 2016, the conversation on multiple religious belonging deepened. Around that time, I received a Facebook message from a colleague who teaches worship and preaching at a Protestant seminary asking about resources for preaching that address Christian-Muslim relations and raise interreligious awareness in Christian preaching. While religious pluralism is a growing phenomenon of society today, its impact and implication is most strongly felt in worship and preaching as sub-disciplines of practical theology.[8] It is not surprising that these disciplines in practical theology take local, lived experiences seriously. It is urgent to seriously regard the deep religious passions expressed in worship if practical theologians intend to genuinely engage the issue of interreligious dialogue and multiple religious belonging.[9]

How do we preach this interreligious reality to the congregation? How do we create a liturgy reflective of these experiences? Do we have a church school curriculum that properly reflects interreligious and multiple religious belonging issues? Is our Christian ritual encouraging believers to maintain their multiple and hybrid religious identities and celebrate the rituals and festivals of two or more religions? Or is our Christian practice opting for a norm, in the name of unity, uniformity, and order?

Dismantling the Dichotomy That Privileges Theory and Christian Supremacy

The main part of this chapter is a response to these questions. In order to do so we will first undertake an investigation of the doctrine of Christian supremacy in light of the reality of religious hybridity and of religious syncretism. This investigation is necessary because "what passes as acceptable worship or worship that is affirmed in liturgical theology"[10] is grounded in a theological claim, the Oneness of God. Once we establish the problem of Christian-centrism, we can make a case to show how liturgies and other practices have contested this notion by demonstrating the evidence of the "multiplicity of liturgical/ritual forms, gestures, theologies, prayers

8. Ibid., 455.

9. Moore, "Toward an Interreligious Practical Theology," an annual lecture of the Center for Practical Theology in Boston University, 2010. https://www.youtube.com/watch?v=8enGhBO1rKU, accessed February 20, 2017.

10. Jagessar and Burns, *Christian Worship*, 5.

and practices enacted everywhere around the globe."[11] This will lead to suggestions for Christian practices.

The normative force in Christian supremacy has been felt from almost the beginning of Christianity. But for the sake of limiting the discussion, let us go back only as far as the Enlightenment. Most Enlightenment thinkers and theologians believed that there was one universal truth or one rational logic that is applicable to all people and things. They were unapologetic about claiming Christian supremacy over other religions. Friedrich Schleiermacher (1768–1834), regarded as "the father of modern liberal theology," who was especially influential in developing modern forms of Protestant theology, for example, held the position that Christianity, in comparison to other religions, is the most perfect of the most highly developed form of religion.[12] While thinkers and theologians like Schleiermacher claim objective truth for Christianity, the ways they compared other religions were far from objectively neutral.

Contemporary to Schleiermacher, Georg F. Hegel (1770–1831) is another philosopher who made a decisive influence on establishing a typology of religion to prove that Christianity is the only universal religion and superior to all others. This typology posited that non-Western religions were primitive and ahistorical while Christianity was the norm, universally valid for all people and capable of sustaining scientific examination of its doctrines. Thus, Christianity is integral and conducive to the developed scientific thought of philosophy and history. Hegel's attitude of Christian supremacy is contested by many postcolonial scholars, including Gayatri Chakravorty Spivak. Spivak puts Hegel's thought in the context of a German identity crisis in the eighteenth century. This context created a narrative: "the 'scientific' fabrication of new representations of self and world that would provide alibis for the domination, exploitation, and epistemic violation entailed by the establishment of colony and empire."[13]

This identity crisis also combined with a rise of a new identity, the upwardly mobile middle class, and the elite males in the age of capitalism, with whom Schleiermacher identified, according to Joerg Riger.[14] Kwok Pui-lan explains why theologians must interrogate Schleiermacher's work from a postcolonial perspective because his theology and philosophy of

---

11. Carvalhaes, "Liturgy and Postcolonialism," 3.
12. Kwok, *Postcolonial Imagination and Feminist Theology*, 193.
13. Spivak, *A Critique of Postcolonial Reason*, 7.
14. Rieger, *God and the Excluded*, 23.

religion is so closely connected to German nationalism, class, race, gender, and colonial fantasy.[15] Germany, unlike Britain and France, did not have colonies in his time, and yet novels, philosophical essays, and political writings around that time bluntly demonstrate their desire to "venture forth, to conquest and appropriate foreign territories, and to (re)generate the self in the process."[16] This desire led Schleiermacher to inculcate Christian supremacy by subscribing a hierarchical view of religion, categorizing Judaism, Islam, and Hinduism as childlike immature religions.[17]

For Hegel, according to Spivak, knowledge as art (religion included) must consist of both sign (spirit) and meaning (knowledge) and demonstrate its congenial relationship. Acquiring this art as knowledge is, however, not a strict epistemology but rather an epistemography, as Spivak calls it, because Hegel demonstrates this art as "a graduated diagram of the coming-into-being of knowledge."[18] According to Spivak, Hegel's understanding of knowledge is graphic and gradual, displaying how knowledge comes into being instead of how one knows and acquires it. Hegel downplays Eastern religions embedded in the art of Persia, India, and Egypt as deviations from true knowledge because they only display signs and lack meaning. Here, meaning as content and sign is regarded as form or shape. For Hegel, these non-Western religions are absent of content that can be used to construct history. That is where his belief came from: "Africa has no history."[19] These external signs are only *unconscious* symbols, remaining in ahistorical or prehistoric realms, even if they hold "*externally* adequate representations."[20]

Hegel's philosophy of dialectics presumes a dichotomy between East and West. For him the West is capable of historical development while the East remains in an ahistorical and primitive state. John Thatamanil challenges Hegel's dichotomy. Building on the work of Arvind Mandair, Thatamanil shows how this dualism emerges from the logic of the universal and the particular, between abstract theory and practical data. In this divide, he writes, "the very dichotomy between a dynamic, historically self-aware West and a frozen and timeless East" is supported by the notion that

---

15. Kwok, *Postcolonial Imagination and Feminist Theology*, 191.
16. Zantop, *Colonial Fantasies*, 2.
17. Kwok, *Postcolonial Imagination and Feminist Theology*, 192.
18. Spivak, *A Critique of Postcolonial Reason*, 41.
19. Benhabib, *Situating the Self*, 213.
20. Spivak, *A Critique of Postcolonial Reason*, 41. Emphasis is in original.

Western Christianity is a religion of history and knowledge with a conceptual power, while other religions are merely "objects to be theorized and not subjects who are agential contributors to theorizing."[21]

Among Christian theological disciplines, practical theology has most persistently and precisely criticized the devastating effect of the binary between theory and practice in privileging a certain kind of knowledge (theoretical, systematic) at the expense of other kinds of knowledge (practical, pastoral). Bonnie Miller-McLemore successfully interrogates this binary as political.[22] Here "political" indicates hegemonic and institutional, as well as value-laden in terms of exerting theory's domination over practice. Acknowledging religious scholars who have challenged the very notion of religion as a Western and colonialist construct, she notes that such a challenge must face theology as well. As long as there is a binary between theory and practice in theological knowledge production at an institutional level, "it is hard to keep it from becoming institutionalized as a hierarchy."[23] This hierarchy is fed by persistent curricular and disciplinary divisions. It is also fueled by the fear of losing academic rigor and intellectual privilege even among those who want to mend the gap and subvert the divisive way of organizing theological knowledge. Tapping into sociology, psychology, and feminist theory, Miller-McLemore notes, *disciplinary amnesia*, as willed ignorance, as she interrogates how this ignorance was funded by this binary that was constructed, maintained, and continues to exert power in the current academia. Thus, we must remember that *disciplinary amnesia* makes it impossible to recognize how this division has ordered and controlled knowledge. This remembrance as a deliverance from amnesia, is a postcolonializing move, Kwok argues, because it helps us decolonize our minds and save ourselves from "the state of unknowing."[24] Another way to recover from our amnesia is, Miller-McLemore adds, to recognize that this amnesia is sustained by the notion that this binary division is "fixed rather than temporary."[25] It means that *disciplinary amnesia* is bound to change. So to arouse this amnesia is to loosen it as fluid, for this binary division is not secure, though it masks as a mighty fortress.

---

21. Thatamanil, "Comparative Theology after 'Religion,'" 240.
22. Miller-McLemore, "The Politics of Practical Knowledge," 196, 204.
23. Ibid., 214.
24. Kwok, "Unbinding Our Feet," 79.
25. Miller-McLemore, "The Politics of Practical Knowledge," 208.

Faustino Cruz, whose academic life has been shaped by his administrative role as dean for over a decade, probes this division further in the tension between scholarship and service in academic institutions.[26] In Christian seminaries, he finds scholarship associated with research, and publication is given much more importance than acts of service, such as advising and mentoring students or chairing committees for the wellbeing of the institutions or volunteering for the church. Yet, Cruz argues that service requires critical "empathic knowing," aiming to integrate thought with action.[27] Empathic knowing denounces the idea that one should pursue scholarship at the cost of serving church and society. Empathic knowing exposes the misleading notion that knowledge is only printed words (privileging publications) and calls for embodied and lived expressions of understanding.

Unbalanced assessments based on a duality of knowledge extend to other ways of knowing as well. Once we privilege literary written knowledge, for example, knowledge based on orality becomes secondary. This is another colonial legacy, as I have discussed elsewhere, because it produces the hegemony of textualism for the colonial authority who controls what is written, kept, and destroyed, while suppressing performative knowledge which is not often written but belongs to the communities of the colonized.[28] That is why postcolonial scholars promote "vernacular" knowledge, which criticizes the Western literary preference of written interpretation. This vernacular knowledge is important, Sugirtharajah argues, because it not only promotes the importance of oral tradition but also recognizes the experience and the language of the household, the local ordinary colonized people including peasants and women.[29] Here we can also note that knowledge in the academia is not free from the matrix of class, gender, and colonialism. That is why when women who are not white are identified as practical theologians, they become further marginalized and more unrecognized, as Joyce Ann Mercer observes.[30] In the academic hierarchy that privileges disciplines of Bible and systemic theologies and white, male scholars, a practical theologian who carries the marginal identities of female, racialized, differently abled, and/or sexual minority must face

26. Cruz, "The Tension between Scholarship and Service," 60.
27. Ibid., 70.
28. Kim-Cragg, "Postcolonial Practices on Eucharist," 78.
29. Sugirtharajah, "Thinking about Vernacular," 94.
30. Mercer, "Feminist and Womanist Practical Theology," 97–114.

multiple hurdles and fight to resist becoming a "poster child" or a "model minority" to keep the "academic walls" from falling.[31]

Theology that is fed by the binary between theory and practice, scholarship and service often becomes a singular theology fueling the totalitarian form of knowledge. Praising the work of Robert Schreiter, Miller-McLemore contends that theologians can accomplish a lot by simply "recognizing theologies as plural" because such recognition "raises significant questions about justice among diverse forms."[32] As much as the dichotomy between theory and practice has been entrenched in theological disciplines, the totalitarian view created by theology of Christianity as a singular and normative religion has continued to entrap us. The compartmentalized disciplinary hierarchy is interlocked with a totalitarian Christian-centrism. Thus, to denounce this notion of the fixed singular Christian identity is theologically imperative and practical theologians have a critical role to play. The following investigation is a small step towards a postcolonial feminist optic that can effectively and positively engage with this practical theological imperative.

Challenging the Logic of the One

European colonialist Christian encounters with non-European and non-Christian people have often produced a fear in the form of religious plurality and theological multiplicity. Thatamanil argues that from its origin the concept of "religion" as a European colonial construct has served to disguise and alleviate the West's anxiety about the East (Rest). The very concept of religion arose when Europe discovered Indian antiquity, including Sanskrit, the East's sophisticated cultural, philosophical, and linguistic embrace of pantheism. This discovery threatened the "ideological foundations of the colonial project by undermining European notions of civilizational separateness and superiority."[33] As a result, Christian theologians had to come up with the idea of religion within the frame of Christian supremacy. In this sense, Christianity is not a religion *per se* other than serving as the center, while other religions are relativized as secondary religions. This construction of religion put Christianity at ease for it culminated in the central gravity of Christianity.

31. Ahmed, *Living a Feminist Life*, 147–48.
32. Miller-McLemore, "The Politics of Practical Knowledge," 203.
33. Thatamanil, "Comparative Theology after 'Religion,'" 241.

The very category of religion, which Europe created, has also led to the creation of a singular Christian identity. Thatamanil notes, "the notion of singular religious identity . . . is generated by and in turn generates the idea that religions are neatly separated by clearly demarcated and impermeable borders."[34] Kwok Pui-lan, agreeing with him, explains that the term religion, and the related field of religious studies and comparative religious scholarship as we know it, is a European colonial categorization that privileges Christianity, while othering non-Christian religions. In this regard, she suggests David Chidester's definition of religion as "intrareligious and interreligious networks of cultural relations" as a way of expanding the narrowly defined view of religion that privileges a singular homogenous Christianity.[35]

Under the guise of scientific, rational objectivity, the creation of a category of comparative religious scholarship was biased, power-laden, and hierarchical. It veiled the real material asymmetries of power between different religious traditions that exist. Therefore, when we engage the issue of multiple religious belonging as an issue of practical theology, we are actually talking about power differentials and dealing with the "theological regulation of gender, class, ethnicity, and political power."[36] Here, theological regulation to claim the one and only Christian truth is done by white people as a superior race, by males as superior to women, by heterosexual as superior to non-heterosexual, by bourgeoisie as superior to peasants, and by the European colonial powers as superior to colonized societies. It was gendered, heterosexual, and racially biased.

Christian supremacy is exercised through this real power in concrete situations. The logic of the One, as Laurel Schneider calls it, is another term for Christian singular supremacist position when we talk about the concept of God. She investigates the power of the logic of the One in order to argue that divinity is beyond the logic of the One. For "divinity *occurs*" and this occurring "pursues incarnation in terms of bodies, the messy variability of bodies."[37] Though such logic as theological discourse was highly metaphysical and abstract, it was aimed to impact on the material conditions in

---

34. Ibid., 243.

35. Chidester, "Anchoring Religion in the World: A Southern African History of Comparative Religion," 155, cited in Kwok, *Postcolonial Imagination and Feminist Theology*, 205.

36. Cooey, "Fiddling While Rome Burns," 47.

37. Schneider, *Beyond Monotheism*, 1–2. Emphasis is original.

Beyond Christian-Centrism

people's lives. Therefore, once theological and religious discourse is separated from other networks of social relations it loses credibility. As a result, religious peace cannot be achieved without involving other issues. That is also why there is never a solely religious matter because religion always plays out in and intersects with other sociocultural, political, and material relations. It is vital to examine Christian privilege from a postcolonial perspective when we engage with interreligious learning.[38] Thus, when we hear, "Oh, that is a religious matter; we cannot talk about it in a secular, thus, non-religious, arena," we know this is actually a highly political decision that serves the interests of certain groups because it "relieves" those of us who buy "into this economy of engagement with complicities."[39] Or when we hear, "Oh, that is not religion; it is only a spiritual practice, or a cultural practice," we know such dismissal comes from a certain Christian-centric point of view and serves to exclude different kinds of beliefs and practices that cannot fit into an inflexible Christian norm.

What then, enables homogenous Christianity and its theology to be normative? What makes heterogeneous and hybrid Christianity abnormal, illegitimate, and even heretic? The logic of the One as the basis of Christian supremacy frames the idea of a universal, unchanging, one, all-powerful God in heaven. Behind this logic of the One, there is "the arrogant notion that . . . any one religious or political group knows all there is to know about what is correct and therefore can dictate the rules to everyone else."[40] This powerful logic of the One establishes the anti-thesis of multiple religious belonging. Establishing this anti and oppositional stance is key to sustaining the logic of the One. It is impossible to be both; it has to be either One or not-One. There is no other. There cannot be many. As a result, the other becomes 'not-one,' as a negative self. From the colonial gaze, the other brought so much fascination, as well as anxiety and fear. Because, as Schneider puts it, "if to be is to be the same, then to be other is a frightful loss of existence."[41] This is where the fear of the other comes. Under the logic of the One, it is impossible to be different. Here being different is understood as being the other, and being the other means not-one, the denial of a self. So if one is the other, being different means death, thus the existence of the other must be erased. It is tragic, even deadly, to admit

38. Kujawa-Holbrook, "Postcolonial Interreligious Learning," 155.
39. Sharp, "Literacies of Listening," 34.
40. Mollenkott, *Sensuous Spirituality*, 63.
41. Schneider, *Beyond Monotheism*, 88.

one's existence is only possible to the extent that the other is to be erased, conquered and subordinated. Turkish-Sephardic-American philosopher Seyla Benhabib captures this tragic history that led to conquest and subordination: "The Orient is there to enable the Occident, Africa is there to enable western civilization to fulfill its mission, the woman is there to help man actualize himself."[42]

This dualistic and deadly machine of the logic of the One has a dilemma, however. Oneness, Schneider argues, is by necessity divided in itself between true and false. If the contradictory realities stand even as an eschatological possibility, the One is dismantled. That is why this seemingly powerful logic of Christian supremacy funds a deep anxiety about identity, the identity of difference. And that is why it also violently denies and suppresses hybridity or contradiction.[43] However, the good news is that this denial and suppression are unstable, because the one who claims truth and sameness needs the other. The logic of the One is not a safe and secure mighty fortress.

To shift the logic of the One to the logic of multiplicity as the springboard of the theological and religious framework of multiple religious belonging is to fully engage religious hybridity that is inherent in Christianity. Using Thatamanil's pointed question, "Can one imagine the possibility of a theology that is aware from the outset that no tradition is itself pure, singular, homogenous, and thus 'uncontaminated?'"[44] Greider in a similar vein argues that this is the fallacy that identifies loyalty and faithfulness with monotheistic faith and practice. Instead, "intrapersonal religious pluralism," which has been created through "colonialism, socialization, choice, or being born into a multireligious family," must be respected without being labelled as a "lack of mature religious commitment or marginalized as threatening religious syncretism."[45]

The logic of multiplicity as a postcolonial theological framework is not opposed to oneness and unity as temporal arrangements. The very term "belonging," belonging to a group, working together among different groups for certain issues, manifesting in coalitions and solidarity work, is one of many obvious examples that supports a need for oneness and unity. But, as Schneider advises, the logic of multiplicity does not

---

42. Benhabib, *Situation the Self*, 15.
43. Schneider, *Beyond Monotheism*, 89.
44. Thatamanil, "Comparative Theology after 'Religion,'" 251.
45. Greider, "Religious Pluralism and Christian-Centrism," 459.

depend upon the ontological status of inexchangeability, *stasis* that denies the world of difference, temporality, particularity, and permeability.[46] To be different is not to be afraid, therefore Keller says, if we understand "difference," is "neither separation nor an identity, but a relation—a differential relation of embodiment."[47]

Furthermore, to claim that no tradition is pure and all theologies are "messy, agonistic, creative . . . [and] multiple" does not mean that one no longer needs to demonstrate "fidelity to its basic commitment to doing theology" which "is informed and enriched precisely by the traditions" one inhabits.[48] In short, one must not need to give up one's own particular religious and theological identity in order to embrace other identities. These identities are never fixed or permanent. Our theological positions are never stuck nor do they remain static. They can be changed, blurred and thus, are permeable. Hereby allowing non-dual and non-fixed stances, the very notion of dichotomy is dismantled. However, to understand identity as permeable, is difficult when identity is viewed as fixed rather than fluid. As long as our religious identity and our theological positions are presented like a rock rather than a liquid,[49] it is difficult to practice a theology of multiplicity or appreciate religious hybridity.

Here, practical theology has a role to play in articulating a fluid Christian multiple identity. Fluidity implies a process rather than an unchanging entity. Practical theology as an academic discipline that strives to provide a "staging ground for action"[50] can contribute to this articulation because practical theology affirms that Christian identity is always constituted by and constantly changes through relationships, encounters, and practices. The following section addresses practical theology's challenge to the binary of theory and practice, by lifting up lived experiences as sources for doing theology.

---

46. Schneider, *Beyond Monotheism*, 199.
47. Keller, "The Flesh of God," 101.
48. Thatamanil, "Comparative Theology after 'Religion,'" 252.
49. Ward, *Liquid Church*. He introduces this term "liquid church" to shift the understanding of the church as a building to movement, pertinent to people's changing identities.
50. Boyer, "The Scholarship of Engagement," 19–20.

Interdependence

Denouncing Colonial Hegemonic Binary between Theory and Practice

Claudio Carvalhaes observes that Christian practices of worship have been inherently multiple and pluralistic but the churches have tried to harness them in the name of norms, forms, prescriptions, and formulas that opt for normative uniformity.[51] What Carhavalhaes's observation implies furthermore is that multiple and pluralistic practices happened first. The efforts to control and harness their occurrence came afterwards. Attention to the order of this process is critical. That is why theologies that deal with these practices, including liturgical theology, are called "primary theology," while doctrinal and systematic theologies are viewed as secondary theology. To put it in the well-known ancient phrase, *Lex Orandi Lex Credendi*, the law of prayer (practice) precedes the law of belief (doctrine).[52] To distinguish primary theology from secondary theology is not to acquiesce to a hierarchy or deny the effect of the secondary theology on the primary theology.[53] It is far from downplaying the importance of theory and the conceptual work of theology. Sara Ahmed's insight is salient here. She critiques theory that bypasses political dimensions and daily experiences by bracketing colonialism, racism and sexism as if people can live outside (or free from) these oppressive realities. Here theory, she argues for, is "lived theory," an approach that "does not separate politics from living."[54] You could do abstract, but "to abstract," Ahmed writes, "is to drag away, detach, pull away, or divert. We might then have to drag theory back, to bring theory back to life." This is where she stresses the importance of theory and the conceptual work, "in which an embodied experience of power provides the basis of knowledge." Theory here "can do more the closer it gets to the skin" because it generates "sweaty concepts" adequate to describe a "situation" as "something that comes to demand a response."[55] Ahmed's point is further illuminated in the insight of Mary McClintock Fulkerson in *Places of Redemption*, where she explores a worldliness of theology for the ordinary which leads toward a practical theology. For this goal, she establishes the primary task

---

51. Carvalhaes, "Liturgy and Postcolonialism," 4.

52. This phrase is coined by the late monk Prosper of Aquitaine in the fifth century. See more in Duck, *Worship for the Whole People of God*, 3.

53. Wainwright, "Theology of Worship," 456.

54. Frye, "Introduction," 13.

55. Ahmed, *Living a Feminist Life*, 10, 12, 13.

of practical theology as "describing a situation," which deserves attention and compels "a response."[56]

The secondary theology (read as systematic and dogmatic theology) has often failed to reflect contradictory beliefs and value commitments. As a result, typical patterns of doing theology occlude ambiguity of practices of the ordinary as a valid source of theological reflection.[57] In short, it is important to note the primacy of lived experiences and practices of people, as a central element of theologizing, integral to both primary and secondary theology. Practices among people at the grassroots level shape and inform theology first, followed by the articulation of why we believe the way we believe. It is imperative to pay attention to the priority of these practices, when they are especially suppressed. Emmanuel Lartey gives wise advice in this regard: "the postcolonializing pastoral leader" should never be "satisfied with solely one perspective on any subject," but actively seek out "other voices, especially submerged, ignored, or rejected voices."[58]

This is also a concrete way to denounce the colonial hegemonic binary between theory and practice, the universal and the particular, meaning and sign, because it serves to explore "how theories are themselves transformed by their practical effects when they are performed in other sites."[59] Examples of sites where the practical effects transform theory can be found in most Asian countries where it is not uncommon for people of faith and people of no faith to visit religious temples other than one's own to worship or for special celebrations. Such practices of fluidly crossing religious boundaries, once people are encouraged to experience them, contribute to navigating to inhabit multiple religious belonging without denying one's own tradition.[60]

Affirming Bodily Fluidity and Theological Leakage

Multiple religious belonging or the affirmation of a multiplicity of theologies is not a new conversation. It has always existed. In terms of its most recent manifestations, practical theology has been responding to the questions about interreligious marriage since the 1960s in the USA.[61]

56. Fulkerson, *Places of Redemption*, 12, 14.
57. Tanner, "Theological Reflection and Christian Practices," 230.
58. Lartey, "Borrowed Clothes Will Never Keep You Warm," 30.
59. Sakai, *Translations and Subjectivity*, 91.
60. Kwok, *Postcolonial Imagination and Feminist Theology*, 540–44.
61. Greider, "Religious Pluralism and Christian-Centrism," 457.

However, a close examination of multiple religious belonging and religious hybridity as a topic for practical theology has barely surfaced. That is why some practical theologians acknowledge that multiple religious belonging and amphibolous faith issues have not yet been explored.[62] Indeed, it has never fully appeared or occurred, highlighted by Schneider's view of divinity as occurring, as an essential topic of practical theology; rather, the conversation around multiple religious belonging, religious syncretism and religious hybridity in the church and academia has been silenced and suppressed.

The reason why religious syncretism and religious hybrid practices have been silenced and suppressed is in part because such practices were deemed messy and chaotic. In an attempt to address this chaos to affirm the realities of ordinary life Miller-McLemore helpfully notes the human tendency to fear chaos and cling to orderliness. Chaos as messiness is associated with "dirt, dust, and debris," the world of devils and destructiveness.[63] While a constant and complete chaos is dangerous and harmful to our well-being, we must acknowledge that chaos was at the beginning of creation in our Genesis biblical narrative and that it has always been part of our life as created beings. Genesis and Revelation, the first and the last books of the Bible, point to the cycle of life where the end is the beginning and the beginning is the end.[64] In fact, earth emerged from the waters as the result of chaotic volcanic activity six billion years ago.[65] When we think about these fierce forces erupting in fiery and chaotic ways, it may conjure associations with popular images of hell covered in fumes and flames. Yet, this is how life began. Instead of the end of life, this chaotic event resulted in the birth of life. "In the beginning God created the heavens and the earth, the earth was a formless void and darkness covered the face of the deep, while a wind from God swept over the face of the waters" (Genesis 1:1–2). All of us came from a formless chaos. The face of the deep was chaotic and messy. This chaotic mess is not evil, as far as the writer and storyteller of Genesis is concerned. Ahmed, affirming messiness as life-giving, also notes that engaging intersectionality in social analysis and scholarship is also messy. As well as postcoloniality, because "a politics of location" is

---

62. Cahalan and Mikoski, eds., *Opening the Field of Practical Theology*, 273.
63. Miller-McLemore, *In the Midst of Chaos*, 17.
64. Beavis and Kim-Cragg, *What Does the Bible Say?* 11.
65. http://www.cbc.ca/geologic/eg_atlantic_coast.html.

"unstable" and "shaped by multiple historical trajectories,"[66] which are often marked by destructive, unpredictable events such as war, famine, climate change, and unknown crises. An individual history is always entangled by these trajectories; that is why a person's identity is messy and unstable, as discussed in Chapters 2 and 3.

The other reason why religious syncretism and religious hybrid practices have been silenced and suppressed is in part because such practices were deemed impure. The association of religious syncretism and religious hybridity with impurity is linked with the biblical understanding of the suitability of priests and impurity of sexuality. Mary Ann Beavis and HyeRan Kim-Cragg have noted that while elucidating the meaning of purity, the Bible does not actually say that impurity, associated with bodily leakage, is negative. They write:

> Purity laws (Lev 17–26) do not pertain primarily to sex, but to bodily states that render persons, especially priests, ritually fit or unfit to engage in acts of worship, especially in the context of offering sacrifices in the temple. Ritual impurity could be incurred through disease, contact with a corpse, bodily discharges (including, but not confined to, menstruation), and sexual activity (which involves bodily discharges for both men and women). Objects as well as people could be considered impure in this sense, illustrating the non-moral nature of ritual impurity.[67]

While the biblical reference of ritual purity is not necessarily related to female sexuality, the link was strongly made to exclude women from the priesthood throughout the years of Christendom. At this time, purity as something noble and virtuous was linked to monotheism. The men were deemed to be of a noble and virtuous nature and thus suitable for religious leadership roles. Here virtue and virility were closely linked in Christian dualistic thought.[68] The labeling of women as impure and unfit for liturgical leadership is often associated with bodily-ness, and specifically blood-leakage. Not long ago there was an uproar of feminist leaders in Korea when a moderator of an ultraconservative Presbyterian church publicly opposed women's ordination on the grounds that menstruation made them unfit to be clergy.[69] The identity of womanhood, marked by leakage of blood,

---

66. Ahmed, *Living a Feminist Life*, 119.
67. Beavis and Kim-Cragg, *What Does the Bible Say?* 132.
68. Jung, "Patriarchy, Purity, and Procreativity," 74.
69. http://www.newsnjoy.or.kr/news/articleView.html?idxno=6502, accessed on

continues to hinder ordination of women in many churches. Another association of women with body leakage is the birth process, which begins with the water being broken, leakage of water from the womb. Breast feeding is also a form of leakage. These are fundamental but not essential body experiences identified with womanhood. Yet, they have served to justify the exclusion of women from all kinds of places including leadership roles in the church. Body leakage has been used to determine women's inferiority to men in Western epistemology, theology and philosophy.[70]

Purity is established as detachment from the bodily-ness, especially fluidity or leakage. It is the leaking of bodily fluids, whether due to menstruation or lactation or sexual intercourse, or skin and other diseases, which has caused the most concern for Jewish and Christian and other religious thinkers for centuries. The escape of liquids from the body is the most visceral and vivid sign of impurity. While it is gendered and sexualized, it is used to support bias against those who are ill and racialized. People with illnesses (e.g., skin disease) were labeled as unclean and impure. Being white is often understood as pure, while non-white people of color are impure. The examination of blood, as discussed in Chapter 2, is closely related to notions of racial and sexual purity and impurity.

Philosophers Gilles Deluze and Felix Guattari denounce the connection of fluidity as illness and undesirability. They point out that "society is always *en fuite*, (leaking and fleeing), and may be understood in terms of the manner in which it deals with its *fuites* (leaks, lines of flight)."[71] What they imply is that leakage could be a sign of a healthy society, though it appears to be messy and even chaotic. This rings true to any embodied beings for whom leakage is an integral part of the healthy life. Panelope Washbourn contends that bleeding in menstruation is "cleansing," nature's way of discharging something it needs to void. Even though it is messy and inconvenient and involves emotional and physical discomforts, menstruation as leakage holds the value of "ambiguity as an ending (of fertility) as well as a beginning (potency for giving birth)."[72] Though it often

---

February 20, 2017. The Moderator of the General Assembly of the Presbyterian Church in Korea, at that time, TaeDuik Lim said, "there is no way that women who are wearing diapers every month can stand on the pulpit and preach." He said this at the seminary chapel, November 12, 2003.

70. Miller-McLemore, *Christian Theology in Practice*, 128.

71. Deluze and Guattari, *A Thousand Plateaus*, 88–89, cited in Schneider, *Beyond Monotheism*, 179.

72. Washbourn, "Becoming Woman: Menstruation as Spiritual Challenge," 250, 256.

involves discomfort, and even causes excruciating pain for some women, it is a healthy and natural process associated with healing and fertility. We do not need to go on to explain what menstruation means and does, or about other fluids including semen and urine, coming out of our body as these and other bodily discharges are generally understood to be fundamental to our well-being.

In terms of highlighting the importance of fluidity in the body, an example of cancer related to blood clots may be instructive. Those of us who have had cancer or have had our loved ones suffering from cancer know the side effect of blood clots. Blood clots are common in cancer patients or any patients that are immobilized. Even if many remain in remission (cancer free), most of them still have to take a blood thinner medication as long as they live because blood could get stuck in the veins. In this case, helping blood flow is a sign of healing rather than causing illness; it is a sign of movement rather than stillness. We cannot romanticize and ought not to be naïve about the destructive nature of leakage and fluidity. When our house leaks, our shelter is in danger. When our dam leaks, our safety is in danger. When we lose blood, we must attend to this urgently. In short, we must acknowledge both truths, when blood clots occur, people can die, and when blood leakage does not stop, this can also result in death.

The biblical references to a purity code as discussed above do not indicate that being impure was sinful, and did not necessarily imply dirtiness. The Bible does not say bad things about bodily discharges because many good actions including caring for the dead, giving birth, having sex with one's partner would inevitably incur leakage. Such occurrence as impurity could be dealt with by appropriate rituals and the passage of time. We, in the course of our biological lives, inevitably cause impurity including menstruation for women and ejaculation of semen for men, or the excretion of blood or pus for those who have skin disease.[73]

To spin the meaning of bodily leakage into that of theological leakage, one may argue that religious hybridity embedded in a theology of multiplicity may be understood as the evidence of a kind of theological leakage. Interreligious marriage and relationships is one example one can name as evidence of social, religious forms of leakage. Their commitment to love and to respect religious differences may be stronger than the rock of Christian-centrism. Their experiences of life together, which are full of negotiations, may create hybrid and syncretic religious practices. They may

---

73. Beavis and Kim-Cragg, *What Does the Bible Say?* 132.

be a threat to those who buttress the mighty fortress of the logic of the One. However, these practices could also become well-spring water to those who are thirsty for messy, porous, incarnational life. To alter the conversation in order to enunciate a new space is to change the view of God who is "no longer an all-powerful, unchanging Lord in the sky." Instead, God is both comforter and "Discomforter" who is "disruptive, disturbing, and even evolving . . . , appearing in unexpected and unplanned places."[74] Perhaps, the logic of the One, the God who is detached, fixed, and static, is one of "the mighty liturgical and theological fortresses" that needs to break down and loosen up.[75]

Even seemingly impenetrable fortresses are vulnerable to leakage, which can cause severe damage and even cause them to collapse. Ahmed speaks of "brick walls" that have been assembled and reassembled over long histories. These walls are more than physical and material barriers. They could be "an atmosphere" or "a gesture." They could be "invisible" to those who do not encounter them in their daily lives. Being stared at, the color-blindness of not seeing, and the issue of passing as discussed in Chapters 2 and 3, could be types of brick walls. One way to break down these walls, says Ahmed, is to make them talk: "if they stay up, we want the walls to talk, to tell our story. A story too can shatter: a thousand tiny little pieces, strewn all over the place. . . . We dwell, we tell. How telling."[76]

Schneider observes that the logic of the One, though powerful, has always faced a persistent resistance from minority theological and devotional traditions throughout the world. Religious syncretism and hybridity have always leaked. There have always been themes that run counter to the logic of the One, resilient infusions of indigenous philosophies, ontologies, and possibilities of divine multiplicity in Christian worship and theology.[77] The anthology *Women at Worship* that was published in 1993, for example, includes diverse practices of ritual: pagan ritual invoking the Goddess, non-denominational women-church that transforms the traditional male-centered liturgy, Hispanic Mujerista liturgy that demystifies the sacred by making it accessible to women, resistant womanist ritual, and reclaiming women's oral tradition in Jewish ritual.[78] These women created the leakage,

74. Miller-McLemore, *In the Midst of Chaos*, 18.
75. Carvalhaes, "Liturgy and Postcolonialism," 12.
76. Ahmed, *Living a Feminist Life*, 220–22.
77. Schneider, *Beyond Monotheism*, 76.
78. Procter-Smith and Walton, eds., *Women at Worship*.

tainting the liturgical fortress, undermining the seemingly tight brick walls. Such disruptive and transgressive practices continue today, found in the Brazilian MCC where Marcos Lord as lay pastor preaches in drag, claiming the space of preaching for the transgender community. Mona West provides other examples such as celebrating World AIDS Day along with Gay Pride and Transgender Day of Remembrance as holy days in the liturgical calendar. Cross-dressing in clerical collars, albs, stoles, leather vestments, boas, mitres, and rainbow stoles is also a hybrid, syncretic, and subversive practice contesting the logic of the One and that of purity.[79]

While we must admit that the logic of the One still dominates theological discourse, we should never assume that the construction of Christian supremacy was seamless. Though silenced, suppressed, and distorted, no one can deny these supple and porous movements of multiple religious hybridity that are running through our biblical hermeneutics, theological traditions and liturgical practices.

Biblically speaking, God's multiplicity is portrayed in the stories in the Bible.[80] For example, the word translated as God in the Priestly creation account (Gen 1:1—2:4a) is *Elohim*, literally means, "gods." That is why God proclaims, "let *us* make humankind in *our* image, according to *our* likeness" (Gen 1:26). In the pre-exilic Israel, the existence of plural gods was the norm, as a well-known commandment demonstrates, "you shall have no other gods *before me*" (Exod 20:3). It is only in the biblical books written after the return from exile (538 BCE), that monotheism in a pure and exclusive sense, is established.[81] One can speculate many reasons for this shift from the multiplicity of God to a monotheistic God in Jewish and later Christian Scriptures. Schneider provides a convincing reason by paying attention to the impact of the exile experiences: "the assault of more than a half millennium of war, exile, and colonization" could be "the conditions that made *exclusive* monotheism both intelligible and persuasive, particularly when what was at stake was cultural survival."[82]

There have also been subversive Christian theological musings on the trinity and the incarnation.[83] The ancient concept of God as Trinity has

---

79. West, "Metropolitan Community Church as a Messy Space," 54.

80. Kirsch, *God against the Gods*.

81. Beavis and Kim-Cragg, *What Does the Bible Say?* 81–84.

82. Schneider, *Beyond Monotheism*, 33–38. The emphasis is original.

83. Kwok, "Jesus/The Native: Biblical Studies from a Postcolonial Perspectives," 75–80.

radicalized the meaning of the divine, the one traditionally understood as the encompassing heavenly monarch that rules from above, to the one completely united with and inseparable from Jesus, incarnate fully in humanity, born in a lowly manger, who lived and died like everyone else, a fellow human being. And this theology of the Trinity is also radical in that God, Jesus, and Spirit are in full communion, without hierarchical order, captured in the term, *perichoresis*, which was developed in the fourth century to describe the dynamic and interdependent relation by embracing three different-yet-equal "persons." Joerg Rieger and Kwok Pui-lan elaborate on this: "In the beginning there is not one single God who then produces a Trinity; in the beginning there is a relationship that models the sort of unity in difference that is also characteristic of the multitude. There is no going back to some primordial unity without diversity."[84] The theological spin around the multitude that is worth noting is its connection of the doctrine of the Trinity to religious pluralism. I have explored this connection with Daoism and Hindu theology elsewhere.[85] Thanks to this relational Trinitarian God we can learn from and appreciate other religious traditions that can in turn be illumined by our own traditions. We tap into other religious traditions neither because we feel our own tradition deficient nor because we desire to appropriate others into our own with a sense of superiority. Rather, we seek to draw from our own deep wells, while also respectfully drawing from other sources of wisdom. This appreciation of others in humility is itself a concrete practice needed for an interdependent practical theology.

Polydoxy is the other theological concept that is helpful in articulating a postcolonial feminist practical theology of interdependence that addresses religious hybridity and Trinitarian relationality. Keller and Schneider define polydoxy as the theology of multiplicity and relation.[86] It points to many paths to truth, recognizing the plurality of religious traditions. Kwok Pui-lan, in a discussion of the future of interfaith dialogue, argues that "polydoxy requires us to debunk and demystify the logic of the One, and especially of monotheism," recognizing the limitation of all our metaphors for God, refusing to call God in any absolute, totalitarian or fixed sense.[87] Rooted in religiously diverse traditions, polydoxy extends its meaning to

---

84. Rieger and Kwok, *Occupy Religion*, 66.
85. Kim-Cragg, "A Plural Mystery for a Plural World," 134–40.
86. Keller and Schneider, eds. *Polydoxy: Theology of Multiplicity and Relation.*
87. Kwok, *Globalization, Gender, and Peacebuilding*, 73.

the cosmos, as the place and the space beyond any geographical and national boundaries. This God of polydoxy is not in line with the traditional attributes of God as divine immutability, divine impassibility, and divine omnipotence, but joining in the view that God moves and dwells in the people's daily lives. In this view our encounter with God is a kind of leakage flowing at times like a mighty river for justice and peace in the world.

Implications of Religious Hybridity for Christian Practical Theology

What are the implications for Christian practical theologians, now and once we affirm heterogeneous and hybrid Christianity as normal, legitimate, and even desirable? One implication for such affirmation is that any book that still purports "a classic and a main resource for much of the liturgical renewal movement can no longer *hold* its basic promise that there is/was a uniform shape of liturgy that can be traced back to this once imagined monolithic thing called the early Christian church or Christian liturgy, in the singular."[88]

Instead practical theology should acknowledge the paradoxical doubleness of doing theology. Feminist liturgical theologians have proposed a kind of "double vision," a vision that "enables women to see the truth of their tradition's ritual practices and also to see what that tradition might become."[89] It is, for example, to recognize that any Christian practice, including Eucharist, carry this doubleness, containing subversive, counter-cultural, and resistant power while at the same time, patriarchal, misogynist, colonial tendencies.[90] In performance theory, doubleness means the play between actual and imaginary, between the real and the mimetic.[91] In ecclesiology, it means that the church inhabits a double reality, as already and not yet. This ambivalent and unsettling doubleness position of ecclesial knowledge and liturgical practice have created both privileged spaces for social entanglement and resistant spaces at the margin—that is, "porous spaces" enchanted by "unknown forms of life, other forms of thinking,

---

88. Carvalhaes, "Liturgy and Postcolonialism," 6. He provides *The Shape of Liturgy* by Gregory Dix as an example.

89. Procter-Smith, "Introduction," 2.

90. Kim-Cragg, "Postcolonial Practices on Eucharist," 82.

91. Craigo-Snell, *The Empty Church*, 20.

other possibilities of the holy and its sacred gestures, different praxes, indigenous resources, resistance processes and people's self-affirmation."[92]

Thus, attention to religious hybridity for Christian life as a task of practical theology is to encourage people to live in a creative, even contradictory tension, holding both without opting for one over the other. Such doubleness also includes learning to reside in the process of moreness, messiness, and mixtures, recognizing that all living beings came from formless void. Thus, we as "body and soul need a soaking from time to time."[93] It is impossible to keep our hands dry and clean if we truly appreciate the fluidity of life as sacred and sources of practical theology. Hybrid suppleness is rooted in the daily life of the people, especially those who are vulnerable, who are on the move, who are poor, colonized, and marginalized as minorities. We will know when practical theology loses its vitality and credibility, once it does not speak to and detach from these people's experiences. As previously mentioned, it holds true to claim that practical theology is primary theology. But it is even more true to contend that practical theology is secondary to the life of a community.[94] Before any theology, before any liturgy, there is life, the messy, supple, and hybrid life in communities. Samir Selmanovic whose life is shaped by interreligious relationships captures this wisdom eloquently: "The sacrament of human life is the sacrament that supersedes our religions. We live before we believe, and we are human before we are religious. Our life together is a temple where we all meet."[95]

As an end, it would be worth pondering the meaning of "apocalypse." Often interpreted as "the end" of the world, "apocalypse" comes from the Greek word *apokalypsis,* which means to "unveil, to disclose, to reveal." It is a disclosure of something hidden. Biblically speaking, and in the cycle of life, a beginning goes hand in hand with an end or a closure. As pointed out earlier, even if Genesis is a beginning, and Revelation is placed at the end, the Bible does not have to take this order in a linear sense. An apocalypse may usher in a new reality. As Keller says, "'The End,' may, paradoxically, dis/close an opening."[96] As argued earlier, our discussion

---

92. Carvalhaes, "Liturgy and Postcolonialism," 13.

93. "My Love Colours Outside the Lines," by Gordon Light (1995) of the Common cup company.

94. Carvalhaes, "Praying Each Other's Prayers," 147.

95. Selmanovic, *It's Really All About God*, 58, cited in Kujawa-Holbrook, *God Beyond Borders*, 124.

96. Keller, *Apocalypse Now and Then*, 2.

of religious hybridity in Christianity is not new. But if this newness is a disclosure of something hidden, and means the beginning of an end of the logic of the One, I propose that our conversation takes newness as an apocalyptic unveiling.

5

Beyond Belonging and Borders

THIS CHAPTER EXPLORES THE theme of belonging and borders by turning our attention to the context of migration and the notion of home. Canada's context will be featured as a space of migration.[1] Attention to the particularity of contexts is central to practical theology's interests. To examine Canada's immigration history, we will employ a social policy method and will relate our findings to histories in the developed world.

Sustained attention to the local and the particular "makes" practical theology's "web of our relationships more apparent" and "grants us . . . a more contextually astute witness."[2] This contextually astute witness enables us to locate twenty-first-century migration in a postcolonial context. In order to properly comprehend global migration today, knowledge of postcolonial legacies is essential. The legacy of colonialism cannot only be understood in a historical way but requires a spatial analysis as well. This holds true of the contemporary phenomenon of migration reality, which is affected by the dynamics of space, as well as time on a global scale.[3] With the help of Scripture, this chapter closely examines the story of the family of Jesus with attention to their experience as refugees.[4] Finally, migration is presented as both a challenge and a possibility, as well as a promise that invites different communities to struggle to live together for the sake of interdependent relationships beyond human-made borders.

1. Razack, ed., *Race, Space and the Law*.
2. Cahalan and Nieman, "Mapping the Field of Practical Theology," 80–81.
3. Soja, *Seeking Spatial Justice*.
4. Kim-Cragg and Choi, *The Encounters*.

Beyond Belonging and Borders
Probing the Uneasiness of "Home"

What is home? Home in the post-colonial world is far from a comfortable and familiar space. Dorothy's magical phrase in the Wizard of Oz, "There is no place like home," would get us nowhere in today's world.

A novel by Toni Morrison *Home* illustrates the contemporary global and postcolonial experience of home.[5] Frank Money, the protagonist in this novel, is a veteran of the Korean War. He returns to his country, the USA, yet struggles to find home because the home he used to know is no longer there. His search for home turns into a quest for his identity. And in the midst of this search, he is led down many winding paths and at one point, spirals downward violently taking someone's life. This moment is full of irony for Frank Money. He had hoped to avoid death because he had seen so much of it in the Korean War. War haunts him like a ghost throughout his journey to find home. The journey towards home ultimately ends in the realization of homelessness. All of us are somewhat like Frank Money. When we hear about the tension around the Korean peninsula, we are tempted to dismiss it as an absurdity happening far away with no bearing on our daily life. When we hear of ongoing conflicts in Syria, Israel and Palestine, Congo, South Sudan, and other places, and the plight of the refugees of these conflicts, it is possible to be gripped by a sense of hopelessness, unsettledness, and helplessness, even though we ourselves might not be directly part of those stories. Along with the sense that events are happening far away, there is a global awareness and immediacy to these events for everyone on planet earth. It is wise to be sensitive to this truth. We must resist, too, the easy and false sense of security that sees such events as "over there." In fact postcolonial discourse can be seen as an attempt to disrupt the notion of "over there" and make the experience of global "others" an ingredient of "our" lived experiences.[6]

Before his death in 2003, Edward Said wrote his last book entitled *Out of Place*. This memoir is loved by many because of his life journey of migration, his experience of finding home away from home, and homelessness in the midst of his most familiar places. It resonates with those of us migrants with similar experiences. In this memoir, Said confesses his "unsettled sense of many identities."[7] Such unsettling complexity of

---

5. Morrison, *Home*.
6. Sharp, "Literacies of Listening," 34.
7. Said, *Out of Place*, 6.

identity is certainly found in those who have experienced physical and geographical migration. However, it can be also experienced among those of us whose work involves national borders. It is also not unlike the experience of those who engage in interdisciplinary work and whose disciplines are undetermined by the unhelpful binary power dynamics in academia.[8]

Migration is a journey undertaken in search of a new home. This search for a new home is one of the strongest forces shaping the world today. We live in a global "age of migration."[9] Active engagements on this topic for practical theology are needed in our classrooms and research. Migration is nothing new; in fact, migration is an ancient human phenomenon. It is a necessity of life. In order to survive and live, any human community, and to some extent, most living creatures must travel and move. Our earth, the very planet that provides us with a home also moves constantly. If the earth stopped migrating, so to speak, life as we know it would end on the planet. While migration is a necessity of life and has always existed, it has not always been easy or safe, especially in recent history. Canadian historian Jennifer Welsh argues that it was "the Second World War that sparked the most pronounced and geographically dispersed example of conflict-related migration, with asylum seekers originating in multiple countries and crossing more than one national border."[10] The scale of migration in the twentieth and twenty-first century is so massive and so global that it affects us all. Its scope and size is unprecedented and increasing at an alarming rate. The data in 2015 shows that the total number of displaced people is about sixty-five million. It has reached the highest level in human history.[11] This is a context of "mass flight."[12] According to a UN report, from 2011 to 2015, the number of people around the globe who were forcibly displaced increased 50 percent. This means on average, twenty-four people were displaced every minute—almost double the typical frequency at which adults breathe.[13] The scale of this phenomenon in recent decades is so big, so fast,

---

8. Miller-McLemore, "The Theory-Practice Binary and the Politics of Practical Knowledge," 190–218.

9. Castles and Miller, *Age of Migration*.

10. Welsh, *The Return of History*, 121.

11. http://reliefweb.int/report/world/unhcr-global-trends-forced-displacement-2015, accessed on December 30, 2016.

12. Welsh, *The Return of History*, 109.

13. http://reliefweb.int/report/world/unhcr-global-trends-forced-displacement-2015, accessed on January 18, 2017.

and so global, that it is characterized as catastrophic.[14] Cognizant of this catastrophic and massive flight of people on a global scale, let us zoom in on Canada to examine social policy on migration.[15] Canada's issues and realities may resonate with most other developed nations including the USA and European countries.

Canada: A Case Study

Canada's national identity, its origin, and its own worldview have been determined and shaped by migration. Canada is a country whose history includes many various waves of immigration. Canada enjoys a reputation throughout the world for being the most multicultural nation and also the most welcoming to immigrants and refugees. It is true that Canada was the first country to create an inclusive immigration and citizenship act, establishing multiculturalism as its official government policy in 1971. But unfortunately this positive assessment of Canada's accomplishments is not the whole story.

Jewish Canadian historian Irving Abella contests Canada's positive reputation. He writes, "It is one of our great national myths that Canada has a long history of welcoming refugees and dissidents, of always being in the forefront of accepting the world's oppressed and dispossessed, of being receptive and hospitable to wave after wave of immigrants, . . . yet as the recent literature in Canadian history has shown, the Canadian record is one of which we ought not to be proud. Our treatment of our native people as well as our abysmal history in admitting blacks, Chinese, Japanese, Indians and during 1930s and 1940s Jews, should lay to rest [this] myth."[16] The study of these groups that Abella lists below shows that the Canadian government, especially in the early part of the twentieth century, was far from hospitable to non-White and non-Christian people. Let us briefly examine these groups.

---

14. Welsh, *The Return of History*, 109.
15. Couture, "Social Policy," 153–62.
16. Abella, "Foreword," vii.

INTERDEPENDENCE

Chinese Migrants: The First Temporary Foreign Workers in Canada

In the year 2017, Canada celebrated the 150th anniversary of its Confederation. In an attempt to create a "White Nation,"[17] four provinces of Nova Scotia, New Brunswick, Southern Quebec, and Southern Ontario, agreed in 1867 to join in forming a new nation. The government passed its first *Immigrant Act* in 1869. British Columbia (BC), the most western province joined the Confederation four years later in 1871. The joining of BC fueled a desire to connect the East and the West through the building of a national rail road. The project of a railroad reaching from coast to coast required workers, and so the government recruited more than fifty thousand Chinese men to come to Canada.

The Chinese workers built the Canadian railroad from British Columbia to Thunder Bay, roughly the halfway point between east and west. In the process of building the railroad, some Chinese workers were killed and many were injured. Though they worked hard and sacrificed a great deal in creating Canada, government policy made it difficult for them to bring their own families over to join them. Once the train tracks were built in 1885, many of the workers were expelled. Those who remained in Canada and wished to bring their families were made to pay a so-called "Chinese head tax," the exorbitant equivalent of two years of wages for each family member. This tax was applied to every new Chinese immigrant and became a barrier to the movement of people from China to Canada. As if this were not enough, other discriminatory policies were applied to dissuade Chinese immigration. These social policies dictated that Chinese immigrants could neither acquire Crown Land nor vote. They could not serve on juries or work in the professions in British Columbia. These government policies were placed in the *Chinese Immigrant Act,* also known as *Chinese Exclusion Act,* which became the first formal race-based immigration restriction law in Canada.[18] Racism toward Chinese immigrants was rampant all over Canada in the early part of the twentieth century. An example is provided in a Toronto newspaper article titled, "Move to Check Smuggling of Chinese into Canada":

---

17. Sociologist and Equity studies scholars Nupur Gogia and Bonnie Slade categorized 1869–1967 as the period of "constructing a White Nation." See their *About Canada*, 19.

18. Ibid., 21.

The average Anglo-Saxon is incapable of distinguishing with any degree of certainty different members of the Chinese race. He only knows that the man before him is a Chinaman, with characteristic eyes, features, pigmentation and gibberish of the Oriental. The difficulty is only increased by the Chinaman's notorious disregard of the truth, and low estimate of his oath. Photographs and body marks should assist greatly in the identification of Chinese criminals and in the administration of justice to these, the most elusive of wrongdoers.[19]

Such orientalist and racist views began to change on the government level in the later part of the twentieth century. The following is one such example of how the official government documented their work and contribution more accurately:

> The building of the Canadian Pacific and Canadian National Railways called for skilled professionals. It called for surveyors and engineers who could plan the routes and grades, experts who could choose the locomotives and rolling stock suited to Canadian conditions, as well as managers who could oversee the complex operations. Then there were people who carried out the orders—thousands of Irish and Chinese laborers were brought into the country for the back-breaking manual work.[20]

It took 120 years for the Canadian government to finally acknowledge that its anti-immigration policy against Chinese people had been racist and to make an official apology to the Chinese community. The government apologized and compensated those who suffered under these discriminatory laws on June 22, 2006.[21]

There are many other discriminatory social policy practices that Canada shamefully exercised against non-White and non-Christian groups. Due to the limited space, I will just name two additional groups. The story of the *Komagata Maru*, is a story of a group of 376 Indian, Hindu, Muslim, and Sikh citizens of British India (they all had British passports) who were refused permission to land in Vancouver on May 23, 1914.[22] The grounds

---

19. The front page of *Toronto Daily News* on January 24, 1913, cited in Gogia and Slade, *About Canada*, 23–24.

20. "Growing Together: A Backgrounder on Immigration and Citizenship," 2.

21. Gogia and Slade, *About Canada*, 24.

22. Kazimi, *Undesirables*. He as film maker also released a documentary called "Continuous Journey" (2004) that captured this event of *Komagata Maru*.

for their rejection were simply racist.²³ Eventually they were forced to return to India. Many did not survive the return trip. Another example is taken from the Second World War, when Pearl Harbor was attacked in 1941. The federal government removed twenty thousand Japanese-Canadians from their homes and sent them to internment camps. Though most of them were born in Canada and had never been to Japan let alone had any connection to the Japanese war effort, they were treated as enemy aliens. Some were even forced to return to Japan and prevented from returning to their Canadian homes.²⁴ These stories are not unique to Canada; Japanese Internment also took place in the USA. Lisa Lowe, for instance, also looks at the example of Asian immigration to the United States to showcase how this kind of racist and discriminatory policy has shaped the nationhood, citizenship, labor and law of the USA.²⁵

African American Migrants: The First Black People on the Canadian Prairie

While the railroad West to East was completed in 1885, the movement to join Confederation took longer in the middle of the country. Alberta and Saskatchewan, neighboring provinces of British Columbia, finally joined the confederation in 1905. In 1910, twelve black families from Oklahoma moved north to settle in Eldon, near Maidstone, Saskatchewan. Led by Joe and Mattie Mayes, they had been attracted to this new province. The province desperately needed new immigrants; thus, they produced and spread promotional literature extolling the prairies as the "Last, Best, West." To Mayes and other black people from the USA, migration offered an escape from racist government laws in the United States and was one more step along the way to freedom. Within a few years they had built a church that they called Shiloh Baptist Church, and Joe became the first minister.²⁶ Eldon was the first Black settlement and Shiloh was the first Black church in Saskatchewan. Between 1905 and 1912, approximately one thousand to one thousand five hundred African Americans emigrated to the provinces of Saskatchewan and Alberta.

---

23. Jones and Perry, eds., *People's Citizenship Guide*, 28.
24. Ward, *White Canada Forever*.
25. Lowe, *Immigrant Acts*.
26. Shepard, *Deemed Unsuitable*, 105.

However, African American immigration declined after 1912, though there were many more African Americans waiting to migrate to the prairies. What was the reason for such decline? The harsh climate with cold and long winter may have been a factor. But the most significant reason might have been racism. One report notes: "White Canadians proved less confrontational and more law abiding than their American counterparts, yet they expressed the same revulsion at the idea of co-existing with black people."[27] That is why the Shiloh people created their own cemetery next to the church; their white neighbors wouldn't allow black people to be buried in their cemeteries. And for years they struggled to get an accessible, non-segregated school. Like other immigrant families, they wanted to secure a better future, requiring a better education for their children. In the end, very much against their wishes, they had to settle for a segregated school. It should be noted, however, that not all white people were inhospitable to the newcomers. The provincial Member of the Legislative Assembly, J. P. Lyle who investigated the school district issue is one such example. He noted the racism and sympathized with the African Americans writing, "It seems to me that their district is not wide enough, and although it might be better to keep them apart, upon their representation I am led to believe that we are doing them an injustice in treating them differently to any other British subject in the country."[28] There were other white people who were like Lyle. For example, the teacher Mabel Lockhart arrived at Silver Fox school at Amber Valley, Alberta, 1931. Upon arrival, she noticed that though the school was racially mixed, there were many people with hostile attitudes towards the black students. She felt a strong urge to address this racism. She wrote, "In order to combat this concept of white supremacy I put forth a special effort to impress on all the children that as far as colour was concerned I regarded them as equals, that behaviour, not colour, was the all important factor in assessing true worth. . . .Whenever credit was bestowed on a white child the same credit was bestowed on a black one . . . whether for effort or achievement."[29] Despite these convictions of White government officials and educators, the Eldon Council would not allow the creation of a racially mixed school district. The African Americans protested and a few white settlers supported them, but the Department of Education

27. http://www.quillandquire.com/review/deemed-unsuitable-the-search-for-equality-in-canada-s-prairie-provinces-by-blacks-from-oklahoma, accessed February 1, 2017. Note that the original was in italics.

28. Shepard, *Deemed Unsuitable*, 110. Emphasis is original.

29. Ibid., 106–7. Note that the original was in italics.

had the power to impose segregation. The heart of the matter was structural racism, which was systematically sanctioned as a social policy.

In order to address this socially sanctioned oppressive policy adequately, Pamela Couture argues for a "strategic practical theology" which considers personal problems as connected to communal and societal problems "in the way in which power in a broader, more encompassing social-ecological sense shapes people's local lives."[30] The case of the Eldon school district is a prime example of where such an approach could have been applied. Particular practices and policies clearly demonstrate that while oppressive practices affect people individually, they are always inseparably linked to legally-justified social systems. For example, many black people faced lengthy interviews and medical examinations by border guards. Without sufficient reasons provided by the guards, many were denied entry. If the government workers could not find an excuse to deny them, they imposed a $50 entrance fee (which is $5000 in today's currency).[31] In short, if practical theology truly seeks to enhance the wellbeing of people's lives, it must address oppressive issues that are structural and systematic and that affect people's personal lives.

The situation in Alberta was not much different. In Alberta, especially around Edmonton, there was so much concern about the tide of African American immigration that various groups organized petitions, with the result that on August 12, 1911, the Wilfred Laurier federal Conservative government drafted and approved the following bill in parliament: "the landing in Canada . . . is prohibited of any immigrants belonging to the Negro race, which race is deemed unsuitable to the climate and requirements of Canada."[32] The Laurier government was shortly thrown out, so it was never implemented as law. Nevertheless, along with various other government initiatives that were implemented to deter African Americans from migrating north, this document helped stem the tide of black immigration.

---

30. Couture, "Social Policy," 157. This term, "strategic practical theology" was coined by Don Browning when he refers a part of practical theology that relates to ministry. See Browning, *A Fundamental Practical Theology*.

31. Gogia and Slade, *About Canada*, 21.

32. Government of Canada, Order-in-Council no. 1324, 12 August 1911, cited in Shepard, *Deemed Unsuitable*, 86. Note that the original was in italics.

Locating Postcolonial Conditions in the Context of Global Migration

The aspects of Canadian history examined above strongly illustrate that from the beginning of the Canadian nation, White European Canadians, especially those with power in the provincial and federal governments, worked very hard to keep non-White people from entering and settling in Canada. But this is not a thing of the past. Efforts to exclude and marginalize racialized people continue in Canada today. Ironically the efforts appear to be futile. This is especially evident when one notices the big cities in Canada today. There are, or soon will be, more non-White people than White people living in Canada's biggest cities. The vast majority of visible minorities (71 percent) are projected to be living in Toronto, Vancouver or Montreal by 2031.[33] This changing face of Canada is partly thanks to the multiculturalism act of 1971. What made this act possible? What was the turning point for Canada? It is abundantly clear that Canada cannot and will not survive, let alone flourish without immigrants. I would argue that the same is true for all countries today. Said asserted more than twenty years ago that the metropolitan centers of the First World need the rest of the world for survival.[34] As mentioned in the introduction of this chapter, migration is a part of human destiny and a necessity of life. Canada is no exception. But even Canada's multiculturalism act in 1971 is closely related to a postcolonial reality, a reality that shapes the world as we know it.

Indian achievement of independence from the British Empire in 1947 was the first event of a series of liberations when most colonized countries of Africa, Asia and Latin America began to secure political independence from the European colonial powers (British, French, Dutch, and German).[35] Most colonized countries in these three continents began to gain their political independence in the 1960s[36] but their struggles culminated in the 1980s in the form of resistance against military dictatorships in Asia and Latin America, and struggles against apartheid in South Africa. Many critical theologies, namely liberation, feminist, womanist, and ecological theologies, were developed during this decade as a way to respond to both

---

33. http://www.statcan.gc.ca/pub/91-551-x/91-551-x2010001-eng.pdf

34. Said, *Culture and Imperialism*, 262–336.

35. Please note that some of Latin American countries achieved independence from Spain earlier than 1947.

36. Ashcroft, Griffiths, and Tiffin, *The Empire Writes Back*, 2.

human suffering and oppression in solidarity with the marginalized. These approaches engaged social issues as a valid theological conversation partner for the work of theology as public theology.[37]

Most colonized countries seeking to establish independent governments in these places faced obstacles of internal conflict and political instability in the later part of the twentieth century and the first part of the twenty-first century. While a formal colonial regime has ended, colonial legacies and struggles have not ended; their past continues to haunt the present. This is what we call the "postcolonial condition" a reality of the present rather than that of the past, although it cannot be understood fully without considering the impact of the past colonial violence. The prefix "post" problematizes the notion of the post read as "after." In reality "imperialism continues without colonies."[38] Postcolonial conditions deliberately confuse temporality and spatiality, challenging the linear notion of progress, while accounting for different geographical struggles and complicated landscapes.[39] These struggles often lead people to leave their homes. From her British perspective Jenny Daggers observes that the postcolonial era is "a time by reverse migration from former colonies into the British metropole, so creating the rich ethnic and religious diversity of the contemporary United Kingdom."[40] The result is the change of space and time, with the massive influx of migration from and within these colonized countries, to European and European settler countries, including Canada.

This hybrid history of Canada, once a colony of Britain and a colonizer to the Aboriginal peoples, is located in this complex tangle of geo-political relations. The ongoing problems of violence, poverty, corruption, and economic political instability in these former colonized countries must be viewed as a part of the colonial legacies, the aftermath of the brutal and oppressive history of colonialism. And the problems, as the Canadian government calls them, around immigration and refugee, are also a part of the colonial legacy with complicated postcolonial conditions that include border security and border control. We must have a broader and more nuanced conversation regarding the demarcation of nation-states as a colonial project, in Canada and other countries. William Cavanaugh introduces the idea of church communities as "alternative social spaces" where nation-states based on enforced national

37. Couture, "Social Policy," 154–55.
38. McClintock, "The Angel of Progress," 295.
39. Kim-Cragg, *Story and Song*, 27.
40. Daggers, "Postcolonizing 'Mission-Shaped' Church," 186.

borders on migrants must be contested. This contestation can be effective, he insists, if we re-discover the Christian identity as a pilgrim identity, "a model of mobility that is not dependent on an imperial gaze."[41] This idea is also shared in non-theological circles by people such as Canadian activist Harsha Walia who urges us to undo border imperialism. She argues, borders and border security are imperialistic because they reinforce the extension and imposition of Western rule by maintaining unequal relationships of political, economic, cultural, and social dominance of the West over its previous colonies.[42]

While unequal, the West is affected by and sometimes challenged by these relationships as the current influx of refugees to colonial cosmopolitan cities demonstrates. Musa Dube rightly points out that we are all subject to the dilemma and the promise of the postcolonial condition. This condition has been created out of "the modern history of imperialism, beginning with the process of colonialism, through the struggles for political independence, the attainment of independence and to the contemporary neocolonialist realities."[43] To properly respond to this condition, we require an ability to connect the past with the present, and to view our particular reality in light of the wider and global realities. This ability is identified by Dube as a call for "a global ethical commitment to liberating interdependence that emphasizes interconnectedness of relationships that recognize and affirm the dignity of all things and people involved."[44] However, this goal of living with "liberating interdependence" is easy to dream but hard to achieve in reality. A challenge of migration remains because the encounters with others are inevitable, but these encounters are never equal. Interrogating this problem is necessary when we discuss migration as a topic of practical theology.

The Problem of the Representation of Others

Whether it is voluntary or involuntary, migration involves an encounter with others. Migration creates a contact zone between those who are already living as the inhabitants of the place and those who are moving into the same place. In many situations, this contact zone becomes a battle zone,

41. Cavanaugh, *Migrations of the Holy*, 42, 79.
42. Walia, *Undoing Border Imperialism*, 24.
43. Dube, *A Postcolonial Feminist Interpretation of the Bible*, 15.
44. Ibid., 18, 186.

resulting in conflicts and leading to violence in some extreme cases, in the form of ethnic cleansing and cultural genocide. As a result, migration involves both displacement of the inhabitants and cultural assimilation from the position of migrants, unless it is a colonial migration, in which case the conditions are reversed.

Kwok Pui-lan, a Chinese migrant living in the USA, sums it up well: "A contact zone is the space of colonial encounters where people of different geographical and historical backgrounds are brought into contact with each other, usually shaped by inequality and conflictual relations. The interaction between two cultures with asymmetry of power is often not voluntary and one-dimensional, but is full of tensions, fractures, and resistance."[45] Algerian postcolonial scholar Frantz Fanon calls this interaction of decolonization as "the encounter between two congenitally antagonistic forces that in fact owe their singularity to the kind of reification secreted and nurtured by the colonial situation."[46] Here asymmetry of power is critical.

The notion of representation is also key. The ones who represent and the ones who are represented is a distinction often made in the contact zone according to who has power. To make the problem of representation worse is to realize that the representation that was made by the powerful is regarded as more accurate than the actual one being represented. Here the powerful representation narrative is at work. A British postcolonial scholar Robert Young who migrated to the USA provides a helpful analogy on this issue: "We recognize a picture of a cozy snow-covered scene as an image of Christmas, although in many places of the world, Christmas actually never looks like that." Even in England, he says, Christmas "is generally a mild day and there is very rarely any snow . . . and yet we keep getting this mode of representation even when we know that the mythical White Christmas is completely untrue."[47] It is not surprising to see that the display of Christmas on the streets of non-Christian countries, with the loud playing of Santa Claus carols, and beautifully wrapped gifts under the Christmas tree, seems to represent Christmas, more so than the actual reality of celebrating Christmas in modest and quiet ways, as cherished by many Christians in typical Christian countries.

Edward Said demonstrates how the Orient was constructed as a systematic representation of the Other by the Europeans as a colonial agenda

---

45. Kwok, *Postcolonial Imagination and Feminist Theology*, 82, 43.
46. Fanon, *The Wretched of the Earth*, 2.
47. Young, *Postcolonialism*, 82.

in order to justify European domination of the world and to strengthen the power imbalance between the West and the Rest including the East.[48] An example of this may be found above in the way Chinese people in Canada in 1900s were portrayed in a newspaper as "criminals" who are "notorious" and "the most elusive of wrongdoers." The very notion of migrant as a villain, a dangerous stranger, treats them as aliens. These evil images of migrants are over-represented. They become a source of fascination and of revulsion. They become a figure, as strangers "stalking the streets," who pose "danger in their very-presence in a given street."[49] Indeed, this over-representation of migrants as villainous, enables narratives that describe their threat to our society or a burden to our economy. Or they steal our jobs. Or they grow terrorism. Such rhetoric is prevalent.

Henry Giroux, as a scholar of critical pedagogy, spins the problem of the representation around a geographical and ontological sense but also a cultural and intellectual sense. While the border-crossing experience is often unsettling, this experience could turn into something subversive and resistant. The process of migration, he argues, "has become a site of pedagogical struggle in which the legacies of dominant histories, codes, and relations become unsettled and thus open to being challenged and rewritten."[50] Giroux's insight encourages practical theologians to equip with internal critiques, unmasking our own complicity and complacency when the issue of representation of others is raised. As an academic discipline, practical theology must be aware of its colonizing privileges by sincerely embodying decolonizing attitudes and practices.[51]

Similar to Giroux, Nam Soon Kang articulates a theology of displacement, border-crossing, and migration experiences. For her, the diasporic stance is not limited to "geographical and historical location," although these are material, and often painful realities that significantly contribute to constructing diasporic consciousness. Rather the diasporic consciousness also includes "epistemological, theopolitical, or metaphorical position or location."[52] To do feminist theology, she infers, is to take a diasporic position because this position "contests traditionally [patriarchal] normative parameters of theological discourse." In a society, she continues to insist, "where

48. Said, *Orientalism*, 202–3.
49. Ahmed, *Strange Encounters*, 3.
50. Giroux, *Living Dangerously*, 40, 50.
51. Sharp, "Globalization, Colonialism, and Postcolonialism," 425.
52. Kang, *Diasporic Feminist Theology*, 3.

heterosexuality constitutes the sexual normativity, this default sexuality puts a sexually minority person in a diasporic position."[53] Kang agrees with James Clifford who clearly stated: "To theorize, one leaves home."[54] Theologizing as theorizing, thus, is diasporic, venturing into spaces of the unfamiliar, by dislodging familiar ways of thinking and practicing. Scriptural hermeneutics also involves diasporic theorizing, especially when reading and interpreting migration experiences in the Bible.

A Hermeneutical Reading of Jesus' Family as Refugees

Before I offer a particular interpretation of the story of Jesus' family, the challenges of interdisciplinary collaboration must be noted as a point of reference. This hermeneutics noted below emerged out of a book project that I shared with a Korean Hebrew Scripture scholar. We both found it a bit of a struggle to re-read together the Bible through the lens of migration.[55] It is not unfamiliar for practical theologians to engage fields of knowledge beyond our own. Interdisciplinary collaboration is a key feature of practical theology.[56] However, this collaboration was definitely an unfamiliar experience of leaving home, traveling in a terrain and through boundaries of thought that were unknown to us both. It was a work of an interdisciplinary collaboration that required a certain level of negotiation and vulnerability. Joyce Ann Mercer calls interdisciplinary work a conundrum, a necessary yet impossible dilemma. She notes that therein lies the difficulty of sufficiently engaging interdisciplinary work, let alone fully accomplishing it. Naming this work as paradoxical and enigmatic is not negative; on the contrary, she argues that interdisciplinary work generates constructive creativity and unsettles one's own ways towards offering different ways of doing theology.[57]

The other challenge of interdisciplinary work for me (more than for my co-author) was to write the book in the Korean language in the first place. It was again another experience of migration in a diasporic position of being unfamiliar in familiar spaces. Because I have been dislocated from

53. Ibid., 17.
54. Clifford, "*Notes on Theory and Travel*," 177.
55. Kim-Cragg and Choi, *The Encounters*.
56. Cahalan and Mikoski, eds., *Opening the Field of Practical Theology*, 4.
57. Mercer, "Interdisciplinarity as a Practical Theological Conundrum," 163–89.

the realm of Korean academic writing for such a long time, it was difficult returning to my mother language for this project. It was like using a stiff muscle again that has not been used for a while. Practical theologians spin the term, "persistent muscular habits,"[58] in order to point to the importance of bodily knowing as depository in which our bodies remember. We develop muscular habits as we practice certain rituals and observe certain customs. Expounding Bourdieu's term *habitus,* Mary McClintock Fulkerson stresses the contribution of the *habitus* as bodily wisdom. "By choosing the term *habitus* instead of habit, which connotes invariant behavior," she writes, "Bourdieu describes a knowledge that is imprecise, yet effective and cumulative.... Thus it is competence that matters—not simply of an abstract sort, but the competence to communicate or respond to *a situation.*"[59] It felt like my dislocated identity and experience took my competence away completely. I felt as if I were going through short term dementia, losing an intellectual/linguistic/cultural capacity that I once had. However, for the sake of responding to a situation of migration, I was relieved to notice that it was not completely forgotten. Slowly but surely, I noticed that my body remembered. Yet, I realized that it was not perfect. Something had indeed been lost. And once again, I had to admit that this is a part of my fractured yet multiply-located identity as a migrant.

One more point of reference to make in doing interdisciplinary writing and research for this particular book is how gender was at play, using migration as a hermeneutical approach to read Scripture. Although my Hebrew Bible scholar colleague and I are both unapologetically feminists, it was not our intention to include women in the Bible as the main focus of the book. However, we had no choice but to choose them as it was mostly women who had migration experiences in the Bible. These biblical women are the ones who left their homes and crossed the borders of land, race, culture, and religion. This affirmed that migration, especially forced migration, is a condition that affects those who are socially weak and economically marginalized. As a result, women in biblical times as well as today end up being migrants. Kathryn Tanner raises this issue of gendered global migration that contributes to religious de-traditioning and changing stereotypical family and gender roles.[60] Tanner's observation has been supported in

58. Witvliet, "Teaching Worship as a Christian Practice," 127.

59. Fulkerson, *Places of Redemption,* 43–46.

60. Tanner, "Globalization, Women's Transnational Migration, and Religious De-traditioning," 544–60.

the research of Gemma Tulud Cruz, a native of Philippines, currently living in Australia. She has examined Filipina women workers in Hong Kong as an example of transnational migration of women due to globalization and how their absence at home de-traditions family and gender roles in the Philippines. At the same time their appearance in receiving countries also changes these roles in their families. Her research demonstrates a need of migration as the locus for theological reflection and articulates an intercultural theology of migration from women's and feminist perspectives.[61]

With this introduction, let us turn to Matthew 2, the only Gospel that describes the family of Jesus as refugees. For Christians, the story of the birth of Jesus is pivotal. The Christian year begins with Advent, the coming of Jesus, culminating at Christmas, the celebration of his birth. "Surely," for Deirdre Cornell, Jesus is "a God who migrated from heaven to be born to a refuge family—to belong to a people painfully and intimately versed in Exodus and exile journeys."[62] This celebration of the birth of Jesus continues in the season of Epiphany, celebrating the manifestation of God in Jesus, which marks a visit to the baby Jesus by the magi. These two consecutive seasons overlap. For Western churches, following the Gregorian calendar, Epiphany is celebrated on January 6, the twelfth day after Christmas. For Eastern churches, following the Julian calendar, Christmas falls on January 7, Epiphany on the 19th of January. Some scholars view these differences as evidence of the religious and theological multiplicities embedded in Christian worship practices and biblical interpretation, as discussed in the previous Chapter 4. The "January 6 feast from Jerusalem, [results] in a double nativity celebration with an emphasis upon the Word Incarnate (John) or the shepherd-oriented birth scene (Luke) on Christmas and the coming of the Magi (Matthew) on Epiphany."[63]

The encounter with the magi changed the course of Jesus' life, and that of his whole family. According to the Gospel of Matthew, the magi are simply described as the ones from the East who followed the star and traveled to find the new born baby who would be the king of Jews. These magi are "others," foreigners, different from Jewish people, probably having different ethnicities, speaking different languages, and having different cultural and religious affiliations. We know so little about them but may surmise that they were knowledgeable people with an interest in stars. We further

---

61. Cruz, *An Intercultural Theology of Migration*.
62. Cornell, *Jesus was a Migrant*, 12.
63. Ruth, Steenwyk, and Witvliet, *Walking Where Jesus Walked*.

note their wisdom related to their ability to read the signs of the times and predict the future. We do not know whether they were all from the same place. It is also not clear how many of them there were, though we think that they had been three because of three gifts they offered to Jesus. With all of these unknowns, however, it is obvious that they were the Other, that is, different from Jesus and his family, non-Jews from another land with strange knowledge and expensive gifts. Their presence in the story recalls Isaiah 2:1–4 and Psalm 72:10–11, passages that foretell a vision of God's just purpose for all the nations.[64] Furthermore, they themselves became the gifts to Jesus and his family, as much as to Jesus' followers who read about them and retell their story even today. One may say that Jesus' first intercultural encounter was with them, although as a brand new baby he would not have been aware of it. The very beginning of Jesus' birth, the very genesis of the Christian story, is in line with intercultural encounters familiar to contemporary people's experience of migration.[65]

Let us put the colonial condition into this mix. The very birth of Jesus cannot be understood without addressing the complex relationship of colonial rule and the resistance of the colonized. Speaking boldly, the entirety of Christian Scripture has a complicated relationship to the Roman Empire and Jewish religious authority represented by Herod, "Rome's loyal puppet king, ally and agent."[66] Ordinary Jewish people's hope and faith, waiting for the coming of Messiah, was met with Herod's fear of this Messiah's coming. Hope and fear serve as two sides of one coin, as one dangerous yet daring story captured in Matthew 2. That is why this visit of the magi is important and why Herod had to call on them to spy: "Go and search diligently for the child; and when you have found him, bring me word" (Matthew 2:8). This spying work of the magi may result in the death of baby Jesus, but it is swiftly subverted and turns into something remarkable, as in their dream they are warned not to go back to Herod. Here we can admire the brave act of the magi against Herod.[67] They were able to trick the false king, while saving and paying homage to the true one (2:11). The verb used to indicate their visit "commonly designates political loyalty and submission to a king."[68] The so-called gentiles, the non-Jews, were the ones who first declare

64. Carter, "The Gospel of Matthew," 69–104.
65. Kim-Cragg and Choi, *The Encounters*, 105.
66. Carter, "The Gospel of Matthew," 80.
67. Kim-Cragg and Choi, *The Encounters*, 111.
68. Carter, "The Gospel of Matthew," 81.

Jesus the true king, the Messiah. They manifested the glory of God, God's life-saving power and mercy. Indeed, Jesus' very life was at the mercy of the Other. In short, Jesus is not only the one who gives love but also the one who receives love. The Parable of Good Samaritan can teach this interdependence.[69] The half-dead in the parable becomes a model of interdependent relationships by becoming the vulnerable recipient of the help of the Other, facing migration realities. This reversed view reorients Christians who have been occupied with maintaining congregational membership of people like themselves while failing to identify with those "beyond one's own particular ecclesial community to the global church as a fuller expression of the Spirit's work in creating and shaping people."[70]

While the liturgical and theological meanings of Advent and Christmas are fundamental to our faith formation and serve our "liturgical homeland,"[71] they can also push us out of our comfort zone. In the season of Epiphany, often celebrated longer than Advent and Christmas together, the story of the magi and the story of the family of Jesus as refugees help us imagine their significant, difficult and long migration journey, and their subversive and courageous act of resistance against colonial power and murderous military violence. The season of Epiphany, which celebrates wisdom, should be informed by a nuanced appreciation of the magi as the migrating Other in a colonial context as we continue our teaching, Christian wisdom, faith formation, liturgy and participation in the life of the church and the world.

Turning back to the story of the family of Jesus, Joseph, Jesus' father, also had a dream right after the magi's visit that warned him to leave his home and flee to Egypt in order to save Jesus from King Herod. Herod's failure to capture and kill Jesus led to the massacre of all infants under two years old in the town of Bethlehem. "God's thwarting of imperial power is only partial, since while it saves Jesus from Herod, Herod murders the baby boys around Bethlehem and Herod's son Archelaus [still] rules," as Warren Carter contends.[72] The imperial power is not completely defeated, and so it began

---

69. Kim-Cragg, "To love and Serve Others," 23–32. My attempt here is to interpret the Parable of the Good Samaritan by arguing that it is not about the Good Samaritan but the Jewish people who would have identified themselves as the one who is half-dead. This parable may be understood as Jesus' teaching of receiving love from the one who is the Other, the one that hearers (Jews in this case) despised.

70. Peterson, *Who is the Church?* 134.

71. Doran and Troeger, *Trouble at the Table*, 23.

72. Carter, "The Gospel of Matthew," 81.

the journey of Jesus' family as refugees. The Gospel of Matthew recounts this long migration, from Bethlehem to Egypt, from Egypt back to the land of Israel, and finally, unable to go back to their home in Bethlehem, from Bethlehem in Judea to a town called Nazareth in the district of Galilee. It is a migration that ends in a home away from home.

One can imagine that during his early formative years in Egypt, Jesus must have encountered people of different customs, languages, and cultures. It is not hard to imagine that his public and official ministry was deeply shaped by these encounters. It is possible that his experience of migration exposed Jesus to many instances when his own life would have been saved and continually cared for by courageous people who like the magi were different from him. Given this experience, it is fair to assume and rationalize why Jesus was so concerned about outsiders and people different from himself. Jesus had experienced life as a refugee, forced to leave home, wandering homeless, unable to return to the place where he was from. John H. Elliott, interpreting 1 Peter, observes that the word used as "aliens" and "exiles" (1:1; 2:11) could be translated as "displaced and dislocated person, the curious or suspicious... stranger." While they are "strangers in a strange land," Elliott asserts, they are simultaneously "at home with God."[73] Jesus like Moses was a stranger in a strange land, yet he was also with God as he was with those who were displaced and dislocated. Yes, Jesus is the One at the crossroads who was "both itinerant and the ultimate divine stranger."[74]

Mayra Rivera, a native of Puerto Rico, living in the USA, talks about God at the crossroads.[75] She shares her own personal experience of being raised in a country that is also the oldest colony in the world. Rivera's colonialized experience and her border crossing experience have informed and influenced her way of doing theology. To her, God is transcendent, but not untouchable, not distant/detached from human struggles and creation's mourning.

Nam Soon Kang takes migration and the reality of displacement seriously in developing her diasporic feminist theology. Her theology seeks to embrace "discourses and practices of theology of living together, and constructs theology of *Mitsein* ('being-with')."[76] Her theology grew out of the experience of displacement as diaspora. She establishes the practice of

73. Elliott, *A Home for the Homeless*, 23–25.
74. Snyder, "Introduction: Moving Body," 10.
75. Rivera, "God at the Crossroads," 202–3.
76. Kang, *Diasporic Feminist Theology*, 37.

being with, living together, in line with the notion of interdependence that this book presents. The late David Ng's wisdom on *koinonia* contributes to this notion as well. In Cantonese *koinonia* is *tuen-kai,* composed of the two words *tuen* meaning responsibility and *kai* meaning solidarity, together referred to belonging to a community. However, belonging is not determined by the like-mindedness of the group. Belonging as *koinonia* means responsibility for and solidarity with others regardless of the cost.[77] *Koinonia* is an "interstitial consciousness" that deterritorializes, undoes unnecessary boundaries, while denouncing "any sense of ownership" of the status quo.[78]

Concluding Remarks

Practical theology offers a critical reflection "about the meaning of faith and action in the world."[79] One of the primary roles of practical theology includes giving "full attention to the structure of situation, its shape and demand, in such a way that the complex of racialized, normalized, and otherwise enculturated bodies and desire are as much a part of the analysis as the presence of biblical and doctrinal elements."[80]

Migration as "the structure of situation" provides practical theology with tools to transform the life of faith into a journey of migration. God invites us to join in this difficult yet exciting journey of encounter with others. We are invited to maintain a stance of openness that leads us to find a new identity. In this migration journey, God is "innkeeper" and "host," who is the "source of that replenishing power which makes possible human conversions," encounters that turn people to "one another."[81]

What does it look like when practical theology takes migration seriously? One of my students provides a salient example of the use of Scripture in order to interpret this contemporary reality of migration that was deeply rooted in her local context of Eldon. Unveiling the migration story near Eldon, Saskatchewan, where the first Afro-American migrants were settled over 100 years ago, she interpreted the story of Hagar,[82] the first African

---

77. Ng, "A Path of Concentric Circles: Toward an Autobiographical Theology of Community," 102.

78. Kang, *Diasporic Feminist Theology*, 37.

79. Poling and Miller, *Foundations for a Practical Theology of Ministry*, 7.

80. Fulkerson, *Places of Redemption*, 21.

81. Kim-Cragg and Tran, "Turning to the Other," 36.

82. Theologian Delores Williams thought-provokingly interprets Hagar as the

migrant slave to appear in the Bible. It is a not-well-known, to put it more bluntly, a-not-very-loved story for Christians. Lifting up the struggles and joys of Hagar brought meaning of faith and action to her congregation in their Lenten journey through Black history month.[83] A postcolonial feminist practical theology with its full potential makes the commitment to learning hidden histories, such as the sad histories of certain migrant groups in Canada, which continue to haunt the present. Such storytelling of migration does not seek to blame or point fingers, but aims to orient the current and next generation to a direction that leads to transformation and just relationships.

A postcolonial feminist practical theology employing social policy methods raises the critical issue of the representation of Others. A postcolonial feminist practical theology equipped with a biblical hermeneutic of border-crossing further affirms the interdependent nature of our identity as humans and as Christians. Encounter with the Other is the heart beat of Christianity, as we have explored in the story of the magi in Matthew. With attention to migration, practical theology will serve to nurture Christians to be better followers of Jesus Christ, the divine stranger whose own life saw times of migration and homelessness. Our identity as Christians is not properly formed unless we dare to encounter and embrace others, including God as the migrant refugee.

---

surrogate figure that resonates with the realities of African American women in the USA. See her *Sisters in the Wilderness*. See also Kim-Cragg and Choi, *The Encounters*, chapter 1.

83. https://www.canada.ca/en/canadian-heritage/campaigns/black-history-month/about.html, accessed on February 7, 2017.

6

Beyond Anthropocentric Borders

BUILDING ON PREVIOUS CHAPTERS, this final chapter proposes that practical theologians think beyond the category of humanity when crafting a Christian response to the needs of today. This suggested approach is influenced by Urie Bronfenbrenner's ecological model of human development which highlights human interaction with the environment.[1] Consideration of the non-human community most acutely demonstrates our "interdependence"—the key theme threaded throughout the entire book. Contemporary lessons from ecology find resonance in the teachings of Jesus. To my mind, one example is the teaching of Jesus that "the last shall be first" (Matthew 20:6). Jesus is referring to the most vulnerable on earth. We may regard other life forms as more vulnerable than ourselves, and yet as we push the limits of the planet's life systems we realize that it is humans who, though thinking themselves as most important, may at last be the most vulnerable.

Humans, especially a few in power from the most powerful countries, have committed massive violence against non-human communities. Insidious and longitudinal forms of structural violence have been enacted as if other life forms are disposable and can be commodified. This structural violence, according to Rob Nixon, is a form of slow violence because it manifests itself bit by bit—it takes a few decades or even a few centuries in some cases to understand the full impact of what is being done.[2] The devastating implications of human over-exploitation and pollution of air, water

1. Bronfenbrenner, *The Ecology of Human Development*.
2. Nixon, *Slow Violence and the Environmentalism of the Poor*.

and soil may not be obvious for generations. That is why we need to learn from indigenous peoples some of whom teach that all of our actions need to consider the effects on the next seven generations of people.[3] That is also why Pope Francis urges us to engage in environmental justice: "What kind of world do we want to leave to those who come after us, to children who are now growing up? . . . Leaving an inhabitable planet to future generations is, first and foremost, up to us. The issue is one which dramatically affects us, for it has to do with the ultimate meaning of our earthly sojourn."[4] He is asking fundamental questions about the purpose of life and asks us to discern how to map our actions as a family tree stretching out into the future. This mapping requires that we look at the world in a certain way. This mapping is always political and is never clear-cut. But it is clear that our map for the twenty-first century cannot be limited to a human-centered norm, in which non-human species are not considered.

Human beings can no longer afford not to address the problem of ecological depletion and destruction.[5] Many human and non-human lives are at stake; some are on the verge of extinction. It is imperative that practical theologians join with other scholars and activists in order to change the course of life on planet earth. Such urgency is not simply because the environmental situations are more dire than ever but also because the environmental issues are often "trivialized or left to the work of a few ecological enthusiasts," as practical theologian Moore noted in 1998.[6] Since then, there have been some contributions in religious education and pastoral theology,[7] but more robust and substantial work is still needed.

When environmental issues are pushed to the margin, all life is pushed to the brink of extinction. We cannot keep on living as if the status quo is acceptable. We need to be aware of the numbness that descends in the face of the hideous realities of massive death or violence. We cannot afford to go into the *de facto* survival mode.[8] We need to invoke the Spirit to come and

---

3. Moore, *Ministering with the Earth*, 53.

4. Pope Francis, *Laudato si'*, point 160, http://w2.vatican.va/content/francesco/en/encyclicals/documents/papa-francesco_20150524_enciclica-laudato-si.html, accessed March 27, 2017.

5. Nixon, *Slow Violence and the Environmentalism of the Poor*, 30.

6. Moore, *Ministering with the Earth*, 2.

7. Chamberlain, "Ecology and Religious Education," 134–50; Mercer, "A Practical Theological Approach to Ecofeminism, 93–106; Martin, "The Human-Nature Relationship: 167–76.

8. Moore, *Ministering with the Earth*, 54.

awaken us. The divine Spirit moves to erase human-made categories that remove us from connection with or responsibility for other life.

Given the urgency of the contemporary ecological crisis, this chapter will focus on three related issues that are integral to ecological and environmental problems. First it examines human-centered worldviews which have been prevalent in Christian theology by engaging in an extensive literature review.[9] Our review of others who have wrestled with humanity's place in the world shows how environmental injustice is interlinked with gender, race, class, and poverty issues. This eco-critical intersectionality is another theoretical framework of practical theology and helps to unmask the mechanisms of global capitalism, environmental racism, ethno-religious conflict, and transnational geopolitics. This examination is a part of practical theology's interdisciplinary engagement and provides perspectives which can lead to strategic and transformational action. Secondly, it draws on specific resources and practices that promote interdependency between human and non-human species, tapping into biblical and theological teachings and visions, especially stewardship and Sabbath. Finally, it identifies the contributions practical theology may bring to the work of ecology and environment. Such attempts are geared toward encouraging the Rain (reign) of God, metaphorically speaking, to fall on the (rain)forest of creation where all life, human and non-human, co-dwell, live interdependently in full bio-diversity as they are mutually nurtured, cared for, and protected.

What Is Going On? Attending to Daily Realities

I live in Saskatoon, Canada, one of the coldest cities in one of the coldest countries in the world. As I write this chapter, I am listening to a weather report claiming that Saskatoon broke the record as having the warmest February since measurements began to be taken.[10] Such record breaking is not surprising anymore because it happens so frequently where I live. News about record-breaking temperatures is not even "news" anymore because it happens everywhere all the time. Unusual weather patterns, including extreme storms, extreme drought, extreme flooding and extreme fires are experienced all over the world in unpredictable but concurrent ways. People

---

9. Osmer, *Practical Theology*, 4.

10. http://globalnews.ca/news/3254217/saskatoon-weather-outlook-record-breaking-heat-then-a-messy-long-weekend/ accessed on February 21, 2017.

Beyond Anthropocentric Borders

talk about the weather,[11] these weird weather patterns. These patterns are unpredictable but not without explainable causes. For example, the reality of deforestation on every continent is startling. One consequence of deforestation is flooding. Nepal, for example, has been deforested and as a result Bangladesh, the neighboring country, now experiences worse floods than ever.[12] But forests also reduce the greenhouse gases that cause global warming which further leads to deforestation and flood, in addition to other consequences. We can talk about this vicious cycle in terms of its impact on the survival of animals and plants as much as people. We have caused the problem and we also suffer from it, although the impacts vary for different groups of people in different parts of the world. Undoubtedly, people who are most marginalized suffer from this environmental exploitation in the most devastating ways. Many indigenous communities, for example, have been forced to leave their homes since they are no longer livable. And yet such displacement and destruction are caused by a few powerful individuals from local governments and transnational companies mostly in the wealthiest part of the world.[13] However, we are not off the hook. Directly or indirectly, all of us have caused such displacement and destruction; thus, we all need to take responsibility.

While the accelerating pace of environmental crisis and degradation that has been occurring in the last decades is new, the ideology of anthropocentrism, the notion that the human species is the center and rightfully the master of the world, is rather old. Rooted in this ideology, says Dieter Hessel, environmental abuse coupled with social injustice is as old as human sin. This sin has become more grievous, he argues, to the point that it has become the most destructive example of *idolatry* in modern times.[14] This idolatry manifests itself in the name of anthropocentrism, individualism, and dualism. These three names are the hallmarks of the Enlightenment thinking and have contributed to the privileging of theory and abstract thinking in the academy at the expense of practice and concern for material realities, including environmental destruction. These are not problems of the academy alone, but also of Christian life with its hierarchal dichotomies between clergy and laity, educated and uneducated, theological professional and ordinary believer. At the annual meeting of

---

11. Keller, "Talk about the Weather," 30–49.
12. Hessel, "Introduction," 4.
13. Moore, *Ministering with the Earth*, 12.
14. Hessel, "Introduction," 14. Emphasis added.

the American Academy of Religion, John Cobb observes that the majority of religious, theological, biblical, and educational discussions proceed as if there were no environmental crisis, sometimes as if there were no natural world.[15] Heather Eaton cannot agree with Cobb more, "One simply has to examine the books, conferences, statements and rituals . . . to be convinced that there are few who say the ecological crisis is a central religious concern. Ten per cent is generous!"[16] Such a weak response to environmental issues in religious and theological studies is another sign of the dichotomy manifested as the separation between public/secular and private/communal religious communities. "Once the life of the modern mind was divided up into academic disciplines," Cobb has suggested, "the work of these disciplines became largely irrelevant to life. . . . The public was offered no participation. 'Lay' thinking has been treated with contempt. . . .This situation as such is anti-intellectual."[17] Cobb followed this critical observation with a hopeful sign of movement in the contributions of ecological and feminist thinking. This kind of thinking, he argued, overcomes false and harmful dichotomies by encouraging the participation of all who are dedicated to the preservation of life, regardless of their expertise. This ecological feminist practice cuts "across all the disciplinary boundaries, throwing a fresh light on all."[18] Speaking at a World Council of Churches' event, Eaton offered as another example of hope, how ecofeminist theology blurs boundaries of "the often-used categories of power and privilege—North or South, elite or marginalized, people of color and white folk, the west and the rest."[19]

Christian theological tradition has been complicit in earth-destroying ideologies. Christianity "has collaborated with [and benefitted from] modern culture to devalue nature and to ignore environmental responsibility, despite strong biblical mandates to serve ecological integrity."[20] A self-critical question needs to be posed to Christian theologians: "How far must theology be reshaped to adequately address ecological and feminist

15. Cobb, "Postmodern Christianity and Eco-Justice," 22, 38.
16. Eaton, *Introducing Ecofeminist Theologies*, 70.
17. Cobb, "Postmodern Christianity and Eco-Justice," 29.
18. Ibid., 39.
19. Eaton, *Introducing Ecofeminist Theologies*, 84. These ten women who gathered to work for ecological justice, representing every continent, blurs the geographical boundaries as a white American living in Chile, a Korean living in the USA, an Indian woman living in Geneva, and a woman from Hong Kong, living in USA.
20. Hessel, "Introduction," 14.

concerns?" Because, Eaton states, "there is a great difference between seeing the ecological crisis as an addendum to the list of Christian concerns and re-examining the fundamental human-earth-Divine relationships."[21] I suggest that anthropocentrism is a fundamental problem contributing to the ecological crisis and harming human-earth-Divine relationships.

A Critical Analysis of Anthropocentrism

The roots of anthropocentrism are deep and old.[22] In Aristotle's *Politics*, men's domination over nature is manifested in a threefold dichotomy: master/slave, man/woman, human/animals. In this dualist thinking, the latter groups, slaves, women, and animals are subordinated to the former group in that hierarchical order.[23] Aristotle's work sustained and reinforced hierarchy (classism), patriarchy (sexism), and human-driven domination of the natural world (anthropocentrism). When Aristotle's philosophy, influential in Western society even today, articulated these dichotomies, it also created a hierarchy of knowledge. Privileged kinds of knowledge, in turn, helped to maintain the monopoly that the male elites have on power. Aristotle, along with other members of the ruling class, believed that this hierarchy was good for the society. Eaton, however, highlights that these were beliefs, and not truths, though they masqueraded as such.[24] Once disclosed as merely deceptions, these beliefs can be denounced and dismissed. But beliefs masquerading as truth are sometimes not easy to unveil. "The binary is tenacious."[25]

Why are such intellectual and philosophical beliefs so hard to erase? Because humans are social-symbolic creatures. People have developed sophisticated language systems that ingrain certain ways of thinking in our consciousness. Sallie McFague, who has researched the powerful roles of metaphors and symbols in theological language uses the example of the metaphors of king or lord to speak of God. As metaphors abstracted from human relations, she says, these images are "in no sense 'descriptions' of God; yet their power is deep and old, their influence inscribed into our

---

21. Eaton, *Introducing Ecofeminist Theologies*, 72.

22. Ibid., 90. She talks about abolishing the hierarchical dualisms in which anthropocentrism is a major one.

23. Plumwood, *Feminism and the Mastery of Nature*, 46.

24. Eaton, *Introducing Ecofeminist Theologies*, 38–39.

25. Slack, "Resisting Eco Cultural Studies," 485.

being from our earliest years. They are, therefore, difficult to discard."[26] Such systems of hierarchy were accepted as the norm during Aristotle's era in the fourth century BCE, and they continue today to some extent. This tenacious past haunts the present because the current knowing is marked by anthropocentric, and hierarchical age-old patterns and beliefs.

We cannot blame only Aristotle or Greek philosophy, for such hierarchies appear in the ancient biblical text as well: "What is man? . . . For thou hast made him a little lower than the angels, and hast crowned him with glory and honour. Thou madest him to have dominion over the works of thy hands" (Psalm 8:5, KJV). This text is repeated again in the letter to the Hebrews: "You made him a little lower than the angels; You crowned him with glory and honor," though here "him" refers to Jesus (2:7, KJV). The problem is not that such texts exist in the Bible; a danger arises when such texts are understood literally and used unequivocally without considering contexts which may inform a better nuanced message. Thus, the problem has to do with interpretation.

Genesis 1:28, "Be fruitful and multiply, and fill the earth and subdue it," is a text that is subject to arguably the most problematic interpretations as far as the ecological crisis is concerned. It has been interpreted to strengthen an anthropocentric view of human domination over nature and has frequently been used to justify slavery, the oppression of women, and the conquest of indigenous peoples in the histories of Western colonial Christianity. The vividness and power of the creation stories in Genesis mean that they are of prime importance for the way we shape our attitudes to the world. These stories orient ourselves to God. They are central theologically because they convey the intention of God and our (human and non-human) covenantal relationship with God.[27] That is why careful interpretation and reinterpretation are needed. Many are attempting such reinterpretations. Pope Francis, for example, has offered an interpretation based on the humility of the human being in the creation story, "We have forgotten that we ourselves are dust of the earth. . . . Our relationship with the environment can never be isolated from our relationship with others and with God."[28]

---

26. McFague, "An Earthly Theological Agenda," 91.

27. Moore, *Ministering with the Earth*, 39.

28. Pope Francis, *Laudato si'*, http://w2.vatican.va/content/francesco/en/encyclicals/documents/papa-francesco_20150524_enciclica-laudato-si.html, accessed March 27, 2017.

In the medieval era, Greek philosophy that devalued nature was less influential. There are some beautiful examples of how Christian leaders in this period attended to the protection of forests.[29] While the earth was understood as female, Christian thinkers and theologians including Hildegard of Bingen and Thomas Aquinas believed that the earth was alive and important as a vital organic whole.[30] However, this religious view was not regarded as credible by scientists who stood on the threshold of modernity. The credibility of Christianity's worldview was put to the test when Galileo claimed that the earth was not the center of the universe, but rather the Sun was. The idea that science was a more reliable source of knowledge than religion also entailed the view that the earth was merely a passive object. While Christianity was in a state of denial regarding Galileo's discovery, science took control, changing our view of the world as an organic whole into one of mechanistic entity. Such a shift was, according to Eaton, "the beginning of the 'death of nature.'"[31]

Francis Bacon as an example of a modern philosopher thought of nature as an "anvil," an inanimate, unfeeling surface upon which humans could hammer all they wanted. He also justified the suppression of weaker human species (e.g., indigenous peoples and women) in the modern era of Europe.[32] A critical review of his work is necessary because it clearly reveals a close link between the domination of nature and women in the name of a mechanical view of the earth that shaped Western European Christianity and the process of modern colonization.[33]

For Bacon, reason—the noble and autonomous virtue that humans seek to achieve— could only truly belong to free men. According to Bacon, it was up to men to unlock the secrets of nature and gain control over it. What is more, he held that this activity was sanctioned by God who created humanity to be fulfilled in the form of the Man of Reason and Man of Knowledge. He wrote:

---

29. Archbishop Eberhard of Salzburg had forbidden the use of the cleared land so that forest could grow again in 1237. Cited in Rasmussen, "Returning to Our Senses," 40.

30. McFague, "An Earthly Theological Agenda," 96.

31. Eaton, *Introducing Ecofeminist Theologies*, 56–57.

32. Rasmussen, "Returning to Our Senses," 53.

33. I have argued this point elsewhere, Kim-Cragg, "A Christian Feminist Theological Reflection on Economy of Life," 170–76.

> Man, if we look to final causes, may be regarded as the center of the world, insomuch that if man were taken away from the world, the rest would seem to be all astray, without aim or purpose. . . . Let the human race recover that right over Nature which belongs to it by divine bequest.[34]
>
> We can, if need be, ransack the whole globe, penetrate into the bowels of the earth, descend to the bottom of the deep, travel to the farthest region of this world to acquire wealth, to increase our knowledge, or even only to please our eye and fancy.[35]

Ecofeminist Carolyn Merchant, reading Bacon, makes the disturbing observation: Bacon describes men's treatment of nature in a way that evokes images of women being raped by men.[36] British feminist theologian Mary Grey similarly analyses Bacon's language and finds echoes of Christian discussions of witch hunts.[37]

> For you [European noble free men] have but to follow and as it were hound nature in her wanderings, and you will be able when you like to lead and drive her afterward to the same place again. . . . Neither ought a man to make scruple of entering and penetrating into these holes, when the inquisition of truth is his whole object.[38]

In fact, one of the most misogynist texts in *Malleus Maleficarum*, translated as "Hammer of Witches," is the best known and the most important treatise on witchcraft. They were intentionally written "to aid the identification, prosecution, and murdering of women as witches," during the Inquisition of witch hunts.[39] The inquisition that swept Europe and expanded to Central and Latin America during the Spanish and Portuguese colonialization from the fifteenth century to nineteenth century is not completely gone from the Christian psyche but still haunts contemporary people's memories with allusions to femicide (killing of women) and gender-based violence. The association of the inquisition with men's hunting for women is frightening. Women who were hunted by men were often interrogated and tortured in the name of finding "the truth." Men go on the hunt for "a woman." This hunting for woman is a game for men. This game

---

34. Ponting, *A Green History of the World*, 48.
35. Merchant, *The Death of Nature*, 249.
36. Ibid., 169–70.
37. Grey, *Sacred Longings*, 14–15.
38. Bacon, "De Dignitate et Augmentis Scientiarum," 296.
39. Eaton, *Introducing Ecofeminist Theologies*, 66. This text was written in 1486.

is portrayed as if it were enjoyable for women. "Man is the hunter; woman the game. The sleek shining creatures of the chase. Who hunts them for the beauty of their skins; They love us for it and we ride them down."[40]

Misogynist thinking is not a thing of the past; it is alive and well in the twenty-first century since gender-based violence is on the rise all over the world today. This age-old image that associates nature with women who are rightfully hunted and violated provides our own generation with "conceptual weapons which can be mined, refined, and redeployed for new uses."[41] It is not surprising to find out that sexual metaphors have been often used to describe the colonized and their land. The colonizer Amerigo Vespucci was said to have "discovered" the land which was named after him. "Ameriga," is however, a feminized version of "Amerigo." A land that was feminine was of course there to be conquered. Christopher Columbus fantasized that the world is not simply round but shaped like a woman's breast.[42] The Enlightenment theologian Schleiermacher's view of the earth as feminine is also revealing: "I lie on the bosom of the infinite world. At this moment I am its soul, for I feel all its powers and its infinite life as my own; at this moment it is my body, for I penetrate its muscles and its limbs as my own, and its innermost nerves move according to my sense and my presentiment as my own."[43] Is this a fantasy of a man who is in total control of a woman during the act of sex? If this is the case, then, this man as the master of human beings is also in total control of the earth and nature. Many postcolonial and indigenous feminist scholars make a convincing claim that colonial expansion was imagined in terms of eroticized male desire. This often translated into the actual rape of the women that the explorers found in the course of their colonial conquests.[44]

Such misogynist ways of thinking were further developed during the height of the colonial period in the nineteenth century. The language of penetration of holes and discovery of nature's secret was actualized in the extractive economies of oil and mining. It is no coincidence that the world's biggest oil corporations were all established in the late nineteenth century and the early twentieth century, the heyday of modern colonialization as

---

40. Seager, *Earth Follies*, 219.
41. Plumwood, *Feminism and the Mastery of Nature*, 43.
42. Kwok, *Postcolonial Imagination and Feminist Theology*, 14, 70.
43. Schleiermacher, *On Religion*, 113.
44. McClintock, *Imperial Leather*, 22; Smith, "Sexual Violence and American Indian Genocide," 31–52.

the Sun never set on the British Empire. These include Esso (1870), Exxon (1882), Shell (1890), and Mobil (1882).[45]

The 1992 Earth Summit in Rio de Janeiro sufficiently raised the ecological issue while highlighting the church's lack of awareness of the problem of global ecological destruction and its connections to other forms of oppression.[46] Finally, two decades later in Busan, the World Council of Churches began to strongly address the interconnection of poverty, wealth, and ecology in *Economy of Life, Peace, and Justice for All: A Call to Action*. This document clearly disclosed the material reality of how the most vulnerable of the earth, including women, children, and non-human creatures, have been affected by the current world order of neoliberal global capitalism. The WCC affirmed that "various aspects of climate, ecological, financial and debt crisis are mutually dependent and reinforce each other. They cannot be treated separately any more. Unprecedented challenges of climate change go hand-in-hand with the uncontrolled exploitation of the natural resources."[47] Eaton claims bluntly that "[t]he players of imperialist globalization or the World Bank do not care whether Wisdom/Sophia was present in Genesis, or that the Christian eschatological doctrines are distorted. But they will care if Christians, inspired and empowered by a new understanding of Wisdom and eschatology, resist efforts of the World Bank . . . to prevent ecological ruin."[48] The implications of practical theology for faithful living with regards to ecological issues are far-reaching, Miriam Martin argues, because these issues "disturb the framework of power across the structures of politics, religion and economics."[49] If practical theology becomes irrelevant to and removed from daily struggles of the ordinary and marginalized people due to environmental crisis, it fails to candidly reveal the matrix of the global economic order, ecological degradation, militarism, and other oppressions. When that happens, as John Reader warns, practical theology will only produce believers that resemble "the living dead."[50]

---

45. Grey, *Sacred Longings*, 15.

46. Moore, *Ministering with the Earth*, 17.

47. *Economy of Life, Peace, and Justice for All: A Call to Action* (WCC, 2012), #10.

48. Eaton, *Introducing Ecofeminist Theologies*, 92.

49. Martin, "The Human-Nature Relationship," 174.

50. Reader, *Reconstructing Practical Theology*, 1. Here "living dead" referred to theology points to familiar frameworks of interpretations that have served us well for many years and continue to haunt our thoughts and analyses, even though they are passing away before our eyes.

We have thus far traced the roots of anthropocentrism. We have laid out the problem of anthropocentrism that goes hand in hand with individualism and dualism. We have also linked anthropocentrism with modern European colonialism patriarchy and misogyny, because there is sufficient evidence of the connection between the treatment of women and nature at the hands of men during the colonial conquest. However, this attempt to trace and link should not presume that hierarchical dualism of human history is homogeneous or unified. Eaton's advice is critical in this regard: "It is crucial to appreciate the dynamism and dialectic between ideas, events and materiality. A monolithic view of these dualisms presents an extremely limited and inaccurate view of history. . . . Many contradictory practices and ideas co-exist, competing for public, political and ideological space."[51] The history of anthropocentrism is uneven, and bumpy and it has been contested and resisted. This gives us cause for kindling hope for an alternative way of life.

Tapping into a Biblical Teaching of Stewardship

Reformed theologian Douglas John Hall invites Christians to be open to the critique from ecologists who consider biblical religion a foe of the earth. As long as Christians remain stuck in the traditional interpretation of Genesis 1:28 such criticism is inevitable.[52] But the problem goes beyond the book of Genesis. Cultural and literary theorist Mieke Bal makes a case in point: "The Bible, of all books, is the most dangerous one, the one that has been endowed with the power to kill."[53] Along with the literal interpretation of the Bible there is a problem of authority. A long tradition in Reformed Christianity is to regard the Bible itself as the authority in matters of faith and life. But combined with a literal interpretation of the text, this gives the Bible the power to dictate our judgments and acts. In fact, in such cases it is not the Bible that has the authority but a privileged group of Christian leaders who act as the interpreting authority, who have claimed the power to say what the texts mean, while demonizing other interpretations as heretical.[54] Thus, searching for biblical wisdom leads us along a thorny path.

---

51. Eaton, *Introducing Ecofeminist Theologies*, 60–61.
52. Hall, *Imaging God*, 195.
53. Bal, *On Story-Telling*, 14.
54. Kwok, *Discovering the Bible in the Non-biblical World*, 17.

It is a path we must take nevertheless because "engaging the Bible is not optional for the Christian community."[55]

Another reformed theologian Dieter T. Hessel remarks "to interpret Scripture and do theological work with the eco-justice eyes—sensitized to both social injustice and ecological peril—has not yet become the church's habit."[56] He further says that "[r]eligion, by definition concerned with binding reality, should foster positive respect for creation and strengthen the links between environmental preservation and social justice," and that this must happen by cultivating habits for a faithful living.[57]

One of the most disastrous aspects of the modern ideology of anthropocentric dualism is the master-slave polemic of human unequal relationships. It has been argued that the first slave was a woman. Many feminists, including ecofeminists, agree that patriarchy is the oldest form of oppression and the root cause of all dominations.[58] This may be debatable, but research has shown that the earliest development of human cities (six thousand years ago with the emergence of agriculture)[59] coincided with the unprecedented control of nature and hierarchical sexual divisions of labor.[60]

A historical asymmetry between women and men, manifested in the master/slave dialectic, is found in Jewish and Christian traditions of biblical interpretation. Paul Santmire boldly claims that the reason why Protestant responses to the environmental crisis have not impacted the public outside the church, let alone convinced or converted the church itself, is the theology of dominion which was the basis of these responses. The problem with this theology is that dominion is interpreted as domination in the Bible.[61] To offer a different interpretation, a Jewish scholar Eric Katz suggests that we examine the meaning of "subdue" in the passage of Genesis 1:28. Citing The Talmud, he says that the phrase "subdue

---

55. *The Authority and Interpretation of Scripture.*

56. Hessel, "Introduction," 13.

57. Ibid., 9.

58. Shiva, *Staying Alive;* Plant, ed., *Healing the Wounds;* Diamond and Orenstein, eds., *Reweaving the World.*

59. Eaton, *Introducing Ecofeminist Theologies,* 50.

60. Miles, *Patriarchy and Accumulation on a World Scale,* 49.

61. Santmire, "Healing the Protestant Mind," 61–62. He recognized that Barth never finished *Church Dogmatics*, especially the part that deals with eschatology. Had he finished it, Barth might have envisioned the world to come in which nature be included as respectful partners.

it" points to a male activity connected to an obligation to propagate the human. While Katz recognizes the power of humanity to use natural resources, he argues that Jewish understanding of this phrase does not support its interpretation as domination of humanity over nature but advocates for a role of human stewardship. Here stewardship is focused on "conservation," rooted in Genesis 2:15, "God took the man and put him in the Garden of Eden to till it and keep it."[62] The theology of Genesis is theocentric; the subject is God and everything belongs to God. As human beings, "we create nothing, we destroy nothing, and we enjoy the bounty of the Earth" that comes from God, for which we give thanks. This theology generates the principle and the origin of Sabbath, "the absence of work and the appreciation of God."[63]

This Jewish theocentric understanding of stewardship and Sabbath can be viewed as a trifocal relationship between God, humans, and creation. Moore puts it this way: "human beings are called to receive from, and participate with the earth in the redemptive work of God."[64] Michael Gilmour's entire book dealing with the Bible and the animals conveys triadic relationships of animals-humans-God as a "triptych."[65] In many cases animals serve as the nexus for an encounter between the divine and the human. Humans are dependent on animals and creation not only for their own survival but also for their relationship with God. Moore similarly points out that God is mediated through creation in the gifts of creation—water, bread, and wine—as tangible and tactile signs of God's grace in the sacraments.[66] Working from this triadic understanding and once we move beyond anthropocentric views, we can even construct practical theology in triune ways. German practical theologian Christian Grethlein organizes his practical theology in a threefold framework: practical theology is doing the work of the human/non-human communication *about* God, *with* God, *from* God.[67]

Speaking of communication about, with, and from God, Catholic theologian and religious educator Gabriel Moran claims the Sabbath as a practice of communion. Sabbath carries two traditions, he writes, "one

62. Katz, "Judaism and the Ecological Crisis," 57.
63. Ibid., 59.
64. Moore, *Ministering with the Earth*, 19.
65. Gilmour, *Eden's Other Residents*, 38, 119, 131, 145.
66. Moore, *Ministering with the Earth*, 45.
67. Grethlein, *An Introduction to Practical Theology*.

that emphasizes doing nothing, the other that gives impetus to action for justice. The one is related to the other, in that, if there is truly to be a quiet rest, then everyone has to have a share of it, not just a few privileged men. The women need rest from the housework, the oxen need rest from plowing, the earth needs to lie fallow. . . . If the *communion* service is not to be a sham, it has to be a reminder to the congregation that everyone, human, and nonhuman, is called to communion."[68]

While it is necessary to tap into this biblical insight of stewardship and the theological view of Sabbath, Eaton cautions that an ecological crisis of this magnitude, which is happening at such a rapid speed, has never existed previously. The Christian biblical and theological wisdom and other religions' wisdoms are not equipped to adequately respond.[69] For we cannot expect to find all the resources to deal with it to come from the Christian Bible or teachings. This limit of our biblical resources forces Christian theologians and educators to reach out to learn from other disciplines, to which we turn next.

Mutual Contributions of Ecofeminism to and from Practical Theology

Long before the term ecofeminism[70] was widely accepted in the academy, women at the grassroots level have been actively raising environmental issues. Ordinary people who are struggling for water and food on a daily basis, and who are affected by war and disasters have addressed the correlation and proposed solutions in intersectional ways. The absence of sewers and safe drinking water, and the accumulation of garbage in cities where most of the human population dwells, is experienced very directly by some. The World Health Organization recently gave a startling report stating that a quarter of all global deaths of children under five years of age are due to unhealthy or polluted environments including dirty water and air, second-hand smoke and a lack of adequate hygiene. The cost of polluted environments is the death of 1.7 million children per year. "A polluted environment is a deadly one—particularly for young children,"

---

68. Moran, *Religious Education as a Second Language*, 153.

69. Eaton, *Introducing Ecofeminist Theologies*, 68.

70. French feminist Francoise d'Eaubonne coined this term in 1974, cited in Eaton, *Introducing Ecofeminist Theologies*, 3.

WHO director-general Dr. Margaret Chan observed.[71] In this treacherous life-and-death situation, the ordinary, especially ordinary women usually carry the heavy load of responsibility for their own survival as well as for the survival of those for whom they care. They are the ones who have given birth to ecofeminism. In this regard, ecofeminism is not an abstract academic discourse but "an insight and a practice"[72] which has arisen from diverse yet ordinary contexts as a direct response to the precarious realities, as an urge for survival and a deep desire to change the world. Where is garbage dumped? Who produces most waste? Who suffers from the lack of drinkable water as well as polluted air? Asking these questions, Brazilian ecofeminist theologian Ivone Gebara invites us to see this suffering from ecological health issues beyond a micro level. In order to adequately respond to these questions we must look at the world at a macro life level in global scales. She continues to invoke our consciousness to think about ecological issues globally yet locally beyond anthropocentric borders. When a war (she is thinking of Vietnam War) kills hundreds of people, we fail to see that the same war destroys the rice fields or rivers serving dozens of villages, because the media and the public, those of us as spectators, are unable to see the destruction of the fields and rivers. Our view is contaminated by anthropocentric bias.[73]

Ecofeminist theology, linking ecofeminism and theology, has made a great contribution to interrogating the root causes of misogyny and the domination of the earth.[74] In this sense, ecofeminist theology is born of daily life, day-to-day practice. This is where practical theology finds a kindred spirit with ecofeminist theology. Joyce Ann Mercer argues that daily and concrete situations are valuable sources for theological reflection. She suggests that practical theology could be a great partner for doing ecofeminist theological reflection.[75]

In many cases, the effect and impact of environmental abuse is only apparent after years of damaging practice. It is important to become aware of the long-term hazardous impact of the things we do on

---

71. http://www.who.int/mediacentre/news/releases/2017/pollution-child-death/en/, accessed April 4, 2017.

72. Eaton, *Introducing Ecofeminist Theologies*, 7.

73. Gebara, *Longing for Running Water*, 27.

74. There are numerous theologians but Rosemary Radford Ruether is one of the pioneers in establishing ecofeminist theology, found in *New Woman/New Earth*. Two decades later, she published a comprehensive work on ecofeminist theology in *Gaia and God*.

75. Mercer, "A Practical Theological Approach to Ecofeminism," 93–106.

generation upon generation, even though it is not visible or obvious in the moment. Theology also explores realities that are neither visible nor obvious in the moment. We seek to explain God as mystery. We know that we cannot limit God to what we understand. *Ficitum non capax infinit* (the finite cannot hold the infinite), insists Calvin. And yet, *Ficitum capax infinit* (the finite bears the infinite), the transcendent is utterly immanent, echoes back Bonhoeffer, supporting Luther.[76] While we cannot totally capture God who is mystery, we experience and articulate God's presence as real and as close as our own breathing. Practical theology, concerned with lived experiences and daily practices, plays a role in raising awareness of nature's less obvious and less visible perils and its relationship with human beings, as it illuminates the divine presence, which is also often invisible and less obvious.

That is why the role of imagination as sources for practical theology is critical. The slow violence done to the most vulnerable people and the non-human world deals with the invisible and inaudible reality of their suffering. We must learn to imagine, being able to see beyond what we can see and hear beyond what we can hear, while being firmly grounded in our reality. Catholic religious educator Harold Horell helps us articulate the role of imagination. Imagination, he explains, is a central part of how we engage in daily learning, while also being central in creating something new. Because imagination involves both regular routines and unexpected surprises, it enables us to be rooted in maintaining our daily lives and at the same time to disrupt such routines. Imagination helps us to see things clearly beyond what we seemingly see. We need to "see the sound"(KwanEum, 觀音), as discussed in Chapter 2. Imagination helps to see "more deeply" "beneath the surface of conscious awareness," he writes. His concluding paragraph is right to the point on the role of imagination. "We can never occupy imagination, but it can occupy us—stretching us beyond what we originally thought possible."[77]

Once occupied by the power of imagination, humans can feel a tree's "flowing veins" hidden under the sturdy bark and hear the sound of "the sucking of the roots" covered under the soil, as Jewish theologian Martin Buber has felt.[78] Buber's imagination seems to find kindred spirits in the Indigenous community in Canada. The following excerpt from a 1913

---

76. Bonhoeffer, "Aufträge der Bruderräte," 42.
77. Horell, "The Imagination of REA: APPRRE," 351–52.
78. Buber, *I and Thou*, 57.

primary school Canadian history textbook ironically captures this resonance in words that seem at the same time to dismiss it as superstition:

> All Indians were very superstitious, having strange ideas about nature. They thought that birds, beasts, and reptiles were like men [sic]. Thus an Indian has been known to make a long speech of apology to a wounded bear. They thought, too, that in lakes, rivers and water fall dwelt the spirits of living beings, and they strove to win the favour of these by means of gifts.[79]

Lutheran theologian Larry Rasmussen argues that modernist Christian theology, influenced by Aristotelian and Platonic dualism, is fatal in its dealings with environmental issues. However, there is a hope for Reformed Christian theology in Luther's thought, Rasmussen contends. "God is *wholly* in the grain," said Luther, "and the grain is *holy* in God."[80] Luther's earthbound panentheistic theology affirms that the creaturely is the one and only place we know the divine in its fullness, while the one and only place is to be understood as partial because we cannot totally circumscribe God. Some ecofeminist theologians are not entirely satisfied with this, however. They see that the categories of pantheism and panentheism only work for conceptual distinctions which may not reflect reality. "Ecofeminism reveals that such theological concepts are too abstract and not grounded in the many-layeredness of human experience. . . . This is one reason why ecofeminists increasingly look to earth sciences and evolutionary cosmology."[81] Cognizant of this challenge to Christian theology which tends to be overly conceptual and abstract, we yet affirm the gift that Christian theology could bring.

Practical theology's epistemology calls for close attention to these experiences which inform, interact, and advance further thinking, theory, and theology and vice versa. Doing this is an integral feature of practical theology. This is where practical theology and ecofeminist theology can be partners. And a few have successfully attempted such partnerships.[82] Eaton argues that ecofeminist theology, especially lifting up multi-religious voices, attends to the daily relationship between women's struggles and natural world's groaning: "issues of toxins in air, water and soil, garbage dumps where people live, economic exploitation from globalization and stories

---

79. Hall, *Imaging God*, 197.
80. Rasmussen, "Returning to Our Senses," 42.
81. Eaton, *Introducing Ecofeminist Theologies*, 89.
82. Filippi, "Place, Feminism, and Healing," 232–42; Clinebell, *Ecotherapy*.

of resistance and celebration. They provide concrete connection between theory and praxis, North and South, affluent and poor, and the actual life and death struggles of the many women of the world."[83]

There is a Korean proverb that says, "as the grain ripens more, it bows down more." It means the more you know the more you know that you do not know everything for sure. It points to the connection between humility and maturity. People with mature knowledge humbly seek the help of others with matters which they do not fully grasp. This humility enables reciprocal and interdependent relationships. It also affirms that we do not have to know everything to solve all the problems in the world! This realization is absolutely needed in engaging the ecological crisis, a problem so huge and so complex that on our own we could never hope to tackle it. The pioneer ecofeminist theologian Rosemary Radford Ruether speaks of inter-connectedness as consciousness: "Human consciousness [is] not what utterly separates us from the rest of 'nature.' Rather, consciousness is where this dance of energy organizes itself in increasingly unified ways, until it reflects back on itself in self-awareness. Consciousness is and must be where we recognize our kinship with all other beings."[84]

A Postcolonial Feminist Practical Theology of Interdependence for Life

Human sin, from the perspectives of ecofeminist theology, is situated within "the interlocking oppressions of ethnicity, colonialism, class, gender, and the domination of the earth."[85] Sallie McFague calls for radicalizing Christian understanding of sin and evil by boldly naming that we are "indifferent, selfish, shortsighted, xenophobic, anthropocentric, greedy human beings" who must repent and who are in need of redemption. The theological task in this regard is "earthy," turning "the eyes of theologians away from heaven and toward the earth" in order to "connect the starry heavens with the earth."[86]

Once this interlocking sin is addressed, doors to liberating interdependence are open, as Dube contends.[87] Ontologically speaking, no living being

83. Eaton, *Introducing Ecofeminist Theologies*, 85.
84. Ruether, *Gaia and God*, 250.
85. Eaton, *Introducing Ecofeminist Theologies*, 79.
86. McFague, "An Earthly Theological Agenda," 87, 89.
87. Dube, *Postcolonial Feminist Interpretation of the Bible*, 199–201.

can sustain its life independently. "It is more elementary than awareness of differences, or than autonomy, individuality or freedom. It is the foundational reality of all that is or can exist,"[88] Gebara says. *Ubuntu*, literally meaning, "I am because we are; I exist because the community exists,"[89] is an African concept of personhood and similarly speaks to the identity of the self that is formed interdependently through community.[90] These insights underscore the fundamental and foundational grounding of the relatedness of personhood. However, this personhood is not limited to the anthropocentric worldview. Gebara contends relatedness is an earthly and a cosmic condition,[91] which is prior to human conditions and goes beyond the human arena.

Returning to the etymology of *"In"* 인 人, which was discussed in Chapter 1, another Korean and Chinese term may be even more illuminating. *"SangSaeng"*상생 (相生), literally translated as "mutual life" or "co-living" also points to a fundamentally interdependent way of life together. Here the second character, *"Saeng" (*생, 生*)*, meaning "life," is neither metaphysical nor mechanical. It points to a biological and existential dimension of life, including the quest and the purpose of life. But it also includes visceral, material matters of life connected with the physical bodily conditions. In this sense, *"Saeng"* is identified with another Korean word, *"Sahm"* 삶, meaning living. This word *"Sahm"* does not have the Chinese letter, but is a vernacular Korean concept, used by ordinary Korean peoples for centuries. It refers to earthy, daily, sweaty, and tenacious living. *"Sahm"* 삶 emphasizes the "physical" and "everyday" life. This concept resonates with practical theology's focus on "living out" knowledge and wisdom. For practical theology, it is not enough to know and teach interdependence; it must be lived out; it must be taught in ways that lead us to practice as an integral part of our daily life and as a spiritual discipline for the span of our life long journey. That is also what a postcolonial feminist practical theology of interdependence aims to achieve. As WCC's *Together towards Life* states, interdependent life is "The whole *oikoumene*, as being interconnected in God's web of life." It further states, "We are therefore called to move beyond a narrowly human-centered approach and to embrace forms of mission which express our reconciled relationship with all created life. We hear the cry of the earth as we listen to the cries of the poor and we know that from

88. Gebara, *Longing for Running Water*, 83.
89. Drucilla, and van Marle, "Exploring Ubuntu," 2.
90. Battle, *Ubuntu*, 1.
91. Gebara, *Longing for Running Water*, 84–85.

its beginning the earth has cried out to God over humanity's injustice (Gen. 4:10)."[92] Again, we need to see the sound (KwanEum) that is in silence.

We must constantly and continually practice this way of life until our body knows and remembers. As mentioned earlier, this is the work of cultivating "persistent muscular habits," which include awareness of such acquired habits, critical appraisal of the habits, and an openness to change them in order to participate in worship and other aspects of the life of the church and society at a deeper level.[93]

Finale as Circling Remarks

This chapter has demonstrated the importance of interdependence for the sake of wellbeing of all living beings. It has attempted to articulate that the subject matter of practical theology is not only human beings but includes non-human beings as well. One of the goals of practical theology is to enhance our ability to respect and care for others. This must be done with the understanding that life is communal and interconnected with all of creation.

Mary Elizabeth Moore in her *Ministering with the Earth* offers detailed descriptions of how all living beings from the tiniest bacteria to the largest Blue Whale are interdependent. Whether we use a scientific language, "the carbon cycle," or a spiritual language, "the circle of life," we meet "the Spirit of Life" in "its interdependent circles of relationship."[94] Indigenous singer Buffy Sainte-Marie, captures this image in the song "We are circling" as she sings of the way humans and non-humans are spiraling, spinning, singing, and growing together.[95] In a similar vein, Mercy Amba Oduyoye from Ghana sings of the circle in her poem:

---

92. *Together towards Life: Mission and Evangelism in Changing Landscapes*: A statement presented to WCC 10th General Assembly, Busan: Korea, 2013, #4, #19.

93. Witvliet, "Teaching Worship as a Christian Practice," 127.

94. Moore, *Ministering with the Earth*, 8.

95. https://www.youtube.com/watch?v=oO8BMg1DW1U, accessed on March 6, 2017.

Beyond Anthropocentric Borders

A Circle expands forever
It covers all who wish to hold hands
And its size depends on each other
It is a vision of solidarity
It turns outwards to interact with the outside
And inward for self-critique
A circle expands forever
It is a vision of accountability
It grows as the other is moved to grow
A circle must have a center
But a single dot does not make a Circle
One tree does not make a forest
A circle, a vision of cooperation, mutuality, and care.[96]

---

96. Oduyoye, "The Story of a Circle," *Ecumenical Review* 53.1 (2001) 97, cited in Kwok Pui-lan, ed., *Hope Abundant*, 17.

Bibliography

Abella, Irving. "Foreword." In B. Roberts, *Whence They Came: Deportations from Canada 1900–1935*. Ottawa: University of Ottawa Press, 1988.
Ahmed, Sarah. *The Cultural Politics of Emotions*. 2nd ed. London: Routledge, 2014.
———. *Living a Feminist Life*. Durham, NC: Duke University Press, 2017.
———. *Strange Encounters: Embodied Others in Post-Coloniality*. London: Routledge, 2000.
Aldrich, Robert. *Colonialism and Homosexuality*. New York: Routledge, 2002.
Althaus-Reid, Marcella. *The Queer God*. London: Routledge, 2003.
Anderson, Herbert. "Loving." In *The Wiley-Blackwell Companion to Practical Theology*, edited by Bonnie Miller-McLemore, 61–69. Chichester, UK: Blackwell, 2012.
Andrews, Dale P. "African American Practical Theology." In *Opening the Field of Practical Theology: An Introduction*, edited by Cahalan, Kathleen A. and Gordon S. Mikoski, 11–29. Lanham, MD: Rowman & Littlefield, 2014.
Anselm. *Basic Writings: Proslogium; Monologium; Gaunilo's on Behalf of the Fool*. Translated by S. N. Deane. Peru, IL: Open Court, 1962.
Anzaldua, Gloria. *Borderlands/La Frontera: The New Mestiza*. San Francisco: Spinsters/Aunt Lute, 1987.
Aristotle, *Generation of Animals*. Translated by A. L. Peck. Cambridge: Harvard University Press, 1943.
Arnold, Rick, Bev Burke, Carl James, D'Arcy Martin, and Barb Thomas. *Education for a Change*. Toronto: Doris Marshall Institute for Education and Action and Between the Lines, 1991.
Ashcroft, Bill, Gareth Griffiths, and Helen Tiffin. *The Empire Writes Back: Theory and Practice in Post-colonial literature*. New York: Routledge, 1989.
Bacon, Francis. "De Dignitate et Augmentis Scientiarum." In *Works* Vol. 4, edited by James Spedding, Robert Leslie Ellis, and Douglas Devon Heath. London: Longmans Green 1875.
Baker, Doris G. *The Barefoot Way: A Faith Guide for Youth, Young Adults, and the People Who Walk with Them*. Louisville: Westminster John Knox, 2012.
———. *Doing Girlfriend Theology: God-Talk with Young Women*. Cleveland, OH: Pilgrim, 2005.
Baker, Doris G., and Joyce Ann Mercer. *Lives to Offer: Accompanying Youth on Their Vocational Quest*. Cleveland, OH: Pilgrim, 2007.
Bal, Mieke. *On Story-Telling: Essays in Narratology*. Edited by David Jobling. Sonoma, CA: Polebridge, 1991.

BIBLIOGRAPHY

Barth, Karl. *Church Dogmatics* 3:4. Translated by. A. T. Mackay, T. H. L. Parker, Harold Knight, Henry A. Kennedy, and John Marks. Edinburgh: T. & T. Clark, 1961.

Bass, Dorothy C. "Eating." In *The Wiley-Blackwell Companion to Practical Theology*, edited by Bonnie Miller-McLemore, 51–60. Chichester, UK: Blackwell, 2012.

Bass, Dorothy, and Craig Dykstra. "Growing in the Practices of Faith." In *Practicing Our Faith: A Way of Life for a Searching People*, edited by Dorothy Bass, 195–204. San Francisco: Jossey-Bass, 1997.

Battle, Michael. *Ubuntu: I in You and You in Me*. New York: Seabury, 2009.

Beavis, Mary Ann, and HyeRan Kim-Cragg. *Hebrews*. Wisdom Commentary. Collegeville, MN: Liturgical, 2015.

———. *What Does the Bible Say? A Critical Conversation with Popular Culture in a Biblically Illiterate World*. Eugene, OR: Cascade, 2017.

Benhabib, Seyla. *Situation the Self: Gender, Community, and Postmodernism in Contemporary Ethics*. New York: Routledge, 1992.

Berger, John. *Ways of Seeing*. London: BBC and Penguin, 1972.

Bhabha, Homi. *The Location of Culture*. New York: Routledge, 1994.

Black, Kathy. *Culturally Conscious Worship*. Nashville: Abingdon, 2000.

———. *A Healing Homiletic: Preaching and Disability*. Nashville: Abingdon, 1996.

Bonhoeffer, Dietrich. "Aufträge der Bruderräte" (Dezember 1939), *Gesammelte Schriften III*. Munich: Chr. Kaiser Verlag, 1966.

———. *Life Together*. Translated by John W. Doberstein. New York: Harper & Brothers, 1954.

Bonilla-Silva, Eduardo. *Racism without Racists: Color-Blind Racism and the Persistence of Racial Inequality in the United States*. Lanham, MD: Rowman & Littlefield, 2006.

Bourdieu, Pierre, and Jean-Claude Passeron. *Reproduction in Education, Society and Culture*. Translated by Richard Nice. London: Sage, 1990.

Boyer, Ernest. "The Scholarship of Engagement." *Journal of Public Service and Outreach* 1.1 (1996) 11–20.

Bronfenbrenner, Urie. *The Ecology of Human Development: Experiments by Nature and Design*. Cambridge: Harvard University Press, 1979.

Brookfield, Stephen D. *The Skillful Teacher*. San Francisco: Jossey-Bass, 1990.

Browning, Don S. *A Fundamental Practical Theology: Descriptive and Strategic Proposals*. Minneapolis: Fortress, 1991.

Browning, Don S., and Bonnie Miller-McLemore, eds. *Children and Childhood in American Religions*. New Brunswick: Reuters University Press, 2009.

Browning, Robert, and Roy Reed. *The Sacraments in Religious Education and Liturgy*. Birmingham, AL: Religious Education, 1985.

Buber, Martin. *I and Thou*. Translated by Walter Kaufman. New York: Scribner's Sons, 1970.

Butler, Judith. *Gender Trouble: Feminism and the Subversion of Identity*. London: Routledge, 1990.

———. *Precarious Life: The Power of Mourning and Violence*. London: Verso, 2004.

———. "Rethinking Vulnerability and Resistance." In *Vulnerability and Resistance*, edited by Judith Butler, Zeynep Gambetti and Leticia Sabsay, 12–27. Durham, NC: Duke University Press, 2016.

Bystydzienski, Jill M. *Intercultural Couples: Crossing Boundaries, Negotiating Difference*. New York: State University of New York Press, 2011.

Bibliography

Cahalan, Kathleen A., and Gordon S. Mikoski, eds. *Opening the Field of Practical Theology: An Introduction.* Lanham, MD: Rowman & Littlefield, 2014.

Cahalan, Kathleen A., and James R. Nieman. "Mapping the Field of Practical Theology." In *For Life Abundant: Practical Theology, Theological Education, and Christian Ministry,* edited by Dorothy Bass and Craig Dykstra, 62–85. Grand Rapids: Eerdmans, 2008.

Caine, Renate Nummela, and Geoffrey Caine. *Making Connections: Teaching and the Human Brain.* Menlo Park, CA: Addition-Wesley, 1994.

Caldwell, Elizabeth. "Religious Instruction: Homemaking." In *Mapping Christian Education: Approaches to Congregational Learning,* edited by Jack Seymour, 74–89. Nashville: Abingdon, 1997.

Cannella, Gaile S., and Radhika Viruru. *Childhood and Postcolonialization: Power, Education, and Contemporary Practice.* London: Routledge, 2004.

Carter, Warren. "The Gospel of Matthew." In *A Postcolonial Commentary on the New Testament Writings,* edited by Fernando Segovia and R. S. Sugirtharajah, 69–104. London: T. & T. Clark, 2007.

Carvalhaes, Cláudio. "Liturgy and Postcolonialism: An Introduction." In *Liturgy in Postcolonial Perspectives: Only One is Holy,* edited by Cláudio Carvalhaes, 1–10. New York: Palgrave Macmillan, 2015.

———. "Praying Each Other's Prayers." In *Postcolonial Practice of Ministry: Leadership, Liturgy, and Interfaith Engagement,* edited by Kwok Pui-lan and Stephen Burns, 137–50. Lanham, MD: Lexington, 2016.

Castle, Stephen, and Mark J. Miller. *Age of Migration,* 4th ed. New York: Palgrave Macmillan, 2009.

Cavanaugh, William. *Migrations of the Holy: God, State, and the Political Meaning of the Church.* Grand Rapids: Eerdmans, 2011.

Chamberlain, Gary L. "Ecology and Religious Education." *Religious Education* 95.2 (2000) 134–50.

Chidester, David. "Anchoring Religion in the World: A Southern African History of Comparative Religion." *Religion* 26 (1996) 141–59.

Chow, Rey. "Between Colonizers: Hong Kong's Postcolonial Self-Writing in the 1990s." *Diaspora: A Journal of Transnational Studies,* 2.2 (1992) 151–70.

Clifford, James. "Notes on Theory and Travel." *Inscriptions* 5 (1989) 177–88.

Clinebell, Howard. *Ecotherapy: Healing Ourselves, Healing the Earth.* Minneapolis: Fortress, 1996.

Cobb, Jr., John. "Postmodern Christianity and Eco-Justice." In *After Nature's Revolt: Eco-Justice and Theology,* edited by Dieter T. Hessel, 22–38. Minneapolis: Augsburg Fortress, 1992.

Cohen, Mark Nathan. *The Culture of Intolerance: Chauvinism, Class, and Racism in the United States.* New Haven: Yale University Press, 1998.

Conde-Frazier, Elizabeth. "Participatory Action Research." In *The Wiley-Blackwell Companion to Practical Theology,* edited by Bonnie Miller-McLemore, 234–43. Chichester, UK: Blackwell, 2012.

———. "Prejudice and Conversion." In *A Many Colored Kingdom: Multicultural Dynamics for Spiritual Formation,* edited by Elizabeth Conde-Frazier, S. Steve Kang, and Gary A. Parrett, 105–20. Grand Rapids: Baker, 2004.

Cooey, Paula M. "Fiddling While Rome Burns: The Place of Academic Theology in the Study of Religion." *Harvard Theological Review* 93.1 (2000) 35–49.

Bibliography

Corky, Alexander. "The Cherokee Stomp Dance: A Case Study of Postcolonial Native American Contextualization." In *Liturgy in Postcolonial Perspectives: Only One Is Holy*, edited by Cláudio Carvalhaes, 267–76. New York: Palgrave Macmillan, 2015.

Cornell, Deirdre. *Jesus was a Migrant*. Maryknoll, NY: Orbis, 2014.

Couture, Pamela. *Blessed Are the Poor? Women's Poverty, Family Policy, and Practical Theology*. Nashville: Abingdon, 1991.

———. "Social Policy." In *The Wiley-Blackwell Companion to Practical Theology*, edited by Bonnie J. Miller-McLemore, 153–62. Chichester, UK: Blackwell, 2012.

Creamer, Deborah. *Disability and Christian Theology: Embodied Limits and Constructive Possibilities*. New York: Oxford University Press, 2009.

Cremin, Lawrence. *American Education: The Colonial Experience 1607–1783*. New York: Harper and Row, 1970.

Cruz, Faustino M. "The Tension between Scholarship and Service." In *Conundrums in Practical Theology*, edited by Joyce Ann Mercer and Bonnie J. Miller-McLemore, 60–89. Theology in Practice Series. Leiden: Brill, 2016.

Cruz, Gemma Tulud. *An Intercultural Theology of Migration: Pilgrims in the Wilderness*. Leiden: Brill, 2010.

Daggers, Jenny. "'Postcolonizing 'Mission-Shaped Church': The Church of England and Postcolonial Diversity." In *Postcolonial Practice of Ministry: Leadership, Liturgy and Interfaith Engagement*, edited by Kwok Pui-lan and Stephen Burns, 183–97. Lanham, MD: Lexington, 2016.

Daly, Mary. *Gyn/Ecology: The Metaethics of Radical Feminism*. Boston: Beacon, 1978.

Davis, Pat. "Okay with Who I Am: Listening to Lesbian Young Women Talk about Their Spiritualities." In *The Sacred Selves of Adolescent Girls: Hard Stories of Race, Class, and Gender*, edited by Evelyn L. Parker, 131–60. Cleveland, OH: Pilgrim, 2006.

de Beauvoir, Simone. *The Second Sex*. Translated by E. M. Parshley. New York: Vintage, 1973.

Dean, Kenda Creasy. *Practical Passion: Youth and the Quest for a Passionate Church*. Grand Rapids: Eerdmans, 2004.

———. "Somebody Save Me: Passion, Salvation, and the Smallville Effect." In *The Princeton Lectures on Youth, Church, and Culture*, 22–23. Princeton, NJ: Princeton Theological Seminary, 2004.

Deluze, G., and Felix Guattari. *A Thousand Plateaus: Capitalism and Schizophrenia*. Translated by B. Massumi. Minneapolis: Minneapolis University Press, 1987.

Diamond, Irene, and Gloria F. Orenstein, eds. *Reweaving the World: The Emergence of Ecofeminism*. San Francisco: Sierra Club, 1990.

Donaldson, Laura E., and Kwok Pui-lan, eds. *Postcolonialism, Feminism, and Religious Discourse*. New York: Routledge, 2002.

Donovan, Mary Ann. "Alive to the Glory of God: A Key Insight in St. Irenaeus." *Theological Studies* 49 (1988) 283–97.

Doran, Carol, and Thomas Troeger. *Trouble at the Table: Gathering the Tribes for Worship*. Nashville: Abingdon, 1992.

Douglas, Jane. "A Turning Point for Reformed Women in Ministry?" *Reformed World* (March 2017) 9–16.

Dreyer, Jaco, Yolanda Dreyer, Edward Foley, and Malan Nel, eds. *Practicing Ubuntu: Practical Theological Perspectives on Injustice, Personhood, and Human Dignity: International Practical Theology* Vol. 20. Zurich: LIT, 2017.

Bibliography

Drucilla, Cornell, and Karin van Marle. "Exploring Ubuntu: Tentative Reflections." *African Human Rights Law Journal* 5 (2005) 195–291.

Dube, Musa. *Postcolonial Feminist Interpretation of the Bible*. St. Louis, MO: Chalice, 2000.

Du Bois, W. E. S. "Of Our Spiritual Strivings." In *The Souls of Black Folk,* included in *The Norton Anthology of African American Literature,* edited by Henry Louis Gates, Jr. and Nellie Y. McKay, 693–99. New York: Norton, 2004.

Duck, Ruth. *Worship for the Whole People of God: Vial Worship for the 21st century*. Louisville: Westminster John Knox, 2013.

Duff, Nancy. "Vocation, Motherhood, and Marriage." In *Women, Gender, and Christian Community*, edited by Jane Dempsey Douglas and James F. Kay, 69–81. Louisville: Westminster John Knox, 1997.

Eaton, Heather. *Introducing Ecofeminist Theologies*. London: T. & T. Clark, 2005.

Economy of Life, Peace, and Justice for All: A Call to Action. Geneva: WCC, 2012.

Edie, Fred. *Book, Bath, Table, and Time: Christian Worship as Source and Resource for Youth Ministry*. Cleveland, OH: Pilgrim, 2007.

Eiesland, Nancy L., and Don E. Saliers, eds. *Human Disability and the Service of God*. Nashville: Abingdon, 1998.

Eisner, Elliot. *The Educational Imagination: On the Design and Evaluation of School Programs*. New York: Macmillan, 1985.

Elliott, John H. *A Home for the Homeless: A Social-Scientific Criticism of 1 Peter, Its Situation and Strategy*. 2nd ed. Eugene, OR: Wipf and Stock, 2005.

Elam, Michele. *The Souls of Mixed Race: Race, Politics, and Aesthetics in the New Millennium*. Stanford, CA: Stanford University Press, 2011.

Erikson, Erik H. *Identity: Youth and Crisis*. New York: Norton, 1968.

Fanon, Frantz. *Black Skin, White Masks*. Translated by Richard Philcox. New York: Grove, 2008.

———. *The Wretched of the Earth*. Translated by Richard Constance Farrington. New York: Grove, 1963.

Feely-Harnik, Gillian. *The Lord's Table: The Meaning of Food in Early Judaism and Christianity*. Washington, DC: Smithsonian, 1994.

Filippi, Linda. "Place, Feminism, and Healing: An Ecology of Pastoral Counseling." *The Journal of Pastoral Care* 45.3 (1991) 232–42.

Foley, Edward, ed. *Developmental Disabilities and Sacramental Access*. Collegeville, MN: Liturgical, 1994.

Foster, Charles. *Educating Congregations: The Future of Christian Education*. Nashville: Abingdon, 1994.

———. *From Generation to Generation*. Eugene, OR: Cascade, 2012.

Foucault, Michel. *Discipline and Punish: The Birth of the Prison*. Translated by Alan Sheridan. New York: Pantheon, 1977.

———. *The History of Sexuality, Vol I*. New York: Pantheon, 1978.

Pope Francis, *Laudato si'*, point 160. Online: http://w2.vatican.va/content/francesco/en/encyclicals/documents/papa-francesco_20150524_enciclica-laudato-si.html.

Frye, Marilyn. "Introduction." In *Are Your Girls Traveling Alone? Adventures in Lesbian Logic*, edited by Marilyn Murphy, 11–16. Los Angeles: Clothes Spin Fever, 1991.

Fulkerson, Mary McClintock. *Places of Redemption: Theology for a Worldly Church*. Oxford: Oxford University Press, 2007.

Ganzevoort, R. Ruard. "Narrative Approaches." In *The Wiley-Blackwell Companion to Practical Theology*. Edited by Bonnie Miller-McLemore, 214–23. Chichester, UK: Blackwell, 2012.

Bibliography

Garland-Thomson, Rosemarie. *Staring: How We Look*. New York: Oxford University Press, 2009.

Gaskins, Pearl Fuyo. *What Are You? Voices of Mixed-Race Young People*. New York: Henry Holt, 1999.

Gebara, Ivone. *Longing for Running Water: Ecofeminism and Liberation*. Minneapolis: Augsburg, 1999.

George, Rosemary Margangoly. *The Politics of Home: Postcolonial Relocation and Twentieth-Century Fiction*. Cambridge: Cambridge University Press, 1996.

Gilmour, Michael J. *Eden's Other Residents: The Bible and Animals*. Eugene, OR: Cascade, 2014.

Giroux, Henry. *Living Dangerously: Multiculturalism and Politics of Difference*. New York: Lang, 1993.

"Glory to God and Peace on Earth: The Message of the International Ecumenical Peace Convocation." WCC, Kingston, Jamaica, 17–25 May 2011.

Gogia, Nupur, and Bonnie Slade. *About Canada: Immigration*. Halifax and Winnipeg: Fernwood, 2011.

Graham, Elaine. *Making the Difference: Gender, Personhood, and Theology*. Minneapolis: Fortress, 1996.

Greider, Kathleen J. "Religious Pluralism and Christian-Centrism." In *The Wiley-Blackwell Companion to Practical Theology*, edited by Bonnie Miller-McLemore, 452–53. Chichester, UK: Blackwell, 2012.

Grethlein, Christian. *An Introduction to Practical Theology: History, Theory, and the Communication of the Gospel in the Present*. Translated by Uwe Rasch. Waco, TX: Baylor University Press, 2016.

Grey, Mary. *Sacred Longings: The Ecological Spirit and Global Culture*. Minneapolis: Fortress, 2004.

Groome, Thomas H. *Christian Religious Education: Sharing Our Story and Vision*. New York: Harper and Row, 1980.

"Growing Together: A Backgrounder on Immigration and Citizenship." Ottawa: Public Affairs Branch Canada, 1995.

Hall, Douglas John. *Imaging God: Dominion as Stewardship*. Grand Rapids: Eerdmans, 1986.

Hamman, Jaco. "Playing." In *The Wiley-Blackwell Companion to Practical Theology*, edited by Bonnie Miller-McLemore, 42–50. Chichester, UK: Blackwell, 2012.

Harris, Maria. *Fashion Me a People: Curriculum in the Church*. Louisville: Westminster John Knox, 1989.

Hauerwas, Stanley. *Suffering Presence: Theological Reflection on Medicine, the Mentally Handicapped, and the Church*. Edinburgh: T. & T. Clark, 1988.

Herbert, Anderson. "Loving." In *The Wiley-Blackwell Companion to Practical Theology*, edited by Bonnie Miller-McLemore, 61–69. Chichester, UK: Blackwell, 2012.

Hess, Mary E., and S. D. Brookfield, eds. *Teaching Reflectively in Theological Contexts: Promises and Contradictions*. Malabar, India: Krieger, 2008.

Hessel, Dieter T. "Introduction." In *After Nature's Revolt: Eco-Justice and Theology*, edited by Dieter T. Hessel, 1–20. Minneapolis: Augsburg Fortress, 1992.

Hill, Lawrence. *Blood: The Stuff of Life*. Toronto: Anansi, 2013.

Hoeft, Jeanne. "Gender, Sexism, and Heterosexism." In *The Wiley-Blackwell Companion to Practical Theology*, edited by Bonnie Miller-McLemore, 412–21. Chichester, UK: Wiley-Blackwell, 2012.

BIBLIOGRAPHY

hooks, bell. "The Oppositional Gaze: Black Female Spectators." In *The Feminism and Visual Culture Reader*, edited by Amelia Jones, 94–104. New York: Routledge, 2003.

Horell, Harold D. "The Imagination of REA: APPRRE." *Religious Education* 111.4 (2016) 349–65.

Isasi-Diaz, Ada Maria. "Solidarity: Love of the Neighbor in 1980s." In *Lift Every Voice: Constructing Christian Theologies from the Underside*, edited by Susan Brooks Thistlethwaite, and Mary Potter Engel, 31–40. San Francisco: Harper and Row, 1990.

Jagessar, Michael N., and Stephen Burns. *Christian Worship: Postcolonial Perspectives*. Oakville, CT: Equinox, 2011.

Jave, Jean, and Etienne Wenger. *Situated Learning: Legitimate Peripheral Participation*. Cambridge: Cambridge University Press, 1991.

Jobling, David. "The Bible and Critical Theology: Best Friend or Unstable Ally?" In *Intersecting Voices: Critical Theologies in a Land of Diversity*, edited by Don Schweitzer and Derek Simon, 154–67. Ottawa: Novalis, 2004.

Jones, Esyllt, and Adele Perry, eds. *People's Citizenship Guide: A Response to Conservative Canada*. Winnipeg: Arbeiter Ring, 2011.

Jung, Patricia Beattie. "Patriarchy, Purity, and Procreativity: Developments in Catholic Teachings on Human Sexuality and Gender." In *God, Science, Sex and Gender: An Interdisciplinary Approach to Christian Ethics*, edited by Patricia Beattie Jung and Aana Marie Vigen, 69–85. Chicago: University of Illinois Press, 2010.

Kang, Nam Soon. *Diasporic Feminist Theology: Asia and Theopolitical Imagination*. Minneapolis: Fortress, 2014.

Katz, Eric. "Judaism and the Ecological Crisis." In *Worldviews and Ecology*, edited by Mary Evelyn Tucker and John A. Grin, 55–70. Maryknoll, NY: Orbis, 1994.

Kawash, Samira. "Terrorists and Vampires: Fanon's Spectral Violence of Decolonization." In *Frantz Fanon: Critical Perspectives*, edited by Anthony C. Alessandrini, 237–57. London: Routledge, 1999.

Kazimi, Ali. *Undesirables: White Canada and the Komagata Maru*. Vancouver: D&M, 2011.

Keller, Catherine. *Apocalypse Now and Then: A Feminist Guide to the End of the World*. Boston: Beacon, 1996.

———. "The Flesh of God: A Metaphor in the Wild." In *Theology That Matters: Ecology, Economy, and God*, edited by Darby Kathleen Ray, 91–107. Minneapolis: Fortress, 2006.

———. *From a Broken Web: Separation, Sexism, and Self*. Boston: Beacon, 1986.

———. "Talk about the Weather: The Greening of Eschatology." In *Ecofeminism and the Sacred*, edited by Carol J. Adams, 30–49. New York: Continuum, 1993.

Keller, Catherine, and Laurel C. Schneider, eds. *Polydoxy: Theology of Multiplicity and Relation*. New York: Routledge, 2011.

Kennedy, William Bean. *The Shaping of Protestant Education: An Interpretation of the Sunday School and the Development of Protestant Educational Strategy in the United States, 1789–1860*. New York: Association, 1966.

Kierkegaard, Søren. *Concluding Unscientific Postscript*. Translated by D. Swenson and W. Lowrie. Princeton, NJ: Princeton University Press, 1941.

———. *The Sickness unto Death*. Translated by Walter Lowrie. Princeton, NJ: Princeton University Press, 1968.

Bibliography

Kim-Cragg, HyeRan. "Baptism as Crossing beyond Belonging." In *Liturgy in Postcolonial Perspectives: Only One is Holy,* edited by Claudio Carvalhaes, 201–11. New York: Palgrave Macmillan, 2015.

———. "A Christian Feminist Theological Reflection on Economy of Life." *The Ecumenical Review* 67.2 (2015) 170–76.

———. "A Plural Mystery for a Plural World." In *Three Ways of Grace: Drawing Closer to the Trinity,* edited by Rob Fennell and Ross Lockhart, 134–40. Toronto: UCPH, 2010.

———. "Postcolonial Practices on Eucharist." In *Postcolonial Practice of Ministry: Leadership, Liturgy, and Interfaith Engagement,* edited by Kwok Pui-lan and Stephen Burns, 77–89. Lanham, MD: Lexington, 2016.

———. *Story and Song: A Postcolonial Interplay between Christian Education and Worship.* New York: Lang, 2012.

———. "Through Senses and Sharing: How Liturgy Meets Food." *Liturgy* 32.2 (2017) 34–41.

———. "To Love and Serve Others (or to Be Loved and Served)." In *Intercultural Vision: Called to Be the Church,* edited by Rob Fennell, 23–32. Toronto: UCPH, 2012.

Kim-Cragg, HyeRan, and Don Schweitzer. *The Authority and Interpretation of Scripture of The United Church of Canada.* Daejeon, South Korea: Daeganggan, 2016.

Kim-Cragg. HyeRan, and EunYoung Choi. *The Encounters: Retelling the Bible from Migration and Intercultural Perspectives.* Daejeon, South Korea: Daeganggan, 2013.

Kim-Cragg, HyeRan, and Joanne Doi. "Intercultural Threads of Hybridity and Threshold Spaces of Learning." *Religious Education* 107.3 (2012) 262–75.

Kim-Cragg, HyeRan, and Stephen Burns. "Liturgy in Migration and Migrants in Liturgy." In *Church in an Age of Global Migration: A Moving Body,* edited by Susanna Snyder, Joshua Ralston, and Agnes M. Brazal, 113–30. New York: Palgrave Macmillan, 2016.

Kim-Cragg, HyeRan, and Mai-Anh Le Tran. "Turning to the Other: Interdenominational, Interethnic, Interreligious Activism and A New Ecclesia." In *Complex Identities in a Shifting World: Practical Theological Perspectives International Practical Theology* Vol. 17, edited by Pam Couture, Robert Mager, Pamela McCarroll, and Natalie Wigg-Stevenson, 127–38. Zurich: Lit, 2015.

Kimelman, Justice Edwin. "Report of a Review of Indian and Metis Adoptions in the Province of Manitoba, Canada in 1980s." Online: https://en.wikipedia.org/wiki/Kimelman_Report, accessed 2 September 2016.

Kirch, Jonathan. *God against the Gods: The History of the War between Monotheism and Polytheism.* New York: Penguin, 2004.

Kittay, Eva. *Love's Labor: Essays on Women, Labor, and Dependency.* New York: Routledge, 1999.

Knowles, Malcolm. *The Adult Learner: A Neglected Species.* Houston: Gulf, 1973.

———. *The Modern Practice of Adult Education: From Pedagogy to Andragogy.* Wilton, CT: Association, 1980.

Kraft, Charles H. *Anthropology for Christian Witness.* Maryknoll, NY: Orbis, 1996.

Kujawa-Holbrook, Sheryl A. *God Beyond Borders: Interreligious Learning Among Faith Communities.* Eugene, OR: Pickwick, 2014.

———. "Postcolonial Interreligious Learning." In *Postcolonial Practice of Ministry: Leadership, Liturgy and Interfaith Engagement,* edited by Kwok Pui-lan and Stephen Burns, 153–65. Lanham, MD: Lexington, 2016.

Kwok, Pui-lan. *Discovering the Bible in the Non-biblical World.* Maryknoll, NY: Orbis, 1995.

Bibliography

———. *Globalization, Gender, and Peacebuilding: The Future of Interfaith Dialogue.* New York: Paulist, 2012.

———. "Jesus/The Native: Biblical Studies from a Postcolonial Perspectives." In *Teaching the Bible: The Discourse and Politics of Biblical Pedagogy,* edited by Fernando F. Segovia and May Ann Tolbert, 75–80. Maryknoll, NY: Orbis, 1998.

———. *Postcolonial Imagination and Feminist Theology.* Louisville: Westminster/John Knox, 2005.

———. "Unbinding Our Feet: Saving Brown Women and Feminist Religious Discourse." In *Postcolonialism, Feminism, and Religious Discourse,* edited by Laura E. Donaldson and Kwok Pui-lan, 62–81. London: Routledge, 2002.

Kwok, Pui-lan, Don H. Compier, and Joerg Rieger, eds. *Empire and the Christian Tradition: New Readings of Classical Theologians.* Minneapolis: Fortress, 2007.

Lartey, Emmanuel T. "Borrowed Clothes Will Never Keep You Warm: Postcolonializing Pastoral Leadership." In *Postcolonial Practice of Ministry: Leadership, Liturgy and Interfaith Engagement,* edited by Kwok Pui-lan and Stephen Burns, 21–32. Lanham, MD: Lexington, 2016.

———. *In Living Color: An Intercultural Approach to Pastoral Care and Counseling.* 2nd ed. New York: Jessica Kingsley, 2003.

Lathrop, Gordon. "The Eucharist as a 'Hungry Feast,' and the Appropriation of Our Want." *Living Worship* 13 (November 1977) 351–61.

Lee, Boyung. "Toward liberating Interdependence: Exploring an Intercultural Pedagogy." *Religious Education* 105.3 (2010) 283–97.

Lee, Jung Young. *Marginality: Key to Multicultural Theology.* Minneapolis: Fortress, 1995.

Liew, Tat-siong Benny. *What Is Asian American Biblical Hermeneutics: Reading the New Testament?* Honolulu: University of Hawai'i Press, 2008.

Locke, John. *Second Treatise on Government.* Reprint. New York: Macmillan, 1952.

Love, Spencie. *One Blood: The Death and the Resurrection of Charles R. Drew.* Chapel Hill, NC: University of North Carolina Press, 1996.

Lowe, Lisa. *Immigrant Acts: On Asian American Cultural Politics.* 6th printing. Durham, NC: Duke University Press, 2007.

Lynn, Robert, and Elliott Wright. *The Big Little School: 200 Years of the Sunday School.* 2nd ed. Birmingham, UK: Religious Education, 1980.

Macadam, Jackie. "Interview with Mary Warnock: A Duty to Die?" *Life and Work* (October 2008) 23–25.

Marshall, Joretta L. *Counselling Lesbian Partners.* Louisville: Westminster John Knox, 1997.

Martin, Miriam K. "The Human-Nature Relationship: Challenges for Practical Theology and Christian Discipleship." *Practical Theology* 8 (2015) 167–76.

Matsuoka, Fumitaka. *Learning to Speak a New Tongue: Imaging a Way that Holds People Together—An Asian American Conversation.* Eugene, OR: Pickwick, 2011.

McCarthy, Maureen Terese. "Nuclear Alternatives: Interracial and Queer Families in American Literature, 1840–1905." PhD diss., Emory University, 2013.

McClintock, Anne. "The Angel of Progress: Pitfalls of the Term 'Postcolonialism.'" In *Colonial Disclosure and Post-Colonial Theory: A Reader,* edited by Patrick Williams and Laura Chrisman, 291–304. New York: Columbia University Press, 1994.

———. *Imperial Leather: Race, Gender and Sexuality in the Colonial Contest.* New York: Routledge, 1995.

Bibliography

McFague, Sallie. "An Earthly Theological Agenda." In *Ecofeminism and the Sacred*, edited by Carol Adams, 84–98. New York: Continuum, 1993.

Mercer, Joyce Ann. "Call Forwarding: Putting Vocation in the Present Tense with Youth." In *Compass Points: Navigating Vocation Princeton Lectures on Youth, Church, and Culture*, 29–44. Princeton, NJ: Princeton Theological Seminary, 2002.

———. "Interdisciplinarity as a Practical Theological Conundrum." In *Conundrums in Practical Theology*, edited by Joyce Ann Mercer and Bonnie Miller-McLemore, 163–89. Theology in Practice Series. Leiden: Brill, 2016.

———. "A Practical Theological Approach to Ecofeminism: Story of Women, Faith, and Earth Advocacy." In *Body Memories: Goddesses of Nusantera, Rings of Fire, and Narratives of Myth*, edited by Dewi Candraningrum, 93–106. Salatiga, Indonesia: Yayasin Jurnal Perempuan and Pusat Penelitian dan Studi Gender, 2014.

———. *Welcoming Children: A Theology of Childhood*. St. Louis, MO: Chalice, 2005.

Mercer, Kobena. "Diaspora Aesthetics and Visual Culture." In *Black Cultural Traffic: Crossroads in Global Performance and Popular Culture*, edited by Harry J. Elam, Jr., Herman S. Gary, 141–61. Ann Arbor, MI: University of Michigan Press, 2008.

Merchant, Carolyn. *The Death of Nature: Women, Ecology, and the Scientific Revolution*. New York: Harper and Row, 1980.

Mignolo, Walter D. *Local Histories/Global Designs: Coloniality, Subaltern Knowledges, and Border Thinking*. Princeton, NJ: Princeton University Press, 2000.

Miles, Maria. *Patriarchy and Accumulation on a World Scale: Women in the International Division of Labour*. London: Zed, 1986.

Miller-McLemore, Bonnie. *Also a Mother: Work and Family as Theological Dilemma*. Nashville: Abingdon, 1994.

———. *Christian Theology in Practice: Discovering a Discipline*. Grand Rapids: Eerdmans, 2012.

———. *In the Midst of Chaos: Caring for Children as Spiritual Practice*. San Francisco: Jossey-Bass, 2007.

———. "The Theory-Practice Binary and the Politics of Practical Knowledge." In *Conundrums in Practical Theology*, edited by Joyce Ann Mercer and Bonnie Miller-McLemore, 190–218. Theology in Practice Series. Leiden: Brill, 2016.

Mollenkott, Virginia Ramey. *Sensuous Spirituality: Out from Fundamentalism*. New York: Crossroad, 1992.

Moore, Mary Elizabeth Mullino. *Ministering with the Earth*. St. Louis, MO: Chalice, 1998.

———. *Teaching as a Sacramental Act*. Cleveland, OH: Pilgrim, 2004.

———. "Toward an Interreligious Practical Theology," an annual lecture of the Center for Practical Theology in Boston University, 2010. Online: https://www.youtube.com/watch?v=8enGhBO1rKU, accessed 20 February 2017.

Moran, Gabriel. *Education Toward Adulthood: Religion and Lifelong Learning*. New York: Paulist, 1979.

———. *Religious Education as a Second Language*. Birmingham, UK: Religious Education, 1989.

Morrison, Toni. *Home: A Novel*. New York: Knof, 2012.

Murphy, Debra Dean. *Teaching That Transforms: Worship as the Heart of Christian Education*. Grand Rapids: Brazos, 2004.

Nandy, Ashis. *The Intimate Enemy: Loss and Recovery of Self under Colonialism*. New Delhi: Oxford University Press, 1983.

Bibliography

Ng, David, and Virginia Thomas. *Children in the Worshipping Community*. Atlanta: Westminster John Knox, 1981.

Ng, David. "A Path of Concentric Circles: Toward an Autobiographical Theology of Community." In *Journeys at the Margin: Toward an Autobiographical Theology in American-Asian Perspective*, edited by Peter C. Phan and Jung Young Lee, 81–102. Collegeville, MN: Liturgical, 1999.

Nixon, Rob. *Slow Violence and the Environmentalism of the Poor*. Cambridge: Harvard University Press, 2013.

Oduyoye, Mercy Amba. "The Story of a Circle." In *Hope Abundant: Third World and Indigenous Women's Theology*, edited by Kwok Pui-lan, 17. Maryknoll, NY: Orbis, 2010.

Okin, Susan Moller. *Justice, Gender, and the Family*. New York: Basic, 1989.

Osmer, Richard R. *Practical Theology: An Introduction*. Grand Rapids: Eerdmans, 2008.

Parker, Evelyn, ed. *The Sacred Selves of Adolescent Girls: Hard Stories of Race, Class, and Gender*. Cleveland, OH: Pilgrim, 2006.

———. *Trouble Don't Last Always: Emancipatory Hope among African American Adolescents*. Cleveland, OH: Pilgrim, 2003.

Parks, Sharon Daloz. *Big Questions, Worthy Dreams: Mentoring Young Adults in Their Search for Meaning, Purpose, and Faith*. San Francisco: Jossey-Bass, 2000.

Peterson, Cheryl M. *Who Is the Church? An Ecclesiology for the 21st Century*. Minneapolis: Fortress, 2013.

Plant, Judith, ed. *Healing the Wounds: The Promise of Ecofeminism*. Toronto: Between the Lines, 1989.

Plumwood, Val. *Feminism and the Mastery of Nature*. London: Routledge, 1993.

Poling, James, and Donald Miller. *Foundations for a Practical Theology of Ministry*. Nashville: Abingdon, 1985.

Ponting, Clive. *A Green History of the World*. London: Sinclair-Stevenson, 1991.

Procter-Smith, Marjorie. "Introduction." In *Women at Worship: Interpretations of North American Diversity*, edited by Marjorie Procter-Smith and Janet Walton, 1–5. Louisville: Westminster John Knox, 1993.

Rasmussen, Larry. "Returning to Our Senses." In *After Nature's Revolt: Eco-Justice and Theology*, edited by Dieter T. Hessel, 40–56. Minneapolis: Augsburg Fortress, 1992.

Razack, Sharene, ed. *Race, Space and the Law: Unmapping a White Settler Society*. Toronto: Between the Lines, 2002.

Reader, John. *Reconstructing Practical Theology: The Impact of Globalization*. Aldershot, UK: Ashgate, 2008.

Reynolds, Tom E. "Invoking Deep Access: Disability beyond Inclusion in the Church." *Dialog: A Journal of Theology* 51.3 (2012) 212–23.

———. *Vulnerable Communion: A Theology of Disability and Hospitality*. Grand Rapids: Brazos, 2008.

Rieger, Joerg. *God and the Excluded: Visions and Blindspots in Contemporary Theology*. Minneapolis: Fortress, 2001.

Rieger, Joerg, and Kwok Pui-lan. *Occupy Religion: Theology of Multitude*. Lanham, MD: Rowman and Littlefield, 2012.

Rivera, Mayra. "God at the Crossroads." In *Postcolonial Theologies: Divinity and Empire*, edited by Catherine Keller, Michael Nausner, and Mayra Rivera, 203–4. Nashville: Abingdon, 2004.

Bibliography

———. *The Touch of Transcendence: A Postcolonial Theology of God.* Louisville: Westminster John Knox, 2007.

Root, Maria. *Racially Mixed People in America.* Thousand Oaks, CA: Sage, 1992.

Ross, Susan A. *Extravagant Affections: A Feminist Sacramental Theology.* New York: Continuum, 1998.

Ruether, Rosemary Radford. *Gaia and God: An Ecofeminist Theology of Earth Healing.* San Francisco: Harper Collins, 1992.

———. *New Woman/New Earth.* New York: Seabury, 1973.

Russell, Letty. "God, Gold, Glory, and Gender: A Postcolonial View of Mission." *International Review of Mission* 93.368 (2004) 39–49.

Ruth, Lester, Carrie Steenwyk, John D. Witvliet. *Walking Where Jesus Walked: Worship in Fourth-Century Jerusalem.* Grand Rapids: Eerdmans, 2010.

Sacks, Oliver. *Seeing Voices: A Journey into the World of the Deaf.* New York: HarperCollins, 1990.

Said, Edward. *Culture and Imperialism.* New York: Vintage, 1993.

———. *Orientalism.* New York: Basic, 1978.

———. *Out of Place: A Memoir.* New York: Vintage, 2000.

Sakai, Naoki. *Translations and Subjectivity: Japan and Cultural Nationalism.* Minneapolis: University of Minnesota Press, 1997.

Saliers, Don E. "Singing Our Lives." In *Practicing Our Faith: A Way of Life for a Searching People,* edited by Dorothy Bass, 179–93. San Francisco: Jossey-Bass, 1997.

———. "Worship." In *The Wiley-Blackwell Companion to Practical Theology,* edited by Bonnie Miller-McLemore, 289–98. Chichester, UK: Blackwell, 2012.

Santmire, H. Paul. "Healing the Protestant Mind." In *After Nature's Revolt: Eco-Justice and Theology,* edited by Dieter T. Hessel, 57–78. Minneapolis: Augsburg Fortress, 1992.

São Paulo Statement: International Financial Transformation for the Economy of Life (2012). Online: https://www.oikoumene.org/en/resources/documents/wcc-programmes/public-witness-addressing-power-affirming-peace/poverty-wealth-and-ecology/finance-speculation-debt/sao-paulo-statement-international-financial-transformation-for-the-economy-of-life.

Schleiermacher, Friedrich. *On Religion: Speeches to Its Cultured Despisers.* Translated by John Oman. New York: Harper Torch, 1958.

Schneider, Laurel C. *Beyond Monotheism: A Theology of Multiplicity.* London: Routledge, 2008.

Seager, Joni. *Earth Follies: Coming to Feminist Terms with the Global Environmental Crisis.* New York: Routledge, 1993.

Selmanovic, Samir. *It's Really All about God: Reflections of a Muslim Atheist Jewish Christian.* San Francisco: Jossey-Bass, 2009.

Senn, Frank C. *Embodied Liturgy: Lessons in Christian Ritual.* Minneapolis: Fortress, 2016.

Senna, Danzy. "The Mulatto Millennium." In *Half and Half: Writers on Growing Up Biracial and Bicultural,* edited by Claudine Chiawei O'Hearn, 12–27. New York: Pantheon, 1998.

Seymour, Jack. *Teaching the Way of Jesus: Educating Christians for Faithful Living.* Nashville: Abingdon, 2014.

Sharkey, Sarah Borden. *An Aristotelian Feminism.* Cham, Switzerland: Springer, 2016.

Sharp, Melinda A. McGarrah. "Globalization, Colonialism, and Postcolonialism." In *The Wiley-Blackwell Companion to Practical Theology,* edited by Bonnie J. Miller-McLemore, 422–31. Chichester, UK: Blackwell, 2012.

Bibliography

———. "Literacies of Listening: Postcolonial Pastoral Leadership in Practice." In *Postcolonial Practice of Ministry: Leadership, Liturgy and Interfaith Engagement*, edited by Kwok Pui-lan and Stephen Burns, 33–48. Lanham, MD: Lexington, 2016.

———. *Misunderstanding Stories: Toward A Postcolonial Pastoral Theology*. Eugene, OR: Pickwick, 2013.

Shepard, R. Bruce. *Deemed Unsuitable: Blacks from Oklahoma Move to the Canadian Prairies in Search of Equality in the Early 20th Century Only to Find Racism in Their New Home*. Toronto: Umbrella, 1997.

Shiva, Vandana. *Staying Alive: Women, Ecology, and Development*. London: Zed, 1988.

Slack, Jennifer. "Resisting Eco Cultural Studies." *Cultural Studies* 22.3 (2008) 477–94.

Smith, Andrea. "Sexual Violence and American Indian Genocide." In *Remembering Conquest: Feminist/Womanist Perspectives on Religion, Colonization, and Sexual Violence*, edited by Nantawan B. Lewis and Marie M. Fortune, 31–52. New York: Haworth Pastoral, 1999.

Snyder, Susanna. "Introduction: Moving Body." In *Church in an Age of Global Migration: A Moving Body*, edited by Susanna Snyder, Joshua Ralston, and Agnes M. Brazal, 1–19. New York: Palgrave Macmillan, 2016.

Soja, Edward W. *Seeking Spatial Justice*. Minneapolis: University of Minnesota Press, 2010.

Spivak, Gayatri Chakravorty. *A Critique of Postcolonial Reason: Toward a History of the Vanishing Present*. Cambridge: Harvard University Press, 1999.

Sugirtharajah, R. S. "Thinking about Vernacular Hermeneutics Sitting in a Metropolitan Study." In *Vernacular Hermeneutics: The Bible and Postcolonialism* 2, edited by R. S. Sugirtharajah, 92–105. Sheffield, UK: Sheffield Academic, 1999.

Swinton, John. *Becoming Friends of Time: Disability, Timefullness, and Gentle Discipleship*. Waco, TX: Baylor University Press, 2016.

———. "Building a Church for Strangers." *Journal of Religion, Disability, and Health* 4.4 (2001) 25–63.

———. "Disability, Ableism, and Disabilism." In *The Wiley-Blackwell Companion to Practical Theology*, edited by Bonnie Miller-McLemore, 443–51. Chichester, UK: Blackwell, 2012.

———. "What's in a Name? Why People with Dementia Might be Better Off without the Language of Personhood." *International Journal of Practical Theology* 18.2 (2014) 234–47.

Tanner, Kathryn. "Globalization, Women's Transnational Migration, and Religious De-traditioning." In *Oxford Handbook of Feminist Theology*, edited by Mary McClintock Fulkerson and Sheila Briggs, 544–60. Oxford: Oxford University Press, 2011.

———. "Theological Reflection and Christian Practice." In *Practicing Theology: Beliefs and Practices in Christian Life*, edited by Miroslav Volf and Dorothy Bass, 228–42. Grand Rapids: Eerdmans, 2002.

Thatamanil, John J. "Comparative Theology after 'Religion.'" In *Planetary Loves: Spivak, Postcoloniality, and Theology*, edited by Stephen D. Moore and Mayra Rivera, 238–57. New York: Fordham University Press, 2011.

The Authority and Interpretation of Scripture: A Statement of The United Church of Canada. Toronto: UCPH, 1992.

Together towards Life: Mission and Evangelism in Changing Landscapes. A statement presented to WCC 10th General Assembly, Busan, Korea, 2013.

BIBLIOGRAPHY

Turner, Mary Donovan. "Reversal of Fortune: The Performance of a Prophet." In *Performance in Preaching: Bringing the Sermon to Life*, edited by Jana Childers and Clayton J. Schmit, 87–98. Grand Rapids: Baker Academic, 2008.

Turpin, Katherine. *Branded: Adolescents Converting from Consumer Faith*. Youth Ministry Alternatives Series. Cleveland, OH: Pilgrim, 2006.

Tye, Karen. *Basics of Christian Education*. Nashville: Abingdon, 2000.

Vanier, Jean. *Befriending the Stranger*. Mahwah, NJ: Paulist, 2005.

———. *Community and Growth: Our Pilgrimage Together*. London: Griffin House, 1979.

Wainwright, Geoffrey. "Theology of Worship." In *The New Westminster Dictionary of Liturgy and Worship*, edited by Paul Bradshaw, 456. Louisville: Westminster John Knox, 2002.

Walia, Harsha. *Undoing Border Imperialism*. Chico, CA: AK, 2013.

Walker, Alice. *The Color Purple*. New York: Harcourt Brace Jovanovich, 1982.

Ward, Pete. *Liquid Church*. Carlisle, UK: Paternoster, 2002.

Ward, W. Peter. *White Canada Forever: Popular Attitudes and Public Policy toward Orientals in British Columbia*. Montreal: McGill-Queen's University Press, 1992.

Washbourn, Penelope. "Becoming Woman: Menstruation as Spiritual Challenge." In *Womanspirit Rising: A Feminist Reader in Religion*, edited by Carol Christ and Judith Plaskow, 246–58. New York: Harper & Row, 1979.

Welsh, Jennifer. *The Return of History: Conflict, Migration, and Geopolitics in the Twenty-First Century*. Toronto: Anansi, 2016.

West, Cornel. *The American Evasion of Philosophy*. Madison, WI: University of Wisconsin Press, 1989.

———. "The New Cultural Politics of Difference." In *The Cultural Studies Reader*, edited by Simon During, 256–67. New York: Routledge, 1993.

West, Mona. "Metropolitan Community Church as a Messy Space for Revisioning the Other Side of Pastoral Ministry." In *Postcolonial Practice of Ministry: Leadership, Liturgy and Interfaith Engagement*, edited by Kwok Pui-lan and Stephen Burns, 49–59. Lanham, MD: Lexington, 2016.

Westerhoff III, John H. "Foreword." In *Children's Ministry in the Way of Jesus*, David M. Csinos and Ivy Beckwith, 9–14. Downers Grove, IL: IVP, 2013.

———. *A Pilgrim People: Learning through the Church Year*. New York: Seabury, 1984.

———. *Will Our Children Have Faith?* New York: Seabury, 1976.

White, James F. *Introduction to Christian Worship*. 3rd ed. Nashville: Abingdon, 2000.

———. *Protestant Worship: Traditions in Transition*. Louisville: Westminster John Knox, 1989.

Wiesel, Elie. *Night*. New York: Hill and Wang, 1960.

Williams, Delores. *Sisters in the Wilderness: The Challenge of Womanist God-Talk*. Maryknoll, NY: Orbis, 1993.

Williams, Patricia J. *Seeing a Color-blind Future: The Paradox of Race*. New York: Farrar, Straus, and Giroux, 1998.

Witvliet, John D. "Teaching Worship as a Christian Practice." In *For Life Abundant: Practical Theology, Theological Education, and Christian Ministry*, edited by Dorothy Bass and Craig Dykstra, 117–48. Grand Rapids: Eerdmans, 2008.

Young, Robert C. *Postcolonialism: A Very Short Introduction*. Oxford: Oxford University Press, 2003.

Zantop, Susanne. *Colonial Fantasies: Conquest, Family, and Nation in Precolonial Germany, 1770–1870*. Durham, NC: Duke University Press, 1997.

Index

A

Abella, Irving, 109, 109n16
adulthood, 5, 10, 15, 15n28, 16, 16n32, 17, 18
Ahmed, Sara, 61, 61n13, 89n31, 94, 94n55, 96, 97n66, 100, 100n76, 119n49
Aldrich, Robert, 40n26
Althaus-Reid, Marcella, 34n1
Anderson, Herbert, 67, 67n37
Andragogy, 16, 16n31
Andrews, Dale P. 78, 78n76
Anselm, 30, 30n77, 31
anthropocentrism, ix, 131, 133, 133n22, 139
Anzaldua, Gloria, 22, 22n51
apocalypse, 104, 104n96
Ashcroft, Bill, 13n19, 115n36
Aristotle, 48, 48n57, 133, 134
Augustine, 70

B

Bacon, Francis, 135, 136, 136n38
Baker, Doris, 37n14, 44, 44n41, 44n42, 44n45
Bal, Mieke, 139, 139n53
Bass, Dorothy, 71, 73, 74
Beavis, Mary Ann, 4, 96n64, 97n67, 99n73, 101n81
belonging, ix, 6, 14, 48, 65, 81, 82, 83, 83n4, 83n5, 84, 90, 91, 92, 95, 96, 106, 114, 126
Benhabib, Seyla, 86n19, 92

Berger, John, 51n65
Bhabha, Homi K., 52
binary, 5, 11, 17, 18, 31, 34n1, 36n4, 41, 87, 89, 93, 94, 95, 108, 108n8, 133
Bingen, Hildegard, 135
Black, Kathy, 31n81, 78n75
Bonhoeffer, Dietrich, 66, 66n34, 144, 144n76
Bonilla-Silva, Eduardo, 77, 77n73
borders, 6, 78, 81n2, 90, 104n95, 106, 108, 114, 116, 117, 117n42, 121, 143
border-crossing, borderlands, 22, 22n51 119, 125, 127
Bourdieu, Pierre, 74, 74n67, 121
Boyer, Ernest, 93n50
Bronfenbrenner, Urie, 128, 128n1
Brookfield, Stephen, 59n6, 65, 65n24
Browning, Don, 61n14, 114n30
Brueggemann, Walter, 38
Buber, Martin, 144, 144n78
Butler, Judith, 11, 11n5, 14, 14n24, 34n1, 41n29, 79n77

C

Cahalan, Kathleen, 4, 4n4, 36, 36n7, 55n85, 65n25, 96n62, 106n2, 120n56
Caine, Renate, 61n12
Caldwell, Elizabeth, 42n34
Calvin, John, 144
Cannella, Gaile, 17, 17n36, 18, 18n43, 60, 60n9, 73, 73n61, 75, 75n70

INDEX

Carter, Warren, 123n64, 123n68, 124, 124n72
Carvalhaes, Cláudio, 85n11, 94, 94n51, 100n75, 103n88, 104n92, 104n94
Castles, Stephen, 108n9
Chamberlain, Gary, 129n7
chaos, 6, 18, 18n40, 24n55, 38n19, 74n64, 96, 96n63, 100n74
Chidester, David, 90, 90n35
Chinese Head Tax, 110
Chow, Rey, 7n6
Christian-centrism, 6, 81, 82, 83n7, 84, 89, 92n45, 95n61, 99
Clifford, James, 120, 120n54
Cobb, John, 132, 132n15, 132n17
Cohen, Mark Nathan, 47n56
colonialism, postcolonialism, 4, 7, 36, 37, 37n9, 40n26, 41, 54, 85n11, 88, 92, 94, 94n51, 100n75, 103n88, 104n92, 106, 116, 117, 118n47, 119n51, 139, 146
communion, 10n3, 24, 35, 70, 71n54, 76, 102, 141, 142
compartmentalized, 3, 62, 63, 78, 89
Conde-Frazier, Elizabeth, 19, 19n45, 20n47, 54, 54n82 60, 60n11
Cooey, Paula, 90n36
Corky, Alexander, 66, 66n65
Cornell, Deirdre, 122, 122n62
Couture, Pamela, 109n15, 114, 114n30, 116n37
Craigo-Snell, Shannon, 103n91
Creamer, Deborah, 28n71
Cruz, Faustino M., 88, 88n26
Cruz, Gemma Tulud, 122, 122n61
cult of normalcy, 71

D

Daggers, Jenny, 116, 16n40
Daly, Mary, 35, 35n3
Daoism, 102
Davis, Patricia, 37, 37n11, 38n17
Dean, Kenda Creasy, 37n14, 39, 39n21
de Beauvoir, Simone, 11
decolonization, 14, 118
Deluze, Guattari, 98, 98n71

dementia, 13, 26, 121
democracy, 25, 27
dialectic, 86, 139, 140
dichotomy, 10, 84, 86, 89, 93, 132, 133
d' Eaubonne, Francoise, 142n70
disciplinary amnesia, 88
disability, xi, xii, 4, 5, 10, 12, 13, 13n15, 13n17, 14, 15, 16, 27, 28n71, 31n81, 32n83, 50, 70, 70n51, 71, 78, 78n75, 79
diasporic, 119, 125, 126n78
displacement, 118, 119, 125, 131
Donaldson, Laura E., 36, 37n9
Doran, Carol, 124n71
double consciousness, 54
double vision, 103
doubleness, 103, 104
Douglas, Jane, 35n4
Drucilla, Cornell, 147n89
dualism, 31, 86, 131, 133, 139, 140, 145
Dube, Musa W., xii, 31n81, 117, 117n43, 146, 146n87
Du Bois, W. E. S., 54, 54n80
Duck, Ruth, 62, 62n15, 65n26, 68n40, 69n43, 70, 71n52, 72, 72n57, 72n60, 77, 77n72, 94n52
Duff, Nancy, 45, 45n49
Dykstra, Craig, 63, 63n19, 65, 65n27

E

Eaton, Heather, 132, 132n16, 132n19, 133, 133n21, 133n24, 135, 135n31, 136n39, 138, 138n48, 139, 139n51, 140n59, 142, 142n69, 142n70, 143n72, 145, 145n81, 146n83, 146n85
ecofeminist, 3, 7, 132, 132n16, 132n19, 133n21, 133n24, 135n31, 136, 136n39, 138n48, 139n51, 140, 140n59, 142n69, 142n70, 143, 143n72, 143n74, 145, 145n81, 146, 146n83, 146n85
ecofeminism, 128n7, 142, 143, 143n75, 145
ecological crisis, 130 132, 133, 134, 141n62, 142, 146
Edie, Fred, 70n49

Index

ego, 12
Eiesland, Nancy, 70n51, 71
Eisner, Elliott, 51, 52n69
Elam, Michele, 41n28, 51, 51n67, 52n70, 52n71, 52n73, 53n75, 53n78, 54n80
Elliott, John H., 125, 125n73
empathic knowing, 88
Enlightenment, 9, 18, 64, 85, 131, 137
environmental racism, 130
epistemology, 13, 39, 86, 98, 145
Erikson, Erik, 39, 39n20
Ex opere operato Ex opere operantis, 69, 70

F

family, ix, 1, 5, 7, 11, 26, 34, 35, 37, 38, 38n18, 39, 40, 41, 42, 43, 44, 45, 46, 48, 50, 51, 52, 54, 55, 56, 67, 76, 81, 92, 106, 110, 120, 121, 122, 123, 124, 125, 129
Fanon, Frantz, 9, 9n2, 13, 14, 14n20, 14n21, 118, 118n46
fear, 5, 22, 27, 41, 49, 57, 72, 74, 75, 76, 87, 89, 91, 96, 123
Feely-Harnik, Gillian, 24, 25n59
femicide, 136
fidelity, 39, 45, 93
Filippi, Linda, 145n82
fluidity, 93, 95, 98, 99, 104
Foley, Edward, 70n51
Foster, Charles, 35n2, 51n66
Foucault, Michel, 60, 69n46, 73, 73n62
Fulkerson, Mary McClintock, 15n26, 20n48, 22, 22n52, 32, 32n86, 94, 95n56, 121, 121n59, 126n80

G

Gaileo, 135
Ganzevroort, R. Ruard, 43, 44n40, 59n7
Garland-Thomson, Rosemarie, 50, 51n63, 54
Gaskin, Pearl Fuyo, 37, 37n12, 42n32, 44, 44n44, 45, 45n47, 46n50, 46n51, 47n56, 50n62
Gebara, Ivone, 143, 143n73, 147, 147n88, 147n91

gender, transgender, xi, 4, 5, 10, 11, 11n5, 12, 17, 34, 34n1, 35, 36, 36n6, 38, 38n18, 40, 41, 41n29, 48, 50, 61, 78, 81, 81n3, 86, 88, 90, 98, 101, 102n87, 121, 122, 130, 136, 137, 146
George, Rosemary Margangoly, 42, 43n35
Gilmour, Michael, 141, 141n65
Giroux, Henry, 119, 119n50
Gogia, Nupur, 110n17, 111n19, 111n21, 114n31
Graham, Elaine, 11, 11n7, 41, 41n29
gratitude, 2, 25
Greider, Kathleen J., 83, 83n7, 92, 92n45, 95n61
Grethlein, Christian, 141, 141n67
Grey, Mary, 136, 136n37, 138n45
Groome, Thomas, 71n55

H

habitus, 121
Hall, Douglas John, 139, 139n52, 145n79
Hamman, Jaco, 17, 17n38
Hauerwas, Stanley, 31, 31n79
Hegel, George F., 85, 86
Hess, Mary E., 59n6
Hessel, Dieter T., 131, 131n12, 131n14, 132n20, 140, 140n56
heterosexism, 36, 36n6, 37, 40
heterogeneity, 43
Hill, Lawrence, 48, 49n59
Hoeft, Jeanne, 36n6
home, homemaking, homeless, ix, 20, 26, 35, 38, 39, 41, 42, 42n34, 43, 43n35, 45, 58, 62, 63, 73, 78, 106, 107, 107n5, 108, 112, 116, 120, 121, 122, 124, 125, 125n73, 127, 131
homosexuality, 40, 40n26, 41, 49
hooks, bell, 53, 53n74
Horell, Herold, 144, 144n77
hybridity, 6, 29n72, 52, 53, 56, 74, 81, 82, 83n4, 83n5, 84, 92, 93, 96, 97, 99, 100, 101, 102, 103, 104, 105

Index

I

idolatry, 131
imagination, viii, viiin1, 8n10, 12, 36n8, 41n27, 43n36, 52n69, 54n83, 85n12, 86n15, 86n17, 90n35, 95n60, 118n45, 137n42, 144, 144n77
independence, xi, 1, 5, 6, 9, 10, 11, 12, 13, 14, 15, 16, 19, 25, 26, 27, 31, 34, 115, 115n35, 117
individualism, vii, 131, 139
InGan, 28
interdisciplinary, 108, 120, 121, 130
intergenerational, 58, 63, 66, 72, 75, 76
interracial, 81, 83
interreligious, xii, 6, 83, 84, 84n9, 90, 91, 91n38, 95, 99, 104
intersectionality, 78, 96, 130
Irenaeus, 32, 32n82
Isasi-Diaz, Ida Maria, 68n39

J

Japanese internment, 112
Jobling, David, 70n50
Jones, Esyllt, 112n23
justice, 17, 29, 35, 38, 38n18, 44, 46, 66, 67, 89, 103, 106n3, 111, 129, 132n15, 132n17, 132n19, 138, 138n47, 140, 142

K

Kang, Nam Soon, 119, 119n52, 120, 125, 125n76, 126n78
Katz, Eric, 140, 141, 141n62
Kawash, Samira, 14n21
Kazimi, Ali, 111n22
Keller, Catherine, 11n10, 12, 12n12, 17n35, 31, 31n82, 93, 93n47, 102, 102n86, 104, 104n96, 131n11
Kennedy, William Bean, 57n2
Kierkegaard, Søren, 17, 17n34, 30, 31, 31n78
Kim-Cragg, HyeRan, vii, viii, ix, xi, 21n49, 25n60, 29n,72, 59n5, 60n8, 62n16, 64,n21, 66n31, 68n42, 72n58, 83n6, 88n28, 96n64, 97, 97n67, 99n73, 101n81, 102n85, 103n90, 106n4, 116n39, 120n55, 121n82, 123n65, 123n67, 124n69, 126n81, 131n82, 135n33
Kin-dom, 68, 68n39, 69, 76
Kittay, Eva, 10, 10n4, 32n88
Knowles, Malcolm, 16, 16n30, 16n31
Koinonia, 126
Komagata Maru, 111, 111n22
Kraft, Charles, 74, 74n66
Kujawa-Holbrook, Sheryl, 81n2, 91n38, 104n95
KwanEum, 55, 144
Kwok, Pui-lan, viiin1, 8n10, 28, 28n70, 29, 29n73, 29n75, 36, 36n8, 37n9, 41n27, 43n36, 54n83, 81n3, 85, 85n12, 86n15, 86n17, 87, 87n24, 90, 90n35, 95n60, 101n83, 102, 102n84, 102n87, 118, 118n45, 137n42, 139n54, 149n96

L

Lartey, Emmanuel T., 44, 44n46, 95, 95n58
Lathrop, Gordon, 66, 66n29
Lave, Jane, 80, 80n79
Lee, Boyung, 31n81
Lee, Jung Young, 24
LGBTQ, vii, 35, 36
liberating interdependence, 31n81, 117, 146
Liew, Tat-siong Benny, 54, 54n81
liminality, 18
lineality, 13
liquid, 49, 93, 93n49, 98
listening, 5, 35, 42, 43, 44, 45, 47, 50, 55, 60, 68, 70, 91n39, 107n6, 130
lived theory, 94
Livingstone, David, 18
Lex Orandi, Lex Credendi, 94
Locke, John, 9, 9n1, 10
logic of the one, 6, 82, 89, 90, 91, 92, 100, 101, 102, 105
Lowe, Lisa, 52, 112
Luther, Martin, 144, 145
Lynn, Robert, 57n2

Index

M

Macadam, Jackie, 26n63
MacIntyre, Alasdair, 62, 63n18
Magi, 122, 123, 124, 127
Magnificat, 67
Malleus Maleticarum, 136
Man of Reason, 135
marginality, 24, 24n56, 24n58, 29, 29n74
Marshall, Joretta, 41n30
Martin, Miriam K., 129n7, 138, 138n49
Matsuoka, Fumitaka, 27, 27n67, 28, 28n69
McCarthy, Maureen Terese, 56n87
McClintock, Anne, 116n38, 137n44
McFague, Sallie, 146, 146n86
Mercer, Joyce Ann, 38, 38n16, 44, 44n42, 44n45, 58, 59n4, 69, 69n47, 72n56, 80, 80n80, 88, 88n30, 120, 120n57, 129n7, 143, 143n75
Mercer, Kobena, 52, 52n70
Merchant, Carolyn, 136, 136n35
Mignolo, Walter D., 8n9
migration, immigration ix, xi, xii, 3, 4, 5, 6, 7, 34, 39, 45, 68n42, 72, 78, 81, 83, 106, 107, 108, 108n9, 109, 110, 111, 111n20, 112, 113, 114, 115, 116, 117, 117n41, 118, 119, 120, 121, 121n60, 122, 122n61, 123, 124, 125, 126, 127
Mikoski, Gordon, 4, 4n4, 36, 36n7, 55n85, 65n25, 96n62, 120n56
Miles, Maria, 140n60
Miller-McLemore, Bonnie, 18, 18n40, 24n55, 38, 38n19, 39n22, 62n14, 74n64, 87, 87n22, 87n25, 89, 89n32, 96, 96n63, 98n70, 100n74, 108n8
minority, 13, 40, 70, 72, 79, 81, 88, 89, 100, 120
misogynist, 103, 136, 137
mixed youth, 35
Mollenkott, Virginia Ramsey, 91n40
monotheism, 81n1, 82, 90n37, 91n41, 92n43, 93n46, 97, 98n71, 100n77, 101, 101n82, 102
Moore, Mary Elizabeth, xi, 15n29, 23, 23n54, 25n62, 27, 28n68, 69, 69n45, 70n49, 75, 75n68, 84n9, 129, 129n3, 129n6, 129n8, 131n13, 134n27, 138n46, 141, 141n64, 141n66, 148, 148n94
Moran, Gabriel, 15, 15n28, 16, 16n32, 141, 142n68
Morrison, Toni, 107, 107n5
multiculturalism, 109, 115
multiple religious belonging, ix, 6, 81, 82, 83n4, 84, 90, 91, 92, 95, 96
multiplicity, 6, 18, 43, 81, 84, 89, 92, 93, 95, 99, 100, 101, 102, 102n86
multitude, 102
Murphy, Debra Dean, 80, 80n78
muscular habits, 121, 148

N

Nandy, Ashis, 18, 18n42
narrative agency, 5, 35, 37, 43
Ng, David, 62, 126
Nixon, Rob, 128, 128n2, 129n5

O

Oduyoye, Mercy Amba, 148, 149n96
Okin, Susan Moller, 38, 38n18
orality, 64, 88
Orientalism, 119n48
Osmer, Richard R., 130n9

P

panentheistic, 145
Parker, Evelyn, 37n13, 37n14, 40, 40n25, 44
Parks, Sharon Daloz, 38n15
participatory action, ix, 19, 19n45, 20n47
Passeron, Jean-Claude, 74, 74n67
passing, 35, 52, 53, 54, 100
patriarchy, 35, 36, 97n68, 133, 139, 140, 140n60
pedagogy, 15, 16n31, 31n81, 58, 59, 119
perichoresis, 102
personhood, 9, 10, 11, 12, 13, 16, 29, 147
Peterson, Cheryl M., 124n70
Piaget, Jean, 75
Plant, Judith, 140n58

169

Index

play, 17, 17n38, 18, 22, 24, 40, 49, 53, 57, 58, 59
Plumwood, Val, 133n23, 137n41
Poling, James, 126n79
Polydoxy, 102, 102n86, 103
Ponting, Clive, 136n34
postcolonial conditions, 4, 115, 116
Power Flower, 76, 77
primary theology, 94, 104
Procter-Smith, Marjorie, 100n78, 103n89
purity, 5, 41, 45, 47, 49, 74, 97, 97n68, 98, 99, 102

Q

qualitative research, 20, 35, 41, 101
queer, viii, xi, 2, 5, 22, 34, 34n1, 35, 37, 38, 39, 40, 41, 43, 44, 50, 54, 55, 56, 61, 76

R

racism, racist, vii, xii, 37, 40, 42, 46, 49, 53, 72, 78, 78n73, 94, 110, 111, 112, 113, 114, 130
Rasmussen, Larry, 135n29, 137n32, 145, 145n80
Razack, Shrene, 106n1
Reader, John, 138
recognition, 4, 13, 24, 35, 43, 53, 54, 55, 56, 89
refugees, 106, 107, 109, 116, 117, 120, 122, 124, 125
regulative norm, 61
religious pluralism, 3, 6, 82, 83n7, 84, 92, 92n45, 95n61, 102
representation, 13, 51, 52, 54, 85, 86, 113, 117, 118, 119, 127
reversal of fortune, 69, 69n44
Reynolds, Tom E., 10, 10n3, 15, 15n25, 67, 68n38, 71, 71n53, 71n54
Rieger, Joerg, 28, 28n70, 29, 29n73, 29n75, 81n3, 85n14, 102, 102n84
Rivera, Mayra, 8n8, 31, 31n80, 32n85, 125, 125n75
Root, Maria, 45
Ross, Susan, 70n49
Russell, Letty M., 81n3

Ruther, Rosemary Radford, 143n74, 146, 146n84
Rux, Carl Hancok, 22, 22n50

S

Sabbath, 7, 130, 141, 142
Sacks, Oliver, 56, 56n86
Sahm, 147
Said, Edward W., 107, 118
Sakai, Naoki, 95n59
Saliers, Don E., 25, 25n61, 63, 64n20, 66, 66n33, 67, 67n35, 68n41, 70n51
SangSaeng, 147
Santmire, H. Paul., 140, 140n61
Schleiermacher, Fredrich, 18, 18n41, 85, 86, 137, 137n43
Schneider, Laurel C., 81n1, 90, 90n37, 91, 91n41, 92, 92n43, 93n46, 96, 98n71, 100, 100n77, 101, 101n82, 102, 102n86
Schooling, 57, 80
Schreiter, Robert, 89
Seager, Joni, 137n40
Selmanovic, Samir, 104
Senn, Frank, 64n22
Senna, Danzy, 41n28
sexual orientation, 4, 34, 36, 37, 38, 61, 76
Seymour, Jack, 37, 37n10, 42n33, 43n38, 53n77
Sharkey, Sarah Borden, 48n57
Sharp, Melinda A. McGarrah, 55, 55n84, 91n39, 107n6, 119n51
Shepard, Bruce R., 112n26, 113n28, 114n32
Shiva, Vandana, 140n58
Slack, Jennifer, 133n25
Smith, Andrea, 137n44
Snyder, Susanna, 125n74
social policy method, 6, 39, 106, 109, 109n15, 111, 114, 114n30, 116n37, 127
Soja, Edward W., 106n3
Spivak, Gayatri Chakravorty, 12, 12n13, 85, 85n13, 86, 86n18, 86n20
stewardship, 130, 139, 141, 142
Stomp Dance, 74, 74n65

Index

Sugirtharajah, R. S., 88, 88n29
sweaty concepts, 94
Swinton, John, 12, 13, 13n15, 13n16, 13n17, 13n18, 14n22, 14n23, 16, 16n33, 26, 26n63, 27n66, 31, 32n83
syncretism, 74, 84, 92, 96, 97, 100

T

tabernacle, 68
Tanner, Kathryn, 95n57, 121, 121n60
Thatamanil, John, 86, 87n21, 89, 89n33, 90, 92, 92n44, 93n48
theology of multiplicity, 6, 81, 93, 99, 102, 102n86
theoria, 31
Thomas, Virginia, 70, 70n17
Trinity, 101, 102
triptych, 141
Troeger, Thomas, 124n71
Turner, Mary Donovan, 69n44
Turpin, Katherine, 37n14, 41, 41n31
Tye, Karen, 60n10

U

Ubuntu, 155, 155n89, 155n90
unlearning, 5, 10, 19, 22, 23, 25, 27, 28

V

Vanier, Jean, 15, 15n27, 26, 26n65
van Marle, Karin, 147n89
violence, vii, 14n21, 26, 27, 116, 118, 124, 128, 128n2, 129, 129n5, 136, 137, 137n44, 144
virility, 12, 97
vocational, viii

vulnerability, 5, 14, 15, 26, 27, 79, 79n77, 120

W

Walker, Alice, 32, 32n87
Walia, Harsha, 117, 117n42
Walton, Janet, 100n78
Ward, Pete, 93n49, 112n24
Warnock, Mary, 26, 26n63
Washbourn, Panelope, 98, 98n72
Welsh, Jennifer, 108, 108n10, 108n12, 109n14
West, Cornel, 19, 19n46, 43n37, 56, 56n88
West, Mona, 101, 101n79
Westerhoff, John III, 19, 19n44, 30n76, 51, 51n64, 64, 64n23
Wettlaufer, Elizabeth, 26, 26n64, 27
White, James F., 24, 24n57, 70, 70n48, 73, 73n63
whiteness, ix, 53, 78
white nation, 6, 110, 110n17
white supremacy, 113
Wiesel, Elie, 32, 32n85
Williams, Delores, 126n82
Williams, Patricia J., 78, 78n74
Wisdom Commentary, xvii
witchcraft, 136
Witvliet, John, 121n58, 122n63, 148n93
WCC, 138, 138n47, 147, 148n92
WCRC, 35, 36
World Bank, 138

Y

yin yang, 54
Young, Robert J. C., 118, 118n47

171

www.ingramcontent.com/pod-product-compliance
Lightning Source LLC
Chambersburg PA
CBHW062047220426
43662CB00010B/1690